EAGLES & DRAGONS

EAGLES & DRAGONS

A HISTORY OF AMERICANS IN CHINA & THE ORIGINS OF THE AMERICAN CLUB HONG KONG

BY **ANDREW COE**

WITH A PREFACE BY
BURTON LEVIN

To Bud and Carolyn,

AC

THE
AMERICAN
CLUB

HONG KONG

EAGLES & DRAGONS
A HISTORY OF AMERICANS IN CHINA
& THE ORIGINS OF THE
AMERICAN CLUB HONG KONG

by Andrew Coe

Andrew Coe's text
Copyright ©1997 The American Club, Hong Kong

ISBN 962-217-484-1

An Odyssey Book
Produced for
The American Club, Hong Kong
by Twin Age Limited, Hong Kong
4/F, No.20 Hollywood Road
Central, Hong Kong
tel: (852) 2868-3822
fax: (852) 2840-1701
e-mail: 100426.3426@compuserve.com

Concept: Magnus Bartlett
Designed by David Hurst
Editors: Hannah Moore & May Holdsworth
Project Manager: Li Suk Woon
Project Coordinator: Anastasia Edwards

Printed in China

LITERARY EXCERPTS

ESSAYS

CONTENTS

AMERICAN CLUB 70TH ANNIVERSARY PUBLICATION SPONSORSHIPS

The American Club would like to extend heartfelt appreciation
to the following sponsors who helped make the
publication of **Eagles & Dragons** possible:

Platinum Sponsor

PROCTER & GAMBLE

Gold Sponsors

UNITED AIRLINES

AMBROUS T. YOUNG

RUSSELL & YOLANDA YEH

MR. & MRS. LARRY CHONG

MR. FRED S. HEENEY

CPC ASIA LTD.

Silver Sponsors

ETAK INTERNATIONAL LTD.

MR. WILLIAM F. DeMUCCI

SYED S. ALBUKHARY

SHUN CHEONG GROUP (HOLDINGS) CO., LTD.

DEAN WITTER REYNOLDS (HONG KONG) LTD.

DR. WILLIAM W. L. SAN

AMERICAN CLUBS INTERNATIONAL JAKARTA, OSAKA, SHANGHAI

DOUG & GERRI HOLTZ

PRESIDENT'S MESSAGE

About a year and a half ago, while talking with some fellow members over cocktails at the Portside Bar, we began to reflect upon the outstanding facilities the American Club offers. This conversation led us to talking about the origins of the American Club. One member of the group, a longtime member and former president, held us spellbound as he reminisced about the days of the St. George's Building and, in particular, an incident involving the move from that building to Exchange Square. This led to the realization there was no written record of events such as this, no account or even archive to record the American Club's 73 years of history.

That oversight has now been rectified. Andrew Coe, assisted by researcher Anastasia Edwards, has woven disparate facts together to produce this history of our club. What is special about this book is that it situates the club's history within the history of China and Hong Kong.

America's presence in Hong Kong and South China began in the 18th century. As the book will relate, the ship *Empress of China* sailed from America to China in 1784, ushering in over two centuries of interaction between the two nations. The American businesses that thrive in Hong Kong today owe a direct debt to the pioneers of the late 18th century who tackled the high seas in their quest for adventure and wealth.

In 1925, there were enough Americans doing business in Hong Kong to justify forming a club "which could serve a dual purpose—social and commercial." As the American population in Hong Kong grew, so did the club's fortunes. The club moved from location to location, improving its premises, food and services to meet the increasing number and demands of its members. The club's growth from the modest first premises in Rutton Building to its present locations at Exchange Square and Tai Tam in many ways mirrors the economic miracle that is the story of Hong Kong.

As 1996 draws to a close we at the American Club look ahead with the people of Hong Kong to the change of sovereignty on July 1, 1997. As we plan for the club's future, our mood is one of confidence and optimism. The American Club will continue to operate according to its mission statement and will strive to ensure the club continues to be a place where Americans and their friends and colleagues can meet. Equally important, the club will maintain the unique and time-honored identity of the American community in Hong Kong.

Thank you, Jack Keenan, for the story that was the seed for this book.

See you at the club,

Mark Blacker

PREFACE
by Burton Levin

Though I was born in the year of the horse, it was a pig that launched me into an involvement with Hong Kong and China that spread over more than 40 years. Reeking of formaldehyde and deceitfully jumbling its veins, arteries and muscles into a confusing mess in revenge for an early death, this dreadful animal defeated my clumsy attempts at dissection and convinced me to abandon parentally-nurtured hopes of a career in medicine. In casting for alternatives, I settled on physical adventure, but soon realized that there was more to life than tossing a ball around. Influenced by two wonderful professors I turned to history, soon focusing on China largely because of the war then raging in Korea.

Thoughts of an academic career were blunted by the realization that I lacked the means and temperament to pursue years of advanced study. Dreams of bringing peace to a conflict-ridden world and the need for a steady income aroused interest in a diplomatic career. To my surprise and my mother's consternation, it took a while for her to grasp the distinction between the Foreign Service and Foreign Legion. I passed the exam and entered for duty in June, 1954. Three weeks later I embarked on my first plane ride to what was then commonly known as Formosa.

I first visited Hong Kong in 1955. Since then I've lived in the territory off and on for 15 years and visited almost annually. The '50s and '60s were a golden era for Americans living in Asia. We basked in the reflected prestige of the most powerful and richest nation in the world. The almighty American dollar and American wages translated into an exceedingly comfortable lifestyle. Necessities, luxuries, spacious housing and servants were great bargains by American standards. Though but a junior officer, in my early visits to Hong Kong I was able to enjoy dining at Gaddi's, shopping at Lane Crawford and a carefree indulgence in nightlife. But there was a disturbing other side of this picture. In Hong Kong as throughout Asia poverty was widespread and life was harsh for most. Beggars,

street walkers, the homeless and malnourished children plagued with skin disease were omnipresent. However used one grew to the surrounding misery there were daily encounters with people living in such pitiful conditions as to provoke deep concern about the human condition.

The impressive growth rate, rapid transformations of skylines and dramatic improvements in the wellbeing and education levels of the peoples of Asia over the past three decades have been well chronicled and need no elaboration. On the personal level, nothing more brings home to me this change than to pay for a cup of coffee in present-day Hong Kong or Tokyo more than I used to spend for a week's living expenses in the Taiwan of 40 years ago.

There have been less remarked changes of greater significance. Mr. Coe's excellent account of the American presence in Hong Kong relates the American Club's grudging acceptance of a handful of Chinese members in the early '50s. This belated small breach of colonial prejudice has widened to the point that such thinking no longer has any significance in Hong Kong. Altruism undoubtedly played a part in this process, but it was the entrepreneurial, professional and educational accomplishments of the Hong Kong people which undermined pretensions of Western superiority. To put it more bluntly, it made far better sense for Westerners to cultivate rather than to antagonize those whose growing wealth and power could help or hinder their own interests.

Change has always been a feature of America's relationship with Hong Kong. As a sign of the importance early America attached to the China trade, we opened our Consulate here in 1843, scarcely a year after the colony was established and 11 years before Admiral Perry's ships opened Japan. The wealth amassed in trade directly with China or through Hong Kong contributed to the cultural flowering of New England in the mid-19th century and provided capital for the construction of our early railroads. The search for wild ginseng to pay for our purchases of tea, silk and other Chinese goods promoted the exploration and settlement of Western New York and the upper Midwest, as well as the dramatic leapfrog of an American presence to the Pacific Northwest. At a time when settlement was still largely confined to the slopes of the Appalachians, these migrations were directly attributable to the abundance of beavers there whose furry skins were a hot item in the China market.

America's busy and profitable ties with Hong Kong were relatively short-lived. With the opening and subsequent flourishing of Shanghai and other treaty ports beginning around the 1860s, America and Hong Kong lapsed into a sleepy relationship. It was not until the early 1950s that a vastly changed America began playing a significant role in a rapidly changing Hong Kong. The first manifestation was substantial American governmental and private contributions of food and other assistance to take care of the destitute refugees pouring into Hong Kong.

Over time the handful of American businessmen in Hong Kong in the '50s was augmented by first a trickle, then a stream, of compatriots attracted by the policies of the Hong Kong government, the industriousness of the people and, subsequently, the territory's key role in trade and financial matters relating to China.

The activities of the American Consulate General mirror the changing weight afforded the territory by the U.S. Government. Beginning with the triumph of communism in China in 1949 and through to the mid-1970s the primary function of the American Consulate General was to cover events in China.

Very little attention was paid to Hong Kong *per se* other than that aroused by such dramatic events as the Cultural Revolution-inspired riots of 1966-67. I served here from 1965-69 as one of the large corps of China watchers. To me and most of my colleagues Hong Kong was little more than a platform from which to imperfectly observe China. We consorted with academics, colleagues in the consular corps and journalists who were similarly preoccupied in trying to find out what was going on in China. We had very little contact with Hong Kong officials or with the business community, Americans included.

All this changed. The opening of American posts in China in the 1970s reduced Hong Kong's China watching importance. At the same time the territory's transformation into an economic power and a major center for trade with a strong emerging China enhanced its intrinsic importance to the United States. By the time I returned to the territory as Consul General in 1981, the Consulate General was far more preoccupied with Hong Kong developments than with those in China.

In the run-up to 1997 and beyond Hong Kong would continue, as it has, to occupy center stage in the Consulate General's scheme of things. I have publicly, loudly and repeatedly proclaimed my optimism about Hong Kong's future. It would take several more pages to present the rationale for my opinion. Suffice it to say that the history of the Hong Kong issue, the major changes underway in China and the political, economic and psychological importance to China of assuring a successful transition to Chinese sovereignty continue to convince me of Hong Kong's future success.

I close with a salute to Andrew Coe for his valuable effort to trace the history of the American Club. The desultory nature of America's involvement with Hong Kong and the relatively small size of the American business community for many decades make for large gaps in this history. One hopes that old-timers reading this account will be spurred to contact the Club to help fill in some of these gaps.

Mr. Coe has made a fine beginning in detailing the course of America's involvement in China and Hong Kong and the activities of the American Club. It's a long, complex, fascinating history. Much of the story awaits further research and I for one hope that we haven't heard the last on the subject.

AUTHOR'S INTRODUCTION

The status and character of Americans in China is mirrored by the history of Hong Kong's American Club. At its founding in 1925, the American Club's role was purely local; this reflected the small American community in the colony as well as the marginality of Hong Kong relative to Shanghai and the other large treaty ports. Since 1949, Hong Kong has been transformed into one of Asia's economic powerhouses; Americans are the dominant foreign community; and the American Club is one of the largest and most important private social institutions in the territory.

Because the American Club is so imbedded in recent Chinese history, we decided to expand this book from a straight club history to a more ambitious look at the club and its place in the history of Americans in China, beginning in 1784. Many of the attributes of the first American/ Chinese relationships—the importance of traders, the American evangelical impulse, the friction between national characteristics—are still evident today. Anyone looking for a guide to the future of American trade and diplomacy in China might contemplate the lessons of the first two hundred years of intercourse between these two countries.

The research and writing of this book have been an adventure, with both joys and frustrations. The bulk of the historical research was accomplished in the United States, where most of the best archives of China-related material are located. The New York Public Libary's Research Collection became the base for the book's writing and research, but we also consulted the collections of numerous libraries and photo archives in Boston, Washington, D.C., New Haven, San Francisco and Hong Kong. One of the surprises of this work was discovering the mammoth archives of missionary-related material deposited in libraries such as Yale University's Sterling Memorial Library and the Yale Divinity School. These photo and information resources have barely been tapped by researchers and could provide material for dozens of publications.

The greatest frustration of working on this book was the lack of information on Hong Kong's American community between 1910 and 1938. The main reason for this gap is that Shanghai was far more important than Hong Kong during these years, and American writers and journalists preferred to write about the booming sin city of the East rather than the staid little colonial outpost. The vast majority of the pre-World War II American population never returned to Asia after the war, so there is very little continuity from this era to the current Hong Kong American community. These decades also saw the founding of the American Club, but almost everything belonging to the early club (except a few hidden mementoes) was destroyed by the Japanese Army, who occupied the club's quarters in the Hongkong and Shanghai Bank Building from 1942 to 1945. If information on the pre-war club exists, it is very well hidden. Let us hope that it is not lost forever.

The great joy in researching this book was meeting numerous old China hands, both American Club members and not, who went out of their way to help me and submitted to hours of importunate questioning. We were disappointed, however, that we did not receive a better response from American Club members after repeated requests for information and photographs. We know that this book's publication will cause a flood of new material, illustrations and anecdotes to be unearthed; their inclusion into this history will have to wait until the next edition or, more realistically, an article in the club news.

We could not have produced this book without the help of the American Club, its employees and its members. When Mark Blacker commissioned this book upon becoming American Club president in the fall of 1995, he perhaps did not realize the length and complexity of this project; we hope we made up for the delay by producing a work of quality and breadth that honors the club's reputation. From the very start, Tom Gorman contributed hours of excellent counsel and dozens of leads that proved invaluable in our research. Club manager Douglas Holtz and membership secretary Johnny Choy went out of their way to help this project and tried to fulfill even our most eccentric requests; Kim Canon read over the manuscript and provided valuable editorial advice.

Dozens of members of the American Club community gave us their time, energy, photographs and memorabilia, among them Larry Allen, Don and Darling Allison, William Anderson, Hal Archer, George Bell, Felix Bieger, Russell Blando, Peg Bordwell, Cathy Braga, Matthew Burvett, Joseph Champagne, Art Chase, Otto Chan, John Colling, James Eckes, Herbert

Edelstein, Stanley Freedman, Sir Kenneth Fung, Sir Sidney Gordon, Donald Greco, Thomas Greer, Donald Griswold, George Hayashi, Anker Henningsen, Sir Y.K. Kan, Ira Kaye, Jack Keenan, Patrick Kroos, George Lau, Burt Levin, Robert Lusher, Neil Mackenzie, Alan Mak, Frank Martin, Michael McCrary, William Mortson, Moira Moser, Richard Mueller, David Murray, Leo Murray, Patrick O'Brien, John G. O'Donnell, Von Oliver, Dr. Francis Pan, John Potter, Mario Prata, Taco Proper Jr., Kaye and Taco Proper Sr., Dick Ross, George R. Ross, Phyllis Ross, Glendon Rowell, Anthony de O. Sales, Robert Sanders, John Shoemaker, Henry Sperry, Henry Steiner, Robert Thompson,Sandra Walters, Y.C. Wang, Fred Westphal, Earl Westrick, Gretchen Willoughby, Andrew Wong MD, Bing Wong and Daniel Zigal.

Numerous other people also helped this project, providing information on both the club and on American and Chinese history, among them Fred Armentrout, Alice Au, James Beeman, Alan Birch, Millie Brown, Colonel Joseph Chan, Caroline Courtauld, Shann Davies, John Deeney, Cliff Dunnaway, Marvin Farkas, Captain James Glover, Charlotte Havilland, R. Campbell James, Tess Johnston, Greenstreet Kan, Vicki Kowalski, Margaret Lee, Mike and Jill Lovatt, Helen Perrell, Joyce Rasmussen, David Roads, Anne and Sandy Schlee, Mark Sheldon, Chaplin Richard Silveira, Carl Smith, Julie Sormark, Russell Spurr, Nora Sun, William Turnbull, Hugh Vickers, Gary Whitney and Diane Woo.

Finally, the author would like to thank Anastasia Edwards for her indefatigable researches through Hong Kong libraries, as well as acknowledge our sterling photo research team of Natalie Coe, Philippa Edwards and Holly Hurd-Forsyte.

Interior of a Fastboat, Canton, *by William Prinsep*

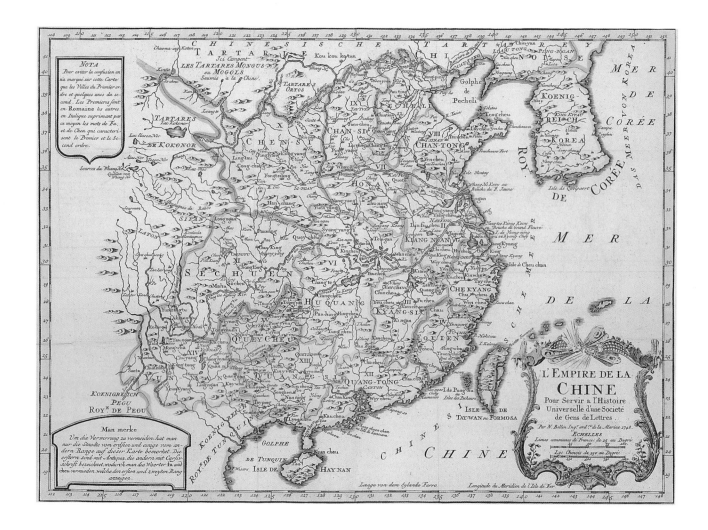

ON THE FIRST AMERICAN SHIP
EMPRESS OF CHINA, CAPT. GREENE

THAT EXPLORED THE ROUT [SIC] TO CHINA,
AND THE EAST-INDIES, AFTER THE REVOLUTION, 1784

With clearance from Bellona won
She spreads her wings to meet the Sun,
Those golden regions to explore
Where George forbade to sail before.

Thus, grown to strength, the bird of Jove,
Impatient, quits his native grove,
With eyes of fire, and lightning's force
Through the blue aether holds his course.

No foreign tars are here allowed
To mingle with her chosen crowd,
Who, when returned, might, boasting, say
They shewed [sic] our native oak the way.

To that old track no more confined,
By Britain's jealous court assigned,
She round the Stormy Cape shall sail,
And, eastward, catch the odorous gale.

To countries placed in burning climes
And islands of remotest times
She now her eager course explores,
And soon shall greet Chinesian shores.

From thence their fragrant teas to bring
Without the leave of Britain's king;
And Porcelain ware, enchased in gold,
The product of that finer mould.

Thus commerce to our world conveys
All that the varying taste can please;
For us, the Indian looms are free,
And Java strips her spicy tree.

Great pile proceed!-and o'er the brine
May every prosperous gale be thine,
'Till freighted deep with Asia's stores,
You reach again your native shores.

Philip Freneau, 1780s

An early map of Asia, ca. 1851, by John Tallis

TARTARS.

RUSSIAN PEASANTS.

PETRA.

The Illustrations by J. Marchant, & Engraved by J. B. Allen.

ASIA.

THE WALRUS

SUN-BIRDS OF INDIA
AND THE PHILIPPINE ISLES

SCALE.

40 100 200   400   600   800   1000 Miles.

Longitude East 90 from Greenwich   110   130   150

The Map Drawn & Engraved by J. Rapkin.

J. TALLIS & COMPANY, LONDON & NEW YORK.

CHAPTER ONE

The New People

Hong Kong in 1996 does not look like a city on the verge. The skyline is a tangle of skyscrapers and cranes, the bamboo scaffolding the only reminder of the Asian earth from which the city arises. Landfill continues its march out into the harbor, whose blue-gray waters are crisscrossed with the wakes of a thousand boats. For almost 20 years, the city has been riding the crest of an economic boom; the impending governmental change seems to be no brake on investment.

From the top floors of one of those skyscrapers—a year ago it was on the waterfront; landfill now makes it a block inland—Hong Kong's American Club has a commanding view of the harbor, Kowloon and the mountain peaks of the New Territories beyond. Peregrine falcons wheel in front of the windows, their brown wings splayed as they circle for prey.

Now 70 years old, the American Club is the largest American social organization in East Asia; its prominence is an accurate reflection of United States influence in the region. Since its founding in 1925, it has prospered and suffered and prospered again, following the fortunes of Hong Kong and China. In the process, the American Club has become an important part of the long and glorious history of Americans in China. This history begins 215 years ago, when Hong Kong was only a barren rock with a few, tiny fishing villages, and the United States was young, poor, and very far away.

Exchange Square, the American Club's present home, is one of Hong Kong's most prestigious addresses

In 1781, the United States of America finally and decisively defeated the British Army at Yorktown. The Americans were free but, they discovered, near destitute. The economy was in ruins, and their markets in the British Empire's trade system had disappeared. Americans had to build up their economy any way they could. Under the circumstances, they were willing to consider dangerous and highly speculative expeditions to find new trading partners—halfway around the world if need be.

1781 was also the year that Captain James Cook's third and final expedition returned to England. Cook himself had been killed in the Hawaii Islands; his crew aboard the ships *Resolution* and *Discovery* continued the voyage, sailing up the Northwest Coast of America, across to Kamchatka, down to Canton and then home via the Cape of Good Hope. Among the crew were two young Americans, John Gore of Virginia and John Ledyard of Connecticut, the first Americans we have records of setting foot in China. Nearly every member of the crew kept a diary of his journey, and as soon as the ships returned, they raced to cash in on their experiences. One of these was Lieutenant John Rickman, with his *Journal of Captain Cook's last voyage to the Pacific Ocean*; another was John Ledyard, whose book was largely based on Rickman's.

Ledyard was an original, one of the first great American travellers. Born in 1751 at Groton, Connecticut, he was congenitally restless. He studied to be a lawyer and soon gave it up; he went to Dartmouth, studied to be a missionary and gave that up, too. Bored at Dartmouth, he built a canoe and sailed down the Connecticut River to the coast, where he planned to become a minister. A few weeks later, he hopped on a ship to England, telling friends he was determined to "ramble for seven years." In London, Ledyard heard that Captain Cook was preparing to embark on his third voyage and quickly secured himself a place as a corporal of the marines. His shipmates said that he had "a passion of lofty sentiment and description"; however, they did not include his writings in the shipboard newspaper because his ideas were "too sentimental" and his language was "too florid."

At the end of his life, an English friend gave this description of Ledyard:

To those who have never seen Mr. Ledyard it may not, perhaps, be uninteresting to know, that his person, though scarcely exceeding the middle size, was remarkably expressive of activity and strength; and that his manners, though unpolished, were neither uncivil nor unpleasing. Little attentive to difference of rank, he seemed to consider all men as equals, and as such he respected them. His genius, though uncultivated and irregular, was original and comprehensive. Ardent in his wishes, yet calm in his deliberations; daring in his purposes, but guarded in his measures; impatient of control, yet capable of strong endurance; adventurous beyond the conception of ordinary men, yet wary, and considerate, and attentive to all precautions, he appeared to be formed by Nature for achievements of hardihood and peril.

In short, John Ledyard was a prototypical American of his day.

Upon returning to London in 1781, Ledyard enlisted on a British warship heading to North America. The ship anchored off the Connecticut coast; Ledyard got shore leave and immediately went AWOL. After visiting friends and his aged mother—to whom seven years before he had neglected to say goodbye—he set out

Robert Morris (1734–1806)

for New York with an idea burning in his fervent brain.

This idea was sparked by his experiences and one line in Rickman's book (which was just beginning to circulate in the U.S.). The setting was Macau, just after the *Resolution* and *Discovery* had left Canton, when a messenger boat caught up with the ships:

"Here they learnt that the skins we had brought with us from the N.W. continent of America were of nearly double the value at Canton, as at Kamshatska."

For less than "sixpence sterling," Ledyard stated in his book, the expedition had bought hundreds of seal and other skins from Indians along the Oregon and Washington coasts and, to their immense surprise, sold them for "100 dollars" in Canton. Ledyard thought that American seamen could replicate this profit by sailing around the tip of South America and up to the Pacific Northwest to buy furs. In Canton, they would exchange the furs for tea—the favorite beverage of Americans—as well as silk and other precious goods and return to the United States to make their fortune.

Ledyard approached merchants in Boston, New York and Philadelphia and finally found a willing ear in Robert Morris, one of the signatories of the Declaration of Independence and the main financier of the Continental Army. Morris commissioned Ledyard to find a ship, but after a year it became obvious that a ship would eventually sail without Ledyard at its helm. Merchants apparently thought him too unreliable for the expedition. In disgust, Ledyard headed back to England and from there embarked on expeditions to Siberia and Africa. After arriving in Cairo, he took ill and died of a self-administered overdose of medicine. He was 38 years old.

While Ledyard was roaming around Russia, Robert Morris's China plans continued apace. With Ledyard gone, he quickly found a ship and hired Captain John Green to command and Major Samuel Shaw as supercargo, or business agent. Dubbed the *Empress of China* (probably to flatter the Chinese authorities), the 360-ton ship departed New York Harbor on February 22, 1784 loaded with 40 tons of ginseng roots and a couple of chests filled with Spanish silver dollars.

The costs for the boat, cargo and crew totalled the then-astronomical sum of $120,000.

This voyage was not an utterly blind gamble. Although they had been barred from trade with Asia by the Honourable East India Company, American colonists had a long tradition of seamanship, including their share of pirates and privateers. In the late 17th century, American pirates such as Captain Thomas Tew terrorized the shipping lanes of the Indian Ocean and captured many rich Mogul ships. American merchants also knew that there was a ready market for ginseng in China, because the East India Company, lacking a source in Europe, had long been shipping the American-grown root to the East.

The *Empress of China* sailed southeast across the Atlantic via the Cape Verde Islands to the Cape of Good Hope. The crew may have seen the ship *Harriet* that had departed Boston two months before the *Empress* and was also bound for

China. The *Harriet* would have won its place in history except that the captain had decided against the risky voyage to Canton and, instead, sold his cargo of ginseng in Cape Town for a modest profit. The *Empress* sailed on, across the Indian Ocean to the Straits of Sunda between Java and Sumatra, where it met two ships belonging to America's French allies, who escorted the vessel through treacherous waters up to Macau. For the first time, the Stars and Stripes, called by the Chinese the "Flowery Flag," waved in Chinese waters.

After presenting the Portuguese authorities with copies of treaties between the United States and the various European powers, the *Empress of China* sailed up the Pearl River to the anchorage at Huangpu 12 miles south of Canton. Their arrival was a surprise to the various European merchants gathered in Canton: They could not believe that a nation so new and on the fringes of the "civilized" world could prepare such an ambitious expedition.

Along the narrow strip of riverfront that was the foreign merchants' quarters, all the European rivalries were being replicated—relations between the French and the English were especially tense—and the Americans' arrival threw a wild card into the game. At first, the representatives of the East India Company, holder of the British monopoly on Asian trade and the largest trading firm in the region, were friendly. When word of the Americans' arrival finally reached London, however, the East India Company directors told their Canton agents to give no help whatsoever. For the Americans, however, China was one place where they were on an equal footing with the European powers.

"Thank God, the intrigues of a Christian court do not influence the wise decrees of the eastern world," wrote a Salem, Massachusetts newspaper correspondent. "Our pretensions there are equal;—nor is it in their power to prevent us sharing the most profitable trade, whenever we have the ability and spirit to build and fit our proper ships for the purpose."

The Chinese, for their part, had trouble understanding who these new arrivals were.

"Ours being the first American ship that had ever visited China," wrote Samuel Shaw in his journal, "it was some time before the Chinese could fully comprehend the distinction between Englishmen and us. They styled us the *New People,* and when, by the map, we conveyed to them an idea of the extent of our country, with its present and increasing population, they were not a little pleased at the prospect of so considerable a market for the productions of their own empire."

Shaw, the *Empress'* business agent, quickly encountered the realities of doing business in 18th-century China. Upon arrival in Huangpu, the ship was boarded by the "hoppo," or Chinese customs official, who immediately asked if the new

(continues on page 24)

Harbor of Hong Kong, *lithograph by Auguste Borget*

SOCIAL INTERCOURSE AND FRIENDLY ATTENTIONS

The factories at Canton, occupying less than a quarter of a mile in front, are situated on the bank of the river. The quay is enclosed by a rail-fence, which has stairs and a gate opening from the water to each factory, where all merchandise is received and sent away. The limits of the Europeans are extremely confined; there being, besides the quay, only a few streets in the suburbs, occupied by the trading people, which they are allowed to frequent. Europeans, after a dozen years' residence, have not seen more than what the first month presented to view. They are sometimes invited to dine with the Chinese merchants, who have houses and gardens on the opposite side of the river; but even then no new information is obtained. Every thing of a domestic concern is strictly concealed, and, though their wives, mistresses, and daughters are commonly there, none of them are ever visible. We dined with four of the cohoang, at separate times, two of whom entertained the French gentlemen and us at their country-houses. On these occasions, the guests generally contribute largely to the bill of fare. Both at Chowqua's and Pankekoa's, the French supplied the table furniture, wine, and a large portion of the victuals. The gardens belonging to Chowqua are expensive; much art and labor are used to give them a rural appearance, and in some instances nature is not badly imitated. Forests, artificial rocks, mountains, and cascades, are judiciously executed, and have a pleasing effect in diversifying the scene. The Chinese, however, discover a vitiated taste in their fondness for water. Every garden must have abundance of this element, and where it does not flow naturally, large, stagnant ponds, in the middle of which are summer-houses, supply the deficiency. Chowqua says that his house and gardens cost him upwards of one hundred thousand taels.

The Europeans at Canton do not associate together so freely as might be expected, . . . the gentlemen of the respective factories keeping much by themselves, and, excepting in a few instances, observing a very ceremonious and reserved behaviour. At the Danish factory, there is, every Sunday evening, a concert of instrumental music, by gentlemen of the several nations, which every body who pleases may attend. This is the only occasion when there appears to be any thing like a general intercourse. On the whole, the situation of the Europeans is not enviable; and, considering the length of time they reside in this country, the restrictions to which they must submit, the great distance they are at from their connections, the want of society, and of almost every amusement, it must be allowed that they dearly earn their money . . . .

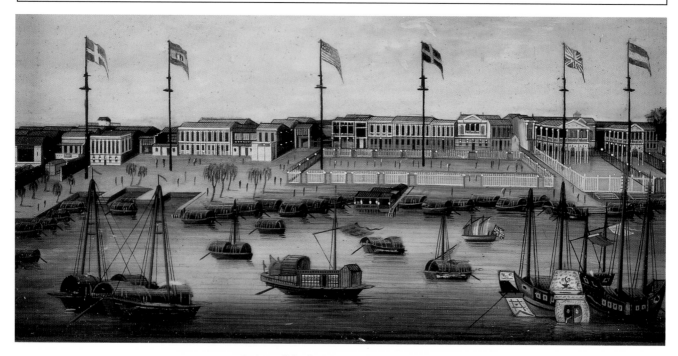

A view of the factories in Canton, ca. 1820

cx

About ten days previous to our leaving Canton, Mr. Randall and I visited the respective chiefs (a ceremony not to be omitted), thanked them for their civilities, and informed them of our intended departure. Invitations from every nation followed, and we were obliged to receive from each another public dinner and supper, the consul of France insisting also upon paying us this honor in his separate right. The attention paid us at all times by the Europeans, both in a national and personal respect, has been highly flattering. From the French it was peculiarly friendly. They aided us in mooring our ship, insisted on our making ourselves at home in their factory, and accommodated us with part of their bank-sall, for the use of which they would not suffer us to make them any remuneration. "If," said they, "we have in any instance been serviceable to you, we are happy,—and we desire nothing more than further opportunities to convince you of our affection."

The Swedes, the Danes, the Dutch, and the Imperialists paid us every proper attention; nor were the English behindhand with them. Besides the gentlemen of the factory, many of their captains visited us, gave invitations, and accepted ours in return. During this intercourse, it was not difficult to discover their jealousy of the French; nor could they conceal their dislike of the good understanding we kept up with them, which would sometimes appear, in spite of their breeding. One evening, in particular, at the English factory, after the company had risen from the table, the chief asked us if we could not take a sociable bottle together. This was a proposition to which we were not disposed to object, as he had always been particularly civil to us. In the course of our *tête-à-tête,* after professing much regard for us, and hoping that our nation and theirs would ever maintain a friendly correspondence, he observed, that there had been a small mistake in the *mode* of our reception, with respect to which he wished to set us right. "As soon as it was known," said he, "that your ship was arrived, we determined to show you every national attention; and when, in company with the French gentlemen, you returned our visit, it was our intention that *you* should dine with us the next day, and the *French* the day after. We were, therefore, not a little disappointed at your coming together, and you may remember we then told you there had been a mistake on your part, for which we were exceedingly sorry; for, trust me, gentlemen," added he, with a smile, "that *we* would not designedly have put you in such company."

-Samuel Shaw,
Memoirs of Major Samuel Shaw

Itinerant Food Vendors, Canton, *by Auguste Borget*

SHOPS, MANUFACTURES, AND ARTS

Shopping in Canton is not like that pastime, which ladies in search of the picturesque are so fond of pursuing in our own good cities. A stranger in China may go from one store to another every day in the year, and never meet a female face in any of them. Men, none but men, he sees at every turn. This might seem excusable in a tailor's stall, but it is too bad when carried into every trade.

The streets, as mentioned before, are extremely narrow. A broad one is no wider than a common alley, and a narrow one might be choked with a single dry goods box. On entering a street, one is completely at a loss to know where to find what he wants. The shops are uniform in size and appearance. They have no broad plate glass windows for the tempting show of goods "selling off at cost," and besides, the extreme similarity of many of the dealers themselves is not a little puzzling. We can tell what commodities are for sale within, only by peeping in at the open doors in a very suspicious and burglar-like manner.

The shops are all built upon a line, principally of wood, sometimes the lower story is of blue brick, and with the doors raised a single step from the street, Not unfrequently the river, which at its mean level is only a few feet below the street, rises and inundates all that part of the city fronting upon its banks. Every avenue is converted into a canal, every pedestrian into an amphibious animal, and the foreigners, whose hongs are built in separate parts of the city, take boats to go from their bed-rooms to breakfast, and throughout the day pursue their business by skimming over the water, and floating in to a silk or tea store, to make their bargains.

~Osmond Tiffany Jr.,
The Canton Chinese,
or the American's Sojourn in
the Celestial Empire

arrivals had brought any "sing-songs"—the wind-up clocks and mechanical toys he was accustomed to receiving as "gifts." Shaw explained that he was from a new country and had not known that these gifts were customary. The hoppo let him off with a warning and reminded him on the next trip not to return without the "sing-songs." This was the Americans' first experience of the "gratuities" and outright bribes—the corruption, as they saw it—without which no business deal in Canton could go forward.

The *Empress* spent two and a half months at dock in Huangpu while Shaw disposed of the ginseng and purchased tea and other wares for the journey home. During this stay, Shaw took copious notes on the ins and outs of doing business in Canton, on the European competition and on Chinese social customs. These notes reveal that the Americans were not naive newcomers but canny businessmen fully aware of their strengths and weaknesses and determined to use them to their advantage. Shaw refused to publish his journals during his lifetime, possibly because he considered them proprietary information most profitably kept to himself.

On December 28, 1784, the *Empress* set sail from Huangpu with a cargo hold filled with tea, silk, nankeen cotton and porcelain. She punctuated her arrival in New York Harbor on May 11, 1785 with a 13-gun salute and caused an immediate sensation. Almost every newspaper in the country printed an article Shaw wrote describing his voyage; politicians urged merchants to follow the *Empress'* example and embark on their own China expeditions; and poets such as Philip Freneau wrote paeans extolling the voyage as an example to the young and vigorous nation. Most importantly, the ship made a profit, estimated by Shaw at $30,727 on the initial $120,000 investment—not the huge reward foreseen by Ledyard, but more than respectable.

Merchants were not slow in following the *Empress*. Between 1784 and 1844, over 516 American sailing ships departed from United States ports bound for Canton. New York was the primary embarkation point, but numerous ships also left from Boston, Salem, Providence, the Connecticut coast, Philadelphia and Baltimore. The United States government considered this trade so important that they drastically lowered all tariffs and duties on the China trade.

The arrival of the *Empress* also began the craze for *chinoiserie*. Anything made in China was the rage. Robert Morris presented George Washington with a set of specially designed China ware, and before long even the humblest household could afford, and had, one or two Chinese tea

Street Traders, Macao, *by George Chinnery*

cups. Women promenaded in gowns made from Chinese silk while cooling themselves with Chinese fans. The houses of the rich had Chinese wallpaper and Chinese furniture upon which rested silver teapots and trays purchased in China. Americans felt that anything associated with China was beautiful, exotic and, compared to similar objects from Europe, cheap.

The majority of ships sailed directly to Canton with cargo holds filled with goods to tempt the Chinese merchants, including ginseng, tar, turpentine, rum, Madeira wine, tobacco and American-made cotton. Others followed Ledyard's advice and sailed up to the Northwest Coast and purchased skins from native tribes to sell in Canton. When the fur stocks became depleted, they turned to the Pacific coast of South America for seals and sea otter and also harvested *bêches de mer* (sea slugs), birds' nests and sandalwood from the South Sea islands.

With the fierce competition, however, the market for these goods was frequently glutted. Until letters of credit became accepted, merchants were forced to carry chests of Spanish silver dollars, seriously depleting their currency reserves. Finding a product for which the Chinese had a consistent demand was a perennial problem; in the early 19th century, following the British lead, American merchants would turn to a profitable but, even then, highly controversial commodity.

Even as American captains learned the route and the location of the reefs and shoals, the voyage remained a dangerous one. A number of ships capsized in storms—a whole genre of Canton maritime paintings was devoted to ships in peril. Pirates were a constant menace; French and British privateers lurked in the sea lanes, and ships were often attacked by powerful bands of Chinese pirates darting out from the coast of Guangdong Province. When tensions

Advertisement for Nathan Dunn's Chinese Museum in Pennsylvania, 1839

CATALOGUE OF
Canton Fans,
GRASS CLOTHS,
AND
FANCY GOODS,
Now landing from the Ship Howard, from Canton,
FOR SALE AT AUCTION,
ON TUESDAY, JUNE 5th, 1832,
AT TEN O'CLOCK,
By Mills, Brothers & Co.
At their Auction Store, corner of Wall and Pearl Streets,
NEW-YORK.

☞ Terms.....Four Months, Debenture in part Pay.
The Sale will commence with a few Articles belonging to the Supercargo.

SNOWDEN, PRINTER,.......58 WALL-STREET NEW-YORK.

between the United States and Britain again rose in the early 19th century, British warships claimed the right to search and seize American ships suspected of harboring deserters (better treatment of crews on American ships had indeed attracted deserters).

On arrival in Canton, American merchants faced a whole new set of problems, generally caused by the difficult relationship between the Chinese imperial government and Westerners. The Chinese Emperor ruled by divine right—the Mandate of Heaven—and this dominion extended not just over China but over the entire human race. All peoples living outside of the Chinese Empire, called the Middle Kingdom, were considered rude tribesmen, barbarians or *fan gui*—"foreign devils." Foreigners were expected to approach the imperial government humbly, with respect and bearing tribute. If they had the supreme honor to appear before the Emperor himself, they had to kowtow not once but three times—something few Westerners would do even for their own rulers.

The imperial government was not so self-centered as to deny the advantages of trade with the West. Since the arrival of Jesuits such as Matteo Ricci in the mid-16th century, the Chinese had been fascinated and a bit perturbed by the wide range of learning and technological innovation coming from Europe, including accurate clocks, faster and more seaworthy ships and maps of the world that revealed far more knowledge than their own. In the 1720s, the government decreed that just one port, Canton, would be open to foreign trade, and that under a series of formidable restrictions.

American ships first had to get a permit from Chinese officials at Macau to sail up the Pearl River. After mooring at Huangpu, they were boarded by the hoppo, the imperial customs officer, who charged them a hefty fee (about $4000 in the early 19th century) that was the same no matter the size of the boat. The freight was off-loaded and shipped up to Canton, where it was stored in one of the foreign "factories"—long buildings that served as warehouses, offices and

The ship Houqua, *ca. 1841, by Thomas Birch (1779–1851)*

Wallpaper fragment showing two boys fighting. Made for export before 1796, such wallpaper reflects America's penchant for Chinese decor at that time

home to the Westerners—until it could be sold. Foreigners could only do business with the *co-hong*, a group of about 12 Chinese merchants (*hongs*), who had the imperial license for this trade and were the actual owners of the factories. They also had to hire a Chinese *comprador*, Portuguese for "buyer," to handle their day-to-day affairs—buying food, etc.—and to limit their association with the local population.

Originally, Westerners could only stay in Canton during the shipping season from October through March; off-season, they had to retire to Macau. In Canton, their movements were tightly restricted. The 13 foreign factories were relegated to a stretch of riverbank just outside the city walls. Merchants could only leave their 1,000-foot-wide quarter with written permission of the hoppo. Western women, even wives, were forbidden, as were weapons and rowing on the river. Three times a month, foreigners were allowed to take an excursion to a nearby garden and Buddhist temple. For the rest of the month, they had to content themselves with strolling up and down the square dividing the factories from the river.

One of the peculiarities of this arrangement was that none of it was secured by formal treaties between China and any of the Western nations. In Canton, there were foreign consuls, generally the most prominent merchants—Samuel Shaw was the first American consul—but no fully-accredited embassies either there or in Beijing. The Emperor was too distant and too exalted to deal with barbarians' problems, so foreign merchants lived and worked at the whim of the endemically corrupt provincial government.

To make matters worse, foreigners could not approach government officials directly but had to do so through one of the hongs—a problematic task if one's problem was with the hong. In criminal matters, they were subject to the frequently arbitrary will of authority. In 1821, Francis Terranova, an Italian sailor aboard an American ship, was accused of tossing overboard a clay pot that struck and killed a Chinese woman in a boat below. The captain and the rest of the American community did not believe he was the culprit; nevertheless, he was tried and found guilty without being able to testify in his own defense. When the American merchants protested, government officials threatened to cut off trade and eject them from Canton.

Linchong's Basket Shop, *ca. 1820*

Inside a Chinese Court at Canton, 1807, *attributed to Spoilum. Until the Treaty of Nanjing granted extraterritoriality to Westerners, Americans were subject to Chinese law*

Chinese fishmonger, ca. 1820

American trading company for the first three decades of the 19th century.

Houqua's name, wealth and reputation as a friend of Americans soon became famous in the United States. Returning merchants hung his portrait in their mansions, and Houqua memorabilia became the star attraction of a China museum that opened in Philadelphia in 1839. Houqua's American ties also led him to invest in the construction of railroads in the western United States; his U.S. agent was Russell & Company, which had bought out Perkins in 1829. After his death, Russell & Company christened one of their ships the *Houqua* as a sign of their respect.

The Americans attributed their success to good business sense, the freedom from government interference and to a different attitude toward other races. The contrast, as always, was with the British. The Americans had no empire; the British had ruled India for over a century and had institutionalized a superior attitude toward the subject races. Transported to Canton, this attitude also governed and often exacerbated their relations with the Chinese, who, as we have seen, also considered themselves the superior race. On his 1784 visit to China, Samuel Shaw recounts the following tale of bargaining with a local shop owner:

The Americans finally gave in—the fact that their ship was carrying illegal opium may have been a factor—and Terranova was executed by strangulation. This was not the first nor the last time the imperial government used this threat to keep foreign merchants in line.

Despite these problems, American merchants in Canton prospered. By the early 19th century, they were the second most prominent trading group after the merchants of the East India Company. The independent American traders who had plied the sea in the late 18th century were gradually replaced by trading companies like Thomas Perkins & Company. Perkins' first Canton representative was John Perkins Cushing, who took charge at age 16 after the intended manager drowned shortly after arrival.

At this tender age, Cushing quickly became one of the most respected businessmen in Canton. He was soon recognized as a just arbiter of disputes, and his word was considered binding. Cushing also became a great friend of Houqua, Canton's richest and most prominent hong merchant. He frequently visited Houqua's mansion, and the merchant tutored him in the intricacies of the China trade. With Houqua's help, Perkins & Company established itself as the dominant

A hong merchant

"I treated him politely every time, and adhered to my first demand, with which he finally complied. After the bargain was settled,—'You are not Englishman?' said he. 'No.' 'But you speak English word, and when you first come, I no can tell difference; but now I understand very well. When I speak Englishman his price, he say, "So much,—take it,—let alone." I tell him, "No, my friend, I give you so much." He look at me, —"Go to hell, you damned rascal; what! you come here,—set a price my goods?" Truly, Massa [Taipan], I see very well you no [have] Englishman. All China-man very much love your country.' Thus far, it may be supposed, the fellow's remarks pleased me.

Justice obliges me to add his conclusion:—'All men come first time China very good gentlemen, all same you. I think two three time more you come Canton, you make all same Englishman too.'"

On issues like race—and politics—the Americans made sure that the Chinese knew that they were *not* British, and this undoubtedly furthered their commercial interests. On the other hand, American traders recognized that the British were the dominant Western power in China, and, at certain times of crisis during the 19th century, they were happy to have their investments protected by the might of the Royal Navy.

For their part, the British keenly felt the threat of American competition. Beginning in 1813, British trading firms in London began to protest against the East India Company monopoly, pointing to the success of the free-wheeling American traders. For example, in the 1820s American merchants were purchasing British woolens in England and selling them in Canton for less than the East India Company. The protests increased in frequency and volume, and in 1834 the East India Company was finally dissolved, due in part to American competition.

America's success with the China trade produced huge benefits back home. Between 1785 and 1845, merchants involved in the China trade were among the richest men in the country and some built the basis of family fortunes that continue today, including the Astor family. China traders built huge mansions in cities like Boston, New York and Philadelphia, and invested their profits in the construction of railroad lines, such as the Michigan Central and the Chicago, Burlington and Quincy systems. The China trade provided American businessmen with capital at a crucial time in their history, and without it, the United States would have been a lesser place.

Sea Battle Between Government Gunboats and Pirates I, *early 19th century, artist unknown*

The China trade was also the spur for the annexation of California, which in the early 19th century was still part of the Spanish colony of Mexico. In 1803, the *Lelia Byrd,* a Salem ship seeking sea otter skins to sell in Canton, landed in San Diego Bay, and United States citizens stepped for the first time on Californian soil. The fur trade was illegal under Spanish colonial trade rules, but neither the Californians nor the Americans had any reservations about pursuing it *sub rosa.* After the sea otter population declined due to over-hunting, merchants discovered a market in Canton for Californian cattle hides and beef tallow, once again purchased on the black market.

After Mexico won its independence from Spain in 1820, the new government opened San Diego and Monterey to foreign trade. American (and British) merchants immediately set up agencies there to purchase hides and tallow for shipment to China. Some Americans married into local cattle-ranching dynasties and soon were among the richest men in the territory. One American trader was Richard Henry Dana, whose 1840 book *Two Years Before the Mast* is written about a hide-collecting expedition on the California coast. As accounts of California's riches began to appear in the East, settlers began to make the arduous trek across the Rockies to the new promised land. In less than a decade, California was part of the United States.

By the 1820s, China traders in Canton were feeling established enough to take some risks. Previously, no passengers had been allowed on the ships except for the supercargo and company personnel bound for China. In 1807, an American ship had defied this ban (the East India Company had refused) and had carried Robert Morrison of the London Missionary Society to Canton as the first Protestant missionary to China. Americans had since followed Morrison's career with intense interest, and now they were themselves determined to "Go . . . into all the world, and preach the gospel to every creature."

The United States had been colonized by devout Puri-

A map of Canton Province, ca. 1655

tans fleeing repression in the British Isles. As a colony and then as a nation, the country was periodically swept by religious revivals that not only intensified believers' faith in Protestant Christianity but led them to conclude, particularly after the Revolution, that their nation had been singled out by God for a special purpose. Missionaries headed west to preach the Word to pagan Indian tribes. When Canton became a regular American port-of-call, it was natural for Christian groups to plan to send not only God's Word but the American ideals of progress and individual freedom to the "heathen Chinee."

In 1829, a devout American trader in Canton named David Olyphant offered to give free passage and room and board to any missionaries wanting to spread the faith. The American Board of Commissioners for Foreign Missions (ABCFM) leapt at the chance. In February of 1830, the first two American missionaries to China arrived—Rev. David Abeel and Rev. Elijah Bridgman. They took up quarters in the Olyphant & Company rooms and began their work. Abeel was chaplain to American residents and seamen, while Bridgman opened a small school for boys. In the eyes of both, however, the real prize was the conversion of the Chinese to Christianity.

A Village on the Canals of Canton, Macao, *by Auguste Borget*

Christianity, in the form of Catholic missionaries (and a few Russian Orthodox priests in the North), had been in China continuously since the 16th century. First Portuguese, then French and Italian priests had had some successes in China; they had opened churches and by 1800 gained at least 200,000 converts spread throughout the country. This number, however, was substantially less than a century before. The Catholic missionaries had been weakened by problems at home, particularly the decline of the Portuguese Empire, the 1773 suspension of the Jesuit order and the constant European wars which drained money and energy from the missionary movement.

Missionaries also faced substantial problems on the Chinese side. At best, the imperial government tolerated them; at worst, they were persecuted and often martyred. Missionaries were the target of rumors accusing them of plotting uprisings and, with more justification, of discouraging converts' participation in seasonal festivals and rites of ancestor worship. In doing this, they broke the crucial familial bonds that were the basis of the Confucian system. Priests were also accused of killing the sick while administering the last rites and then stealing the body parts for arcane and evil ceremonies. Facing ignorance, prejudice and imperial oppression, the American missionaries had an uphill battle ahead of them.

If you judge Elijah Bridgman and David Abeel by the number of Chinese converts, they were utter failures. After five years, they had none. Their influence, however, was much greater in other areas. Known as "Zion's Corner," their rooms in the Olyphant & Company section of the American factory became a center of the Western Christian community. In addition to running his school, Bridgman began to print a magazine called *The Chinese Repository* which contained news not only on missions but on Chinese events and culture. Copies reached the United States and became a basis for the field of Sinology, then in its infancy. Abeel left Canton after a year, visited the East Indies and then embarked on a lecture tour of the United States and Europe to drum up support for missions to China. By the mid-1830s, a trickle began that soon turned into a flood.

Poontinghua's Garden at Puntong, Canton,
mid-19th century

Temples of Macao, ca. 1830, by William Prinsep

By far the most renowned—among both the foreign and Chinese populations—early American missionary in China was Dr. Peter Parker. Parker had graduated from Yale with dual divinity and medical degrees and the conviction that it was his "duty and privilege" to become a missionary in China. In 1834, the ABCFM sent him out on an Olyphant boat to tend to the medical and spiritual needs of the American community in Canton. One year later (with less than a week's experience in a New York eye hospital), he opened his famous Ophthalmic Hospital treating the numerous eye complaints of Canton's Chinese community.

Crowds began lining up at the hospital gate the night before, and both rich and poor were treated equally. Parker did not charge fees, and all gifts, even the most lavish, were refused. He had particular success treating cataracts and tumors that Chinese traditional medicine had no way of destroying. His achievements were chronicled by the famous local artist Lamqua, who painted a series of before-and-after paintings depicting patients with large tumors and then with the growths gone.

Through his practice, Parker became friends with numerous provincial government officials. In the 1840s, he accompanied the American envoy Caleb Cushing to negotiation sessions with those same officials and helped the United States gain an extremely favorable treaty, which, among other things, allowed Americans to build "Temples of Worship." His wife, Harriet, also became the first American woman legally allowed to live in Canton.

By the late 1830s, the American missionaries were busy and organized, banding together with the British to strengthen their work. Their most important task was to translate Christian works into Chinese. Robert Morrison had begun that work; now they completed the translation of the Bible and also published Chinese versions of Aesop's Fables, histories of Europe and the United States and, as always, religious tracts. Another group, the Morrison Education Society, opened a school for Chinese pupils and began to make plans to send Chinese students to the United States or one of the British colonies. Encouraged by Peter Parker's success, the Medical Missionary Society found a permanent home for the Ophthalmic Hospital in one of Houqua's buildings and convinced the doctor to open a branch hospital in Macau.

At the same time as these successes, the American missionaries were placed in a difficult position by one, highly-profitable aspect of the China trade: the importation of opium into China. On the one hand, the missionaries agreed with the imperial government: Opium was evil. On the other, their position in Canton depended on the profits of their patrons, the importers of that same opium. The missionaries tried to intervene between the Chinese and the for-

AN OPIUM CLIPPER

As we anchored in Macao roads, we saw a heavy armed brig going about two knots to our one. She overhauled us, and went past like a flash, dropped her anchor, rounded to, and fired her guns.

She had no name on her stern, and we concluded that she was an American government brig. In an instant her yards were swarming with men, and the sails were furled in man-of-war time and precision. We soon learned that she was an opium clipper, carrying twenty heavy guns, and a crew to match.

Besides the men and officers, the smuggler employs a "schroff" or assayer, a native whose music has been the jingle of dollars, and whose sight is so keen that he can look further into a lump of sycee silver than any ordinary gazer.

The vessel makes sail with a freight of the "pernicious drug," and wherever an opportunity presents along the line of the coast, she anchors, and a trade is at once begun with the Chinese, who are always ready for the bait.

The chests are brought up on deck, the opium examined, and paid for in the unalloyed metal, the schroff turns over every piece, and hammers into it with an iron spike, and having thoroughly tested and valued it, the bargain is made, the opium sent over the ship's side, and the vessel proceeds on her errand. If the location is a good one, and the flats bite fast, the clipper remains several days dodging about the same spot, and if the government junks are disposed to meddle and look too curiously into her affairs, the ports are thrown wide open just to show her spunk.

-Osmond Tiffany Jr.,
*The Canton Chinese, or the American's Sojourn
in the Celestial Empire*

eign merchants, ineffectually, and in 1839 the disagreement came to a head.

The British had been exporting opium to China since the 1720s. At first, the quantities had been relatively small and the quality low, the drug generally coming from Turkey and the nearby countries of Asia Minor. However, the problem for foreign merchants had always been finding a commodity for which there was a market in China. They could not afford to continue sending casks of Spanish dollars in ever-increasing quantities. In opium, they had a product that the Chinese not only wanted but to which they were addicted.

The British seized on this opportunity by developing extensive poppy fields in their Indian colony. The East India Company ships sailed directly from India to Canton with holds filled with opium chests. This naturally distressed the imperial government, which had been campaigning to abolish the use of the drug. In 1796, they outlawed the trade and use of opium but to no avail; captains merely bribed the authorities or off-loaded their cargo to smuggling ships at the island of Lingding 40 miles downstream. Opium became the most profitable export to China, and the basis for the East India Company's profits. At the height of the trade in the 1836, the British alone exported to Canton over 23,000 chests of opium each weighing 130 to 160 pounds—over three million pounds worth.

American merchants never reached these levels; nevertheless, they were second to the British in the volume of their opium exports to China. The opium was generally purchased in Turkey and then sent to New York, where it was loaded on ships heading to Canton. American ships bound for China also picked up Indian opium on consignment from British firms. Because of these mixed shipments—and the fact that merchants did not advertise their illegal trade—it is hard to total American involvement in the opium trade. The best guess is that around 10 percent of opium brought to Canton was carried on American ships.

Numerous American trading companies, most prominently Russell & Company, depended on the opium trade. The Americans justified this business by saying, essentially, that if it was good enough for the East India Company, it was good enough for them. Aside from the missionaries, however, there were some prominent merchants in Canton who actively campaigned against the trade. The anti-opium campaigns of David Olyphant (one might have guessed) and his partner, Charles King, almost caused them to be ejected from the community.

By 1838, the Chinese Emperor had had enough. Hundreds of thousands of his subjects were addicts, including many soldiers in his own imperial army; corruption from the opium trade had weakened his hold over the bureaucracy; and now more precious silver was flowing out of China than in. He appointed an imperial commissioner to stop the opium smokers and smugglers and end the importation of opium by Western ships.

When Chinese officials in Canton heard of Commissioner Lin's impending arrival, they decided to prove that they were taking their duties seriously. They arrested the owner of an opium den, brought him to the square in front of the foreign factories and prepared to strangle him to death. When the Western merchants saw what was about to happen, they realized that the Chinese were trying to humiliate them. They quickly gathered together and, with American trader William Hunter as their spokesman, went to confront the official. The square was their recreation ground, they said, duly leased from the local government, and they would not allow it to be desecrated. All this land was property of the Emperor, replied the mandarin, and he was carrying out orders from senior provincial officials.

At this point, a group of British sailors appeared in the square and decided to make a preemptive strike. They attacked the jailers and any Chinese within reach and destroyed the official's tent, table and tea service. The Chinese party hurriedly departed down a side street, where they summarily dispatched the prisoner. They also organized a counter-attack; within a short time the factories were besieged by a mass of people described by Hunter as "many thousands of vagabonds, who kept an incessant attack on windows and gates with stones and brickbats."

The siege lasted into the evening, and the Westerners were just preparing to sally out to defeat the mob, when William Hunter and Gideon Nye, another American, managed to reach the mansion of their friend Houqua by sneaking over the rooftops. Houqua dispatched a messenger to the local magistrate, who sent a troop of soldiers to disperse the mob with whips and the power of imperial authority. The next day, the factories returned to business as usual, at least on the surface.

Below the surface, however, the incident had exposed ugly and dangerous tensions. By interrupting the execution, the Westerners had shown their contempt for Chinese authority. The subsequent riot had exposed the hatred the local population felt for the foreign devils. The situation could only get worse.

Commissioner Lin arrived in Canton in March, 1839 and within a week had issued an order that Chinese and foreigners must stop their trade in opium and hand over all stores of the drug. Despite the pleading of the hong merchants, including Houqua, the traders refused—the drug was not

(left) William C. Hunter;
(below) A view of Hong Kong

theirs, they said, only being held on consignment. In retaliation, Lin ordered the arrest of Lancelot Dent, of Dent & Company, one of the leading opium traders. When the foreigners refused, Lin upped the ante. The Chinese staff were ordered to leave the factories; the river opposite the square was blocked by an line of war junks; and soldiers in the square and surrounding streets kept the foreigners penned in the factories. No foreigners were allowed to leave, and, worse, no business would be transacted until every last chest of opium was surrendered. Faced with Commissioner's hard-line approach, there was little doubt that this would eventually happen.

The siege lasted six weeks, during which the Westerners had to feed themselves, wash their clothing and sweep the factory floors—tasks to which they were completely unaccustomed. After repeated failures at boiling eggs and cooking rice, the American traders managed to survive on food smuggled in by Houqua's coolies. Indeed, with their forced confinement and copious supplies arriving every evening,

they suffered more from over-eating than from the lack of food. At night, the Chinese soldiers banged gongs and drums, keeping up such a racket that the traders could not sleep. Despite their privations, however, the Americans did not see the siege as a penalty but as an opportunity.

They were not the main targets of Commissioner Lin's campaign—the British were. During the siege, the foreign community was led by Captain Charles Elliot, the British Chief Superintendent of Trade in Canton, who had agreed that the British government would take responsibility for all opium owned by British merchants—and all opium held on consignment by American traders. For the merchants this was welcome news, because now they could petition the British government for compensation on their losses.

The Americans sent their consul, Peter Snow, to inform Commissioner Lin that the opium was not theirs but belonged to the British. Neither the United States nor any of its colonies has ever produced opium, he said, and made a weak pledge never to engage in future trafficking. Somehow, Lin never discovered that the Americans still held 50 cases of Turkish opium, which, one assumes, were later discreetly sold. The British, on the other hand, had to promise never to deal in opium on penalty of death, and 16 of its most prominent traders were forever banned from doing business in Canton.

Finally, on May 20 almost three million pounds of opium were destroyed by mixing it in huge trenches with water, salt and lime and then washing the resulting sludge out to sea. The only Westerner invited to this ceremony was an American, Charles King, as a sign of respect for his anti-opium stand. Instead of solving the opium problem, however, Lin's actions had only made it worse.

Lin lifted the ban, expecting the trade in legal goods to resume, but Captain Elliot ordered all British citizens to retire to Macau. By confining the Crown representative, Commissioner Lin had insulted the British nation. Not only that, the opium merchants were demanding repayment for their losses and the legalization of the opium trade to Canton and to the rest of China as well. The British decided that the only way to force the imperial government to recognize their claims was to use the might of the Royal Navy.

Meanwhile, Canton was abandoned—except by the Americans. Having established good relations with Commissioner Lin, they were free to stay and do business. Business was very good. British trade to China did not stop; now the Americans, led by Russell & Company, acted as Canton agents for British traders. In doing so, they frequently straddled the boundaries of legality: On arriving at Macau, the ship's flag was changed from British to American, with only a dubious bill of sale acting as proof of ownership. The ship then sailed up to Huangpu to sell its goods. The British got their profit, and the Americans raked in fat commissions. Commissioner Lin was aware of what was happening and protested; however, far more serious events were demanding his attention.

In July, a group of drunken sailors ashore in what is now Kowloon killed a Chinese man. Commissioner Lin demanded that the British give up the culprit; Elliot refused and Lin sent a troop of soldiers toward Macau to oust the British. Rather than risk the lives of women and children, Elliot placed the entire British community, numbering several hundred, on a fleet of ships and sailed for Hong Kong on August 15, 1839. From this point began the British occupation of Hong Kong Island.

While the Americans traded, the British and Chinese continued to fight. A dispute over the food and water supply to the British led to a September 4th naval battle in Hong Kong harbor in which five junks were sent to the bottom. The British set up camp on Hong Kong Island, and their troops had numerous small skirmishes with Chinese soldiers and peasant militias on the mainland.

Finally, in June 1840, the British fleet arrived; its most celebrated ship was the *Nemesis,* a steam-driven vessel which, together with other steamers, devastated the antiquated Chinese navy. Over the next six months, the fleet blockaded the Bogue (the mouth of the Pearl River), destroyed numerous Chinese forts, captured Zhoushan and even threatened Beijing by appearing off the nearby port of Tianjin. The Emperor, through his emissary Qishan, persuaded the British to return south, where they were willing to negotiate. Before discussions began, Captain Elliot destroyed the Chinese forts at the Bogue as a way of emphasizing his power.

By the end of January, 1841, Elliot had forced the Chinese to sign a draft treaty ceding Hong Kong to Britain and agreeing to the withdrawal of the British from Zhoushan and the payment of six million Spanish dollars as restitution for the destruction of the opium. The treaty marked the beginning of Britain's century-long position as the dominant Western player in China.

For now, the Americans followed a dual track in China: On the one hand, they would cultivate the imperial government, pointing out how they, unlike the European powers, respected Chinese law and in negotiations preferred friendly discussion to force. On the other, they were only too happy to follow in the wake of British might, taking advantage of new openings for trade and establishing long-lasting relationships with British firms.

CHAPTER TWO

The Treaty Ports

On the morning of January 26, 1841, the British flag was raised on Hong Kong Island. Captain Charles Elliot unilaterally declared Hong Kong a British possession. Neither the British nor the Chinese governments were happy with his choice. The Emperor naturally did not want to give up a piece of his realm; back in London, Lord Palmerston described Hong Kong as "a barren island with hardly a house upon it." The British had wanted an island but had been hoping for something larger and not so close to the Chinese mainland —Taiwan would have been perfect. As soon as London heard the news—months after the fact—Elliot was fired.

While Elliot's replacement, Sir Henry Pottinger, sailed east, the British began to settle on their island. Palmerston

Aberdeen Street Looking North, 1846, *by Murdoch Bruce. The American flag probably belongs to Russell & Co.'s premises*

was exaggerating; it was not totally barren, and a handful of houses did dot the shores. The largest settlement was a fishing village of 2,000 Hakkas at the site of today's Stanley, and about a dozen smaller hamlets dotted the coast. Nearly all of the inhabitants were dirt-poor fishermen, except for a few stone cutters at a small quarry on the east side of the island. Inland—uphill—the island was all rock, scrub and, in the ravines, jungle. Waterfalls coursed down the hillside; there would be enough water for the settlers. Hong Kong's main—some said only—attraction was the harbor, with its deep water anchorages protected from typhoons by the island's mountainous ridge. It would do, for now.

The land at the north side of Hong Kong Island was divided into lots and sold to merchants and property speculators. One merchant was Charles Gillespie, lately of Macau, who became the first American resident of Hong Kong. Gillespie was hired by Captain Thomas Larkins to be manager of his godown at 46 Victoria Avenue (soon to become Queen's Road). In July 1841, Gillespie was advertising the godown as a sort of general store selling textiles and a variety of provisions and building supplies from wine to nails. He was also hired by the American traders in Canton to be their Hong Kong agent. By early 1842, he had erected an elegant home called Jorrocks Hall across the street from the godown. Gillespie's boom was short-lived; within a year he was forced to sell his house and retreat to Canton to escape from creditors.

Other American pioneers in Hong Kong were Rev. Jehu Lewis Shuck and his wife, the pious (some would say sanctimonious) Henrietta, who had arrived in China in 1836. A Baptist, Shuck had been snubbed by the other Protestant missionaries in Macau and Canton. He had his revenge by actually converting a Chinese man to Christianity, but the convert back-slid into traditional beliefs after 18 months, returning the number of converts by American missionaries in the 1830s to zero.

British missionaries had already scouted out Hong Kong, but when Shuck arrived in early 1842 he immediately began constructing the island's first Christian church on Queen's Road and another in the Bazaar, the heart of the Chinese quarter. Shuck also followed in the journalistic tradition of other American missionaries and founded Hong Kong's first newspaper, the *Friend of China,* which published its first issue on March 24, 1842. The *Friend of China* quickly came out against the opium trade; its pro-opium competitor, the *China Mail,* appeared in 1845, bankrolled by the English firm of Dent's, among others.

Like her husband a native of Virginia, Henrietta Shuck was the first American woman to live in Hong Kong. Her brand of Christianity admitted no compromises, and she quickly acquired a reputation for getting in theological arguments with the less dogmatic British citizenry. In 1842, she started a small school to educate her own children that also took in Chinese boys and girls. Within two years it was housed in a new building and taught over 30 students. Mrs. Shuck died in childbirth in 1844, but her contribution as the pioneer of education in Hong Kong is commemorated by the naming of the Henrietta School.

While the infant colony took its first steps, tensions continued to be high between Britain and China. It soon became obvious that the Emperor would not accept the agreement with Elliot. The Chinese negotiator, Qishan, was returned to Beijing in chains. Elliot sent his fleet up the Pearl River again, forced his way past the Chinese defenses and occupied Canton. Local officials were forced to sign a new, more onerous treaty; the British could now resume trade to Canton and, more openly, the shipments of opium. For London, however, this was not enough. Elliot's demands had always been too low, they thought, and his methods too desirous of avoiding bloodshed. In August 1841, Elliot's replacement, Sir Henry Pottinger, arrived with greatly improved naval firepower at his heels.

(continues on page 50)

A VILE SINNER

I had a long conversation, yesterday afternoon, with an English gentleman, who is intelligent in the things of this world, but manifests a woeful ignorance of the plan of redemption. He told me he believed that there is a God, a heaven, but *no hell;* and that was *'fudge'* concerning the punishment of the wicked hereafter. He made many such harsh and wild remarks. I told him plainly what I knew, and what I thought he might expect, except he should repent of his sins, and seek pardon from a merciful but just God. He thought me a fanatic, and I thought him what is worse. He rose to leave, after some time, and said, 'Well, Mrs. Shuck, I'll leave your delusion—'tis all a dream.' Said I, 'Happy for you were it so'; and we parted, when I most devoutly prayed to God to cause him to see himself a *vile sinner.*"

–J.B. Jeter,
*Memoir of Mrs Henrietta Shuck:
The First American Female Missionary to China*

PERMANENT AMERICANS

The Wild East of Hong Kong's early years, as colorful and hazardous as the Wild West, drew a steady stream of Americans to these shores, missionaries seeking souls, merchants seeking trade, soldiers and sailors, beachcombers, honest laborers, and more than a handful of downright villains. Some stayed for a few days, and some for a few decades, but several hundred will stay in Hong Kong forever—"permanent residents" of the old colonial cemetery in Happy Valley.

Hallowed and blessed is the memory of the good. So reads the epitaph of Henrietta Shuck, first woman missionary in China. She was born in Virginia in 1817, the daughter of a Southern Baptist minister, and departed for Macau shortly after her marriage to Reverend Jehu Lewis Shuck in 1835. Henrietta was not allowed to accompany her husband to Canton, but she started a mission school in Macau for Chinese children, girls as well as boys, a progressive idea which made her something of an innovator. In March 1842, the Shucks moved to the booming new town of Hong Kong, where the Reverend helped set up the *Friend of China,* the colony's first newspaper. Henrietta seems to have spent much of her time nursing other missionaries as well as running her school and household, but her own health had been broken by a serious illness in 1838 and the rigors of frequent pregnancy—in 1844, she died at age 27, after giving birth to her fifth child in eight years.

The cemetery at Happy Valley, however, was not estab-lished until the following year. Thus, Henrietta Shuck was buried in the City of Victoria's original graveyard, in Wanchai where St. Francis Yard now stands. It was not until 1889 that her bones were moved to their present resting place in Happy Valley, together with about fifty other burials from the colony's earliest years.

The lethal combination of debilitating climate and a host of endemic or epidemic diseases brought many other Americans, like Mrs. Shuck, to an early grave in Hong Kong. Some were Americans who had never actually seen "home," like little Jeannette Jordan off the ship *Fanny Fern,* buried on July 9, 1863, aged three; or Bessie Haskell, daughter of the sometime American consul in Huangpu, born at sea in 1859, dead in Canton in 1869, and buried in Hong Kong. But many others who arrived with high hopes in adulthood found that age did not protect them; in those days, Hong Kong could be hazardous to anyone's health, old or young, rich or poor.

A cluster of Americans who died in the second half of 1870 illustrates the point. In July, an inquest was held on John Henry Thompson, cook and steward off the American ship *Lawrence,* who collapsed suddenly at a modest boarding house frequented by his compatriots; his death was attributed simply to chronic diseases of the heart and lungs. In August, Police Constable William West died of apoplexy—a brain hemorrhage or stroke—after participating in a police sweep of the hills behind Central. He was only 20, but a stout young man; he was thought to have over-exerted himself because of the "chaffing" of his fellow constables. In October, Edward Marsden Martin of New York City, presumably a prosperous businessman, died of consumption at the respectable Stag Hotel, several cuts above the lowly establishment where John Henry Thompson died.

On November 5th, the prominent ship- and dock-owner James B. Endicott died at the age of 56. Born in Massachusetts, descendant of the first governor of that state and member of a great shipping family, Endicott had survived the hazards of life in Hong Kong, Canton and Macau for thirty-seven years but typhoid claimed him in the end. He was a close associate of

The Protestant cemetery, Happy Valley, ca. 1873

(continues on next page)

Thomas Hunt of Salem, one of the pioneer dock-owners at Whampoa, and the employer of little Bessie Haskell's father. Hunt died in May of the same year—1870—but he had the relative good fortune to do so in Salem.

If illness didn't kill you, the sea might. Naturally, almost by definition, few shipwreck victims receive a decent burial ashore; but Elizabeth Abbe of Boston managed this difficult feat in 1863. A doctor's wife, she survived the wreck of the *Hotspur* and drifted for many days in an open boat until picked up by the *Victor Canning* in February, and brought to Hong Kong; but the long exposure, working on a system already frail from illness, was ultimately fatal, and she was buried in Happy Valley on April 4th.

In the close quarters of the sailing ships, it was all too common for violence to break out, or tyranny to go too far. On the appropriate date of July 4, 1857—the same day as the American pirate Eli Boggs came up for trial in the same dock—the captain, mates, carpenter and steward of the American ship *John Wade* were tried for murder. The victim was Jacob Lauder, a seaman on the same ship, interred in Happy Valley the previous month. The evidence showed "a most revolting series of cruelties perpetrated on the deceased and all the crew, principally by the second mate," but the court was lenient—the carpenter and steward were acquitted, and the others found guilty of manslaughter and sentenced to transportation, presumably back to the States.

Piracy had been rampant in South China waters for centuries, and posed a grave threat to the commerce of the new colony. On September 23, 1866, for example, the American schooner *Lubra* was captured by pirates in a vicious attack that left two crewmen dead: the captain, Benjamin P. Howes, and a seaman named Nichols. Details are sketchy, but the ship must have been released soon after she was looted, since Howes and Nichols were buried in Happy Valley only two days later. At least one of their attackers was brought to justice, a pirate named Leong Sin Kit, who was tried in November for piracy and murder, and hanged in December. In a sad footnote, the grave of Captain Howes was reopened on November 12th to receive the body of his infant daughter, Genevieve.

Naturally, the American and British navies did not stand idly by while pirates preyed on the local shipping. In 1855, when the steam frigate USS *Powhatan* was in Hong Kong for repairs, the first great Anglo-American counterstroke was organized. Men and boats from the *Powhatan* joined the steam sloop HMS *Rattler* in attacking a powerful fleet of some thirty armed pirate junks off Kuhlan Bay on August 4th, sinking ten and killing upwards of 800 pirates, at the cost of four dead Englishmen and five dead Americans. Three of the latter—John Pepper, Benjamin Adamson, and Samuel Mullard—were buried in Happy Valley, the others presumably at sea. The

names of all nine were recorded on a monument that stood at the corner of Leighton and Morrison Hill Roads, and was the gathering point for funeral processions until it was relocated in a largely military section inside the cemetery during this century.

Of course these were not the only USN personnel to achieve a burial ashore in Happy Valley. The first was John Goodwin, off the steam frigate USS *Susquehanna,* on August 9, 1853. He was rapidly joined by five of his shipmates, and over the next years by four from *Macedonian* (1853-1855), four from *Vincennes* (1854-1855), three others from *Powhatan* (1855), eight from *Levant* (1856-1857), four from *San Jacinto* (1856-1858), nine from *Hartford* between 1860 and 1875, and many others in ones and twos from a further score of ships.

But of the many American sailors buried in Hong Kong, the most eminent was Rear Admiral Ralph Chandler, Commander-in-Chief of the USN forces on Asiatic Station from 1886 until his death on February 11 1889, aged 59. Born in New York, he served the navy for more than forty years, not only in battles and blockades, but in coastal survey and scientific enterprises, notably the Transit of Venus Expeditions in 1874/75.

This long and distinguished career came to an end with shocking suddenness. Chandler sailed into Hong Kong on his flagship *Marion* on a Friday, taking rooms for himself and his wife and daughter at the Hong Kong Hotel. On Monday morning, he shrugged off a vague illness to keep an engagement with the governor, but suffered what was described as a fit of apoplexy just before arriving at Government House. True to type, he attempted to carry on with his official duties—but by the afternoon he was comatose, and by 9:15 in the evening, despite the ministrations of a doctor summoned by His Excellency and Lady des Voeux, he was dead.

On Wednesday, he was buried. Business shut down from midday for the occasion, flags hung at half-mast, bands played, guns were fired in parting salute. His procession was described as the most impressive ever seen in the colony, while the "largest crowd ever assembled in the cemetery" gathered at his graveside. This is difficult to imagine now, as his grave is modest and lies in a quiet backwater.

Two early 20th-century Americans lie close together on the same terrace of Happy Valley, and both died by misadventure. Elmer Hammond, aged 30, a Pentecostal missionary stationed in Causeway Bay with his wife and two children, was travelling home from Canton on the newly opened Kowloon-Canton Railway on the morning of June 15th, 1916. An hour out of Canton, the express rounded a curve to find forty feet of rail had been torn up ahead of it; the train ran off the rails, the first two carriages telescoped, and the wreck smashed to a halt. It was not an accident—two hundred armed brigands rushed out of hiding to terrorize and loot the shocked passengers, escaping with a hefty haul in cash and valuables. It is unlikely, however, that Hammond ever saw the brigands; he was travelling in the third class carriage nearest the engine, and sustained fatal chest injuries when the train crashed off the rails.

Buried close to him two years later was Peter Herbert Gandall, aged 24, a young man from Honolulu who had followed his father into the Hong Kong and China Gas Company. On February 26, 1918, he joined a large and festive crowd at the Happy Valley racecourse for the second day of the races, and was unfortunate enough to be taking his lunch in one of the temporary mat-shed stands along one edge of the track. Just before the three o'clock race began, the mat-sheds swayed and then collapsed like a row of dominoes; moments later, the highly flammable ruins caught fire. Peter Gandall was one of nearly six hundred victims of the disaster.

Finally, an American who was not buried in Hong Kong, but most likely became a "permanent resident" anyway. Although Charles Newman asked to be shipped back to San Francisco for burial, he probably lies in an unmarked grave in the old Magistracy compound, where executed murderers were customarily interred.

Newman, a watchman, was not a member of the respectable community of 1890s Hong Kong. At the time he committed murder, he was living in sin with a woman named Louisa Lockhardt, down among the insalubrious tenements of Wanchai. In the early evening of August 8, 1878, he was seen on the street eating ice cream with his good friend Silvano Gutierrez; an hour later, screams and crashes were heard in his rooms, and a distraught Newman burst into the street. "Oh, we have all gone to hell, all flying in the air," he said, before leading a constable upstairs to show him Louisa unconscious and Gutierrez dying, bleeding from numerous hatchet wounds. Louisa survived, but Gutierrez was buried in Happy Valley the same night.

Newman's trial in December 1878 was a classic of Victorian reticence. Although the victim's trousers had been found around his ankles, Miss Lockhardt's contention that she and Gutierrez had simply been chatting while Newman went out to fetch their supper was not seriously questioned. The "crime of passion" mitigation was not allowed; the jury took barely three minutes to find Newman guilty. Newman accepted his death sentence calmly, asking only, in a "firm and natural tone," to be buried in San Francisco. In the two weeks remaining to him, a grieving Louisa Lockhardt visited him repeatedly in prison; and for her sake, he amazed everybody by converting to Catholicism. He approached his execution on December 19, 1878 "in a firm and manly manner," shook hands with the hangman, and struggled very little at the end of the rope—"though life was not extinct for nearly five minutes." The newspapers were guardedly impressed.

~ REBECCA BRADLEY

View of Amoy, ca. 1845

View of Hong Kong Harbor and Victoria Peak, ca. 1862

EUROPEAN LIFE IN CHINA

Of cooleys, the most faithful and deserving of them all, attached to Russell & Co.'s establishment, Old Qui is really entitled to a special paragraph. Qui, a man of sixty, which some call the prime of life, is so identified with the interests of Europeans, and has lived so long in the same hong, that he seems to be part and parcel of it. When strangers come or depart, he hurries with or for baggage to the square, counts each piece, is sure that it is right, and takes a fatherly interest in every portmanteau.

If visitors come to stay a while, he makes himself known, and his short name is never forgotten; he keeps a sharp eye on every one, and now and then ventures an opinion on the weather, saying, "He more colo to-day sir." He wears a large slouched hat, and usually introduces his bare feet, surmounted by trouserless calves, into very roomy shoes, and when it rains, into wooden slippers, that clatter musically as he moves. He has on more than one occasion proved his zeal in the cause of the foreigners, and once displayed considerable coolness and bravery during a riot. Before I reached China a disturbance had occurred, which rose from a very singular circumstance.

A new flagstaff of immense length had been brought out in a United States man-of-war, and planted in the centre of the American garden. At the end of this mast, the pole was affixed, which was smaller, of course, and could, if necessary, be lowered through the cross-trees. On the top of this staff, a neat vane had been affixed but a short time, when the wind happened to blow from the north, and of course the vane pointed its arrowy dart directly towards the city. The superstitious Chinese, of the lower order, at once conceived that evil was designed by the mysterious indicator, as if this airy demon was in the act of pointing invisible fiends to their devoted city, and they rose *en masse*.

The Europeans decided that it would be as well to yield to the deep-rooted fears and terrors of the populace, and the upper staff was offered to be lowered for the purpose of removing the vane. While this was being performed, a rope parted, and the tall pole came down by the run. The rabble growing with each instant more excited and insolent, filled the square, and burst into a perfect storm of fury. The vane struck against something and flew off, and the crowd made a rush for it. But Old Qui, who had all the while been watching the proceedings intently, now flew among the brawlers, knocked some half dozen over, grabbed the cause of all the mischief, and waving it over his head, while shouting in triumph, dashed with it into the hong, leaving the baffled scoundrels speechless with rage. For this act he was liberally rewarded, made the pet of the establishment, and if not "the glass of fashion and the mould of form," was for a while at least "the observed of all observers." He kept pretty close for some time, and did not venture into the streets until the affair had well blown over, as he might have found his neck in an uncomfortable collar, had he been recognized . . . .

Butterfield & Swire's shipping staff in Shanghai in 1883. Americans in South China could also rise to prominence in British companies. Henry Bridges Endicott (left, standing) at one point became Butterfield & Swire's highest paid employee.

&

The important meal over, unless the business is very pressing, the partners, and clerks too, usually take leisure for an hour or so, and repair to the water. Some pass through the square and ground beyond it, and betake themselves to a little mud bank, which is, or was during my visit, decorated with a consoo house, and styled Jackass Point. On the verandah are a number of sets, some composed of large stones set upon three legs, and forming cool resting places. From this point an excellent view of the river is obtained, and it is always a lively sight to see the varying craft flit by, some gay as banners, green paint, carving and gilding can make them, and others stout, sober, and business-like, working slowly past. On the bank are groups of clerks playing leap-frog and hop-scotch, if the day is sufficiently cool, and if very hot, standing still looking at the vessels, and talking to the boat girls. The more sober partners order the hong boat, which is precisely like the dollar boat already described, and go up the river. They sit down and look out of the windows until all the boats are passed, and when they come to the Macao passage they anchor for half an hour, and have a comfortable snooze. Many of the young men go out on the river every evening in their own boats, either sailing or pulling. There are several classes, and no one need send to England or America for them; once give the Chinese builder his model, and he forthwith goes to work. In a very short time he has a beautiful boat, equal, from stem to stern, to the best European cutters or wherries, and so light, that he can almost take it up and bear it to the water. There are several builders close to the factories, who are employed nearly all the time in filling orders for the foreigners. They display the most admirable judgment in uniting strength and speed; one sailing vessel, built on the model of the Newport sail-boats, eclipsed any one there, and would have done honor to Narragansett Bay. Of cutters the American Fah-kee (nation of the flowery flag, as the Chinese call us,) bore away the bell. She was an eight-oared boat of remarkable beauty, the pet of the hongs, and had been victorious in several closely contested races. With the American ensign waving in the wind, she would cut through the water with such ease and lightness, that she seemed as if endowed with life, and tripping joyfully.

The boat races always took place above the city in the Macao passage, from near its entrance down to the old fort on the little island in the middle of the stream. The hour chosen was just at sunset, when the latest hues of the day threw a glorious light upon the scene, and numbers of the foreigners and Chinese came to witness the contest. The umpires' boats were placed at proper stations, the emulous racers came to the tow line minus suspenders, straps, standing collars, and check reins of every sort, and arrayed in neat flannel jackets, which, however, they dispensed with at the last moment.

They are ready, with mouths shut tight and backs bent over, a pistol is fired and off they go, straining every nerve. The foreigners' friends on either side encourage them by loud shouts, the boat rounds the turning point of the race, the interest never flags, (as reviewers say,) the goal is reached, and one comes in a winner. Then the pistols go off in dozens, and, perhaps, a Chinaman on the stern of a cargo boat, who had forgotten his devotions for the moment, bangs upon his gong with tremendous force, as a salvo shot and a chin chin joss at the same time.

Then the flannel jackets are put on again, and all set their faces towards home, the winners in excellent humor with themselves and every body else, and the losers as happy as they can be under the hard fate they suffered. But they console themselves by saying, if so and so had happened, the result would have been the other way, and firmly making up their minds that they were going to gain the victory next time. Back they all go, and then comes the uncorking of beer, followed at night by a cosy supper, during which the unfortunates continue to forget their troubles, and become so exhilarated that they are convinced that they are as good as the victors at any moment. Thus with an abundance of wine, fun, songs, toasts, and speeches, all of course unrivalled, several hours pass by, during which time they all become such good friends, that they come to a unanimous determination, namely, to see each other home, which proves to be a matter of some trouble. And the next morning two or three of the losers, with bad headaches, (from the fatigues of rowing,) slink into China street to the smith's to buy the silver cup they were so sure of winning, that they had never thought of the pattern.

~Osmond Tiffany Jr.,
The Canton Chinese,
or the American's Sojourn in the Celestial Empire

ELI BOGGS, PIRATE

With pirates like Eli Boggs, legend and history tend to intermix. We know for certain that he stood trial before Hong Kong's Supreme Court on July 4, 1857. The London *Times* correspondent, George Wingrove Cooke, was there. He wrote of Boggs:

"His name would do for a villain of the Blackbeard class, but in form and feature he was like the hero of a sentimental novel; as he stood there in the dock, bravely battling for his life, it seemed impossible that that handsome boy could be a pirate whose name had for three years been connected with the boldest and bloodiest acts of piracy."

Boggs commanded a fleet of 14 pirate junks. He stole only opium and silver—except on one occasion when he purloined a box of candy belonging to a Mr. Carvalho. There was no evidence that he had ever killed anyone.

He claimed in his defense that he had been framed by Ma Chow-wong, a fish merchant and

bumboat owner, and Daniel Caldwell, a senior police officer. He said that they were the real culprits. He even wrote a poem about it.

The judge seems to have believed him. Boggs was declared not guilty of murder, but guilty of piracy. His punishment was deportation. It was a bewilderingly light sentence—little more than a slap on the wrist.

Ma Chow-wong was arrested and charged with piracy. It appears that he and Caldwell were running an extortion racket. If pirates like Boggs did not pay their protection money, Caldwell would either arrest them or inform the Royal Navy, which would run them down. Caldwell was eventually dismissed.

Boggs languished in Victoria Gaol for months because no merchant ship was prepared to give him a passage back to America. Eventually he got a berth and vanished into history.

~ARTHUR HACKER

There had been more skirmishes between Chinese militias and British troops in the countryside around Canton. In response, Pottinger destroyed the forts at the Bogue and stationed troops in Canton. Then he went north with his fleet to capture Xiamen, Ningbo, Zhoushan (for the second time) and Shanghai. After sailing up the Yangtze, China's main artery of trade, he advanced toward Nanjing, capital of China during the Ming dynasty. With the British at the walls of Nanjing and preparing to attack, the imperial government sued for peace.

On August 29, 1842, the Treaty of Nanjing was signed on the H.M.S. *Cornwallis.* In it, the British would try to resolve all their difficulties in dealing with China. Hong Kong Island would become a British possession "in perpetuity," and five Chinese cities—Canton, Xiamen (Amoy), Fuzhou (Foochow), Ningbo and Shanghai—would be open to British traders and their families. The co-hong system was abolished, and the British could trade with whomever they pleased. The imperial government would pay $6 million as compensation for the destroyed opium and a further $15 million to repay outstanding co-hong debts and for British military expenses. The only conspicuous omission was the legalization of the opium trade: The issue was too dangerous politically in both London and Beijing.

For the Americans, largely based in Canton, the new treaty was a threat. Rumors flew that Britain and China had signed a secret clause saying that only British ships could engage in the China trade, and all others would be expelled. Ever since the 1839 opium crisis, American merchants had been petitioning Washington to recognize the importance of their trade and give them political and military backing. The United States Navy's East India Squadron, formed to protect American trade in the Western Pacific, had been stopping in Macau and Canton every few years beginning in 1819, but it was not enough. Now they wanted a concerted effort to protect their interests.

The China trade merchants back home in Massachusetts and Boston took up the cause. In March 1840, Congressman Caleb Cushing rose in the House of Representatives and proclaimed:

"I have, it is true, thought that the present contingency—when the Americans in Canton, and they almost or quite alone, have manifested a proper respect for the laws and public rights of the Chinese Empire, in honorable contrast with the outrageous misconduct of the English there—and when the Chinese government, grateful for the upright deportment of

Factories in Canton

the Americans, has manifested the best possible feeling toward them—I have thought that these circumstances afforded a favorable opportunity to endeavor to put the American trade with China on a just and stable footing for the future."

As soon as word of the Treaty of Nanjing reached Washington, preparations began for an American mission to Beijing. Its head was Caleb Cushing, who travelled with a careful set of instructions from President Tyler and much advice from the China trade merchants. In February 1844, Cushing arrived in Macau at the same time as a French ambassador on the same mission. They were met by mockery from the British government. The *Times* of London wrote:

"Laughter has already begun at the appearance of two ambassadors sent thither before it was known that they would be received, on order to gain a purpose which was granted before they appeared. They now have no grounds for negotiation and must return to their own country in order to be laughed at at home and abroad."

At first it appeared that the British were right. The rumors of only British ships being allowed to trade were unfounded; the Chinese had announced that the treaty ports would be open to all. And the Chinese flatly rejected Cushing's request to travel to Beijing and negotiate with the Emperor. Nevertheless, Cushing persisted; he added the veteran missionaries Peter Parker and Elijah Bridgman to his advisers and entered into discussions with Qiying, the newly-appointed governor of Guangdong and Guangxi provinces.

The meetings took place during a particularly tense time in the relations between American merchants and Canton's unruly Chinese population. Just before the arrival of Caleb Cushing, the American consul had placed an arrow-shaped weathervane atop the flagpole in front of the American factory. The local population decided that the arrow was the cause of the drought then afflicting the region, and a mob went to tear it down. Luckily, the consul decided to remove the weathervane, ending the conflict. Shortly thereafter, an American killed a Chinese man who was part of a gang that attacked him. The local authorities demanded the American give himself up, but Cushing ordered that a jury of Americans try their compatriot. They found that he had acted in self-defense, and Qiying accepted this verdict, perhaps influenced by the fact that three American warships were anchored at Macau and Huangpu.

After two weeks of negotiations, on July 3, 1844 the American and Chinese governments signed their first treaty in Wanghia Village just outside Macau. The Americans had gained all the concessions of the British (except the establishment of their own colony) as well as terms that made trade easier and less expensive. In the five treaty ports, they were allowed to construct churches and hire Chinese scholars to teach them the Chinese language, two clauses highly important for the missionaries. The treaty solved the problem of the arbitrary Chinese justice system by introducing extraterritoriality: Americans who committed crimes in China —except for trading in opium—could now only be tried by American consuls or other officials. The Chinese and Americans then agreed to review the terms of the treaty in 12 years' time.

Even the British had to admit that it was an improvement on the Treaty of Nanjing. They were especially pleased, because their own treaty with the Chinese had a most-favored-nation clause: If China signed a treaty with any other foreign power that had more advantageous terms, those terms would also apply to the British. The British government would take full advantage of that clause in the decades to come.

Meanwhile, the gold rush to the treaty ports had already begun. Beginning in the 1830s, merchants and missionaries had scouted them out on semi-clandestine trading voyages, frequently to sell opium. In the interval between the signing of the treaty and the actual opening of the ports, they had been visited by both British and American traders to make contact with local merchants and, if possible, steal a march on their competition.

The treaty ports were officially opened between July 1843 and June 1844; they had not been picked at random. Each had been chosen for its access to the interior, high volume of trade and availability of relatively open land that could be used as a foreign quarter. It was important that this be easy to defend, preferably with a body of water separating it and the Chinese city. After their Canton experiences, the Westerners were determined to have their own communities separate from the Chinese population and administered by

Honam, opposite Canton, *artist unknown*

Sieving of Tea Leaves,
mid-19th century, by Tingqua

their own laws and legal institutions. The opening of each port began with the arrival of the British consul, generally on a warship, accompanied by various military officers, merchants and missionaries. Hot on their heels came the Americans.

In 1840s China, the dominant American firm was still Russell & Company, followed by A. Heard & Company (founded by two ex-Russell partners in 1840) and Olyphant & Company. The Americans traded in many of the same goods as they had in Canton, with some important differences. Tea and silk were still significant, but less so. Cotton had become much more important, not just exports of heavy nankeen cotton but imports of American cotton into China, threatening the sales of the British-made product.

Americans' involvement in the opium trade also continued, although they were still far behind British firms such as Jardine, Matheson & Company, and Dent & Company. Russell & Company directors denied their direct involvement; however, British traders often chartered their boats to ship opium, among other products. The smaller trading firms, including Heard, had less refined scruples. Using fast ships, they could easily outrun the antiquated Chinese navy and their British competitors on the India route and earn hefty profits. With nearly the whole coastline between Shanghai and Macau open to trade, business was very good.

In the traders' wake came the first full-time American consuls. Washington had finally decided to professionalize its Far Eastern diplomatic corps, beginning to replace the old honorary consuls, usually respected merchants, with salaried employees from the United States. Unfortunately, these were often political patronage appointees rather than trained diplomats. They were also woefully underpaid; they had to support themselves by fees extracted from American citizens and by cutting deals of often dubious legality. In the following decades, a number of consuls were sent home in disgrace after official investigations.

For the major ports—Canton, Shanghai and Hong Kong —the consuls were happy to accept the position. In Xiamen, Fuzhou and Ningbo, however, the appointees, hearing of the poor prospects in those places, managed to secure other jobs that precluded their heading to China. A full-time United States government representative did not arrive in Fuzhou until 1854, and occupancy of Ningbo's position was sporadic for decades.

The arrival of the U.S. consul meant that other foreign powers, i.e. the British, had to begin to show respect for burgeoning American power. Shanghai's first consul, Henry Wolcott, immediately raised the American flag outside his residence in the heart of the British concession. The British representative immediately protested to the American minister, Commodore Biddle, who happened to be in port aboard the U.S. warship *Vincennes*. Biddle rejected the demand, stating that under the extraterritoriality clauses of their treaty, they were only subject to U.S. laws. This source of conflict was removed when the consulate built its residence outside British jurisdiction.

The treaty ports quickly sorted themselves into a hierarchy of commercial importance. Canton, still the base of most American firms, continued to thrive despite the difficult relations with the Chinese population. Quickly up-and-coming was Shanghai, the northernmost treaty port, which lay near the mouth of the Yangtze River halfway between Beijing and Canton. Here traders had access not only to the entire China coast but to the 150 million Chinese who Westerners estimated lived in the interior. Shanghai

had long been an important trading center, particularly for cotton textiles, much of which had been shipped to Canton and sold by the co-hong. In 1844, the British secured rights to a patch of marshy ground along the Huangpu River three-quarters of a mile north of the Chinese city. Within months the major trading firms had offices along the waterfront, among them Russell & Company and A. Heard & Company, and business grew exponentially.

After Shanghai, in descending order of importance, came Xiamen, Ningbo and Fuzhou. At each, the British founded the foreign settlements apart from the Chinese. Xiamen and Fuzhou's communities were built on Gulangyu and Nantai islands, while in Ningbo the settlement was constructed on the opposite side of the river, all sites separated by water from the Chinese city. Despite initial hopes, busi-

A VISIT TO THE HONG KONG COLONY

I was agreeably disappointed in Hong Kong; it was not the dog's hole I had heard of.

The steep hill, as I have before observed, is excavated several hundred feet, and the barren sand reflects the solar heat and burns into the eyes with torrid glare. But in the evening one can drive along the street with pleasure, or seated in a sedan chair be carried by cooleys. The houses lie on each side of the way, and between the buildings on the water side one may catch glimpses of the blue water and the white sails.

On the other side the hills tower abruptly, and several ambitious tenements are perched high in air. The houses are usually large, vast rooms are necessary in such a raging climate, and towards the water are built deep latticed porches.

The houses up the hill are inaccessible to carriages, paths are cut, winding like Alpine passes, and it is pleasant at sunset to struggle up one of these defiles, and gain the little level garden surrounding the aerial mansion. Beneath lies the town, its white walls glittering in the departing splendors of day, while along the whole line of road the people flock to enjoy the hour.

Further onward lies the beautiful sheet of sheltered waters, blue as the heaven above, and dotted with the anchoring ships or restless sails. Beyond the peaks of opposite islands glow in the purple light, and are reflected in the waves that creep to their green declivities.

But we must not grow too sentimental; with a white jacket and a segar, nothing is more delightful than sitting in a marble-paved verandah, with a keen sighted spy-glass, and to look every now and then lazily at a ship, and eagerly at a woman with a taking figure.

The Governor General's house is placed on one of these eminences overlooking the town, and with a military guard and flagstaff to denote it.

As the town was rapidly increasing when I was there, go where you would your ears were met

The families of Russell & Company lived luxurious lives, . .

ness in these three cities remained substantially below expectations. Unlike Shanghai, the local merchants had little experience with trade and production for global markets.

In 1846, visitors found no Americans in either Xiamen or Fuzhou and only American missionaries in Ningbo. American ships stopped at these ports a few times a year on voyages up and down the coast, often selling rice from Manila, but the volume of business did not warrant the full-time presence of any American merchants. In the late 1840s, Xiamen slowly began to pick up, after merchants heard of demand across the Pacific for one commodity of which China possessed seemingly limitless supplies: cheap human labor.

Another foreign settlement in the doldrums was Hong Kong. Conceived as a shipping and warehouse station for British merchants, it was far from the nearest markets. The only firms that found the island profitable were the British opium traders, who used the island as a safe and convenient transshipment point. The burgeoning Chinese population was made up of peddlers, laborers and criminals drawn from the nearby mainland by the lure of a quick dollar. Crime proliferated, and no Westerner went out alone after dark.

The small number of Americans living in Hong Kong looked longingly at the treaty ports. In his letters back to Washington, Frederick Busch, the American consul in the mid-1840s, repeatedly wrote "nothing of interest to dispatch," complaining that no American ships had stopped in there for months and all the business was in Canton and Shanghai. For the American merchants in Canton, Hong Kong was a "dog's hole," where no business was transacted and the British enacted the somnolent rituals of empire.

---

with the clink of hammers and chisels, and your eyes were in danger of sparks of stone at every corner. The buildings were run up and finished with magic ease; one day the cellar would be dug, and the next the roof was being chunamed.

It was not that the houses were hurried and slighted, but that such numbers of Chinese were at work, that, like bees, the hive was soon ready for honey. The intense power of the sun drives all the workmen to shelter, and before a house is commenced a staging of bamboo is erected and covered with matting. As the building rises the bamboo poles are run up story by story, the matting elevated, and the whole house completely protected from the glare of day until the last nail is driven.

Many of the buildings are of a kind of sandstone easily worked when first quarried, but becoming harder the longer it is exposed to the weather.

The English have made, as is usual with them, most excellent roads around the island, and have also introduced a strong police force. At night one always walks attended by a cooley carrying a lantern, and at the distance of every ten paces a policeman is stationed, and the light of the lantern shows him armed to the teeth.

The shops in Hong Kong are of the most wretched order, there being no rich natives on the island, and the Europeans being supplied from several shops kept by English, and in which the wares of London are retailed at enormous profits. But the ravening wolves most successful in Hong Kong are the hotel keepers. Their houses are of the first order, over-run with rats and mosquitoes, and they manage to charge more and give less than any other "publicans and sinners." They go upon the Grahamite principle of buttering bread, they put as little as they can on, and scrape as much as they can off.

-Osmond Tiffany Jr.,
The Canton Chinese,
or the American's Sojourn in the Celestial Empire

. . . here, the American daughter of one family poses on her pet donkey

Many of the American missionaries who had moved to the new colony now sought richer fields elsewhere. Shuck returned to Canton, where he remarried and spent the rest of his life, while the others spread out among the treaty ports.

In 1848, gold was discovered in the hills of California, and miners desperately needed cheap labor to work the seams. Word reached Hong Kong first and quickly spread through the countryside of Guangdong Province. The poor Chinese of South China were no strangers to emigration; they had been heading to greener pastures in Southeast Asia for centuries. In the 1840s, the British had shipped thousands of Chinese laborers to their Australian colony. Much of this trade was transacted in conditions the same as or even worse than slavery; the Chinese phrase for it meant the "pig trade" and laborers were "piglets." Despite the trade's evil reputation, Cantonese and Fujianese villagers began to ship out for California.

The first Chinese reached San Francisco in 1848; by the next year the trickle turned into a flood. Returnees regaled friends and families with tales of life in the "Mountain of Gold"—California—at elaborate homecoming feasts they threw in their own honor. Soon thousands of Chinese were travelling to Hong Kong by junk or overland to catch a boat to the promised land. Much of this business was organized by Chinese merchants, who chartered American boats and had the emigrants sign labor contracts to pay for their passage, usually as miners or railway workers.

The trip across the Pacific was uncomfortable at best. It was often the first time the American captain and crew had to deal with large numbers of Chinese, and cultural clashes were common. One American captain, worried about "sanitary conditions," tried to force his passengers to cut off their queues and scrub themselves with brooms. The emigrants rebelled, killing the captain and running the ship aground near Taiwan. Conditions were worse on ships leaving Xiamen, the second most frequent embarkation point, where there were no British regulations to control the trade. Callous captains occasionally sealed their Chinese passengers below decks with minimal food and water. When they arrived at port, many of the Chinese were not surprisingly dead. American ships also took part in the transportation of Chinese coolies to Cuba and Peru, where conditions were far worse than California.

An unexpected side effect of this trans-Pacific trade was the arrival in China of Americans who were not merchants, missionaries, diplomats or military. In 1853, Shanghai's American consul wrote to Washington:

> "There are now in this port (Shanghai) at least one hundred and fifty sailors ashore, men of all nations, who go into the Chinese city and drink and riot and brawl, daily and nightly. . . . The United States having assumed jurisdiction over their own citizens in China, are expressly bound to compel them to keep the peace, and this cannot be done as long as there is no place to confine the delinquents in, except a loathsome hole inhabited by the foulest lepers, and in itself so weak that a man of American energies can kick his way out in a few minutes."

CONSUL HYATT'S REPORT ON THE LOG OF THE COOLIE SHIP WAVERLY

"Oct. 27—'At 6 A.M., commenced heaving up anchor and made all sail and proceeded down towards Cavita where we came to anchor. At 11 A.M., the coolie cooks came aft, and refused to cook any longer without they could get their wages paid down every month. I promised them I should do all I could, when I got on shore, but that would not satisfy them; and all the coolies came aft, with the intention to kill me, and Mr. Meeks got the men all aft, and got the arms on deck and then commenced to show fight—which killed about four or five and drove them all down below, between decks. In the afternoon, at 3 o'clock, being obliged to get water on deck, we went down and found that they had broke the lock on the sister hatch, and had got hold of some of the provisions; there was one of them who was very impudent, and I killed him. At 4 P.M., we heard that they were breaking off the forward hatch, and two of them then stood on the steps, tried with all their strength to come on deck—but shoved them down again. Washed the ship inside and outside; at 8 P.M., set the watch with one officer and six men. I think we should have had no trouble with the coolies, if we only had a good interpreter and doctor for them on board; for that is the greatest trouble in carrying coolies, and by having had lots of Chinese on board is very fatal.'"

~Eldon Griffin, *Clippers and Consuls*

Many of these men were riff-raff drawn to the opportunities in California and, after a night's carousing in San Francisco bars, "shanghaied" onto American ships heading to China. In Shanghai they deserted, becoming the basis for the population of drunks, adventurers and mercenaries causing headaches for American consuls for over a century.

The clipper ships did not only carry Chinese bound for contract labor. Chinese students were now beginning to make the journey, as American missionaries finally began to see the fruits of their labor. Direct evangelization had not worked; education and, to a lesser extent, medicine had. Wherever they went, the missionaries had opened schools, and Chinese began to see the advantages of Western education for their children, particularly if they were poor. The Westerners were rich, powerful and technologically advanced; maybe some of that would rub off on the Chinese.

Chinese steerage passengers aboard the Pacific mail steamer Alaska, *bound for San Francisco*

As children progressed through the mission schools, many were converted to Christianity. The missionaries then found places for them in American secondary schools and universities. When they returned, they were instrumental in bringing Western thought and technology to China. The first Chinese to graduate from a U.S. university was Yung Wing, born into a poor family near Macau. He arrived in America in 1847 and graduated from Yale in 1854. A decade later, the imperial government commissioned him to go to the United States to purchase steamship and arms-making technology, forming the basis for a modernized Chinese military.

Some of the mission school graduates became evangelizers in their own right. The Western missionaries had had little success in approaching the unconverted directly; their increased visibility in the community had led to more tensions with the Chinese and further cultural clashes. Now they would use agents who understood the language and cul-

Chinese schoolboys on their way to America. Hong Kong, 1872

View towards Flagstaff House, Hong Kong, with Murray Barracks to the left, *ca. 1846, by George Chinnery*

ture—just as traders used compradors—to achieve far greater penetration of the Chinese community. Evangelization, however, had consequences that no missionary could have predicted.

One could argue that American missionaries were the trigger for the Taiping Rebellion that killed over 20 million Chinese and almost toppled the Qing Empire. According to Professor Jonathan Spence, in 1836 Reverend Edwin Stevens (another Yale graduate) distributed a Chinese-language tract titled "Good Words for Exhorting the Age" in Huangpu. He placed one of the tracts, written by Leang Afa, the first Chinese agent of Protestant missionaries, in the hands of Hong Xiuquan, an examination candidate working as a village school teacher. Hong glanced at the pamphlet and then left it in his hut. A few years later, however, after a series of examination failures, Hong had a vision of speaking with an older, golden-haired man and a

young man whom he called "Elder Brother." Hong re-read the pamphlet and in a flash of inspiration realized that the two men were God and Jesus and that he must be Jesus's brother.

When Hong began to convert the villagers and advocate the destruction of Confucian shrines, the local authorities ran him out of town. Hong went to Canton, where for two months he studied scripture under Isaacher Roberts, a Baptist missionary from the mountains of Tennessee with a reputation for fiery sermons and uncompromising faith. In 1847, Hong wandered to the wilds of Guangxi Province and began gathering converts, many of them Hakka tribespeople; by 1850 they were an army 20,000 strong. After Hong preached the violent downfall of the Manchu "devils," the imperial government sent an army to oust him from the mountains. The Manchu commander was killed, their army defeated, and shortly thereafter Hong declared himself

Heavenly King of the Taiping Tianguo, or the Heavenly Kingdom of Great Peace.

The Taiping army marched northeast sacking cities of gold and armaments and gaining thousands of recruits. In March of 1853 they scored their greatest victory; they captured the old capital of Nanjing and slaughtered every Manchu man, woman and child within its walls. For the next 11 years, Hong and the Taiping ruled a large territory comprising much of Jiangsu, Anhui and Zhejiang provinces. The rules of their kingdom included segregation of the sexes; bans on opium, drinking and dancing; and a revolutionary program of land redistribution. Unfortunately, they did not develop the bureaucracy to implement their plans, as the leadership spent most of its time devising plots against each other and Hong retreated into his own private world of concubines and religious visions.

From their base in Shanghai less than 300 miles east of Nanjing, Westerners watched the Taiping rebellion with a mixture of fear and admiration. In 1853, it looked like the Taiping were heading toward Shanghai after capturing Nanjing; instead, they veered north toward Beijing, and the merchants breathed a sigh of relief. However, they had to deal with another Chinese rebellion close at hand.

In October the Shanghai local government was toppled by a loose group of secret societies and disaffected laborers known as the Small Swords. When the imperial customs officials fled town, no one was left to collect the dues. After much argument—the Americans and French were suspicious that the British were trying to seize a commercial advantage —the Western merchants agreed to create a foreign-run customs inspectorate to collect imperial duties, an institution that continued after the suppression of the Small Swords in 1855. The lesson of both these rebellions was that Westerners had to strengthen the extraterritorial provisions of their treaties

The arsenal at Nanjing, ca. 1868

with the Chinese and build parallel institutions that would not be threatened by the continuing weakness of the imperial government.

Many Westerners, particularly Protestant missionaries, also saw much to admire in the Taiping. The missionary role in Hong Xiuquan's career was well known—in 1853 he invited Isaacher Roberts to visit him, but the American consul refused to grant permission—and they could see shards of their teachings in his eccentric doctrines. (Western Catholics, almost all French, abhorred the Taiping for doctrinal reasons.)

Robert Maclay, an American Methodist missionary in Fuzhou wrote:

"We are not yet in possession of sufficient data for a thorough analysis of this wonderful movement. Enough is known, however, to show that it is a direct result of Protestant missionary operations, and that as a religious system, notwithstanding its great and lamentable defects, it is far in advance of the hoary heathenism of China."

WHIPPING AN ENQUIRER

An incident occurred at Ngu-kang which will furnish some illustration of our work in China. One Sunday afternoon we commenced our usual service in the house of one of the brethren. The room was crowded, and many were standing about the door.

We had sung the opening hymn and kneeled for prayer, the entire congregation kneeling with us. I had uttered only a few sentences of the prayer when whir-*whiz*-WHACK came a blow so close to my face that for a moment I felt sure it had been aimed at me. Somewhat startled, I opened my eyes, and there, right before me, stood a strapping field-woman, armed with a stout bamboo cane. She seemed frantic with rage, and poured her blows with furious energy upon the shoulders and back of a young man kneeling at my side. Her voice, never musical I should suppose, was now gratingly harsh, and pitched on a particularly high key, so that the volleys of objurgations and curses with which she interlarded her

blows fell on the ear like rapid discharges of fire-crackers. A moment's thought explained the character of this unexpected episode in our services, and, as all the congregation remained quietly kneeling, I determined to continue my prayer notwithstanding this unwelcome disturbance. The execution of this purpose was more difficult than I had anticipated. The woman was in a towering passion, her arms and tongue moving with astonishing velocity, and, in self-defense, I found myself compelled to lead the devotions of the sanctuary in an elevation of tone and a prolixity of address quite unusual with me. The storm, however, gradually subsided. Finding that the meeting was going forward in spite of her disorderly proceedings, the woman began to restrain herself, and the young man, acting on the advice of the brethren near him, arose from his knees and accompanied her from the place. After our exercises were over the brethren gave the following explanation of the disturbance: The woman was the mother of the young man she thus publicly chastised. The son had become interested in Christianity, and began to attend our meetings. His mother opposed him, and threatened to beat him if he did not change his course. On the Sunday preceding the above occurrence the mother had dragged him out of the prayer-meeting and gave public notice of intention to beat him if he ever dared again to disobey her commands on this subject. Greatly to the surprise of the brethren the young man appeared in the congregation on the present occasion, and hence the scene that ensued. Shortly after this I left China, and have not yet learned the final issue in the case, but hope and pray that the young man may persevere in his desire to become a Christian.

~Rev. R.S. Maclay,
Life among the Chinese with Characteristic Sketches and Incidents of Missionary Operations and Prospects in China

St. John's Cathedral, Hong Kong, ca. 1873. The view here is from the courtyard of Messrs. Augustine Heard & Co.'s premises

Unlike the imperial government, they knew, the Taiping were disciplined and efficient—they even paid their troops on time. A number of Americans in the dockside rabble of Shanghai ended up as mercenaries fighting on the side of the Taiping.

Led by the British, the Westerners also saw the Taiping Rebellion as an opportunity to press for further concessions from the imperial government. In 1854, they asked for a treaty renegotiation, basing their demand on the 12-year clause in the American treaty, but the Emperor refused. In 1856, the British saw another opportunity when the *Arrow*, a Chinese boat flying the British flag, was boarded and searched by imperial customs officers. The British responded by shelling and then capturing Canton and exiling its viceroy to Calcutta. They were joined in this military venture by the French navy, which wanted revenge for the massacre of Catholic missionaries in Guangxi. Then the British once again sailed north, capturing the Dagu forts outside Tianjin and threatening that city and Beijing. In June 1858, the Chinese capitulated and signed the Treaty of Tianjin.

Now all of China would be open to travel and trade, and nine new treaty ports were opened up, seven on the coast (including two on Taiwan) and three inland. Foreign ambassadors would be allowed to take up residence in Beijing, and all official communications would be in English, reducing the problem of misinterpretation inherent in separate versions of treaties. Taxes would be reduced, and, finally, opium was recognized as a legal item of trade—despite Chinese anti-opium laws still on the books. Due to the most-favored nation clauses in their treaties, these terms also applied to the Americans and French.

Even though they signed the treaty, the imperial government did not want to comply with it. The presence of foreign ambassadors in Beijing—and the implications that had for the status of the Emperor (would they kowtow or not?)—was the clause that most stuck in their throat. When their minister was refused entry, the British navy again attacked the now-heavily-defended Dagu forts. This time the British were beaten back, and their commander was wounded and nearly captured. He was saved by Josiah Tattnall, captain of a "neutral" American navy ship hovering nearby, who justified his deed with the shout: "Blood is thicker than water!"

Determined to avenge their humiliation and teach the Chinese a lesson that they would never forget, the British under Lord Elgin marched on Beijing. On October 18, 1860, they sacked the Summer Palace and burned it to the ground,

an act of retribution which indeed deeply shocked the Chinese. The Emperor fled north, to another summer palace at Rehe, forcing his brother to reaffirm the treaty and some onerous new clauses. The Chinese would also pay substantial war reparations, open Tianjin as a treaty port and cede Kowloon to the British in perpetuity.

The events of 1858-60 redrew the Westerners' map of China and their relationship to the imperial government. There were now 16 treaty ports where they could build extra-territorial settlements, and they had access not only to Beijing but to every other part of China. With greatly increased commercial interests, the Westerners suddenly realized they had a stake in China's well-being.

Foreigners were now among the most important businessmen in nearly every major Chinese trading center. They owned (actually leased) valuable property and modern port facilities; they controlled an ever-increasing share of the coastal trade; and, under the Maritime Customs Service, they were actually imperial employees collecting tariffs due the Emperor at most important ports. They were a privileged class in China and saw that they had more to gain from protecting the Emperor than trying to topple him. There was money to be made.

Despite these new opportunities, the Americans could not take full advantage of them. American trade with China had steadily increased from 1841 on. Then, in 1860, it became obvious that civil war was about to erupt between the States. Ships were diverted to military uses, and factories were re-tooled for the production of war material. China trade financiers back in New York or Boston now had more pressing demands on their time, and many of the smaller American trading firms lost their backing and were forced to close. The U.S. government also lost its clout, as the Navy's East India Squadron was ordered to return home. For the next few decades, the Americans in China were even more dependent on the protection of the British Empire.

Most of the Americans were now based in either Hong Kong or Shanghai. After an 1858 fire destroyed most of the foreign factories in Canton, the majority of them had moved down to Hong Kong, where they did not have the constant threat of the rebellious Canton citizenry. In Shanghai, the American Settlement spread along the banks of the Huangpu river just across Suchou Creek from the International Settlement (previously the British district). Those American firms that remained were generally the larger ones. Russell & Company and A. Heard & Company still had elegant office/warehouse complexes in Hong Kong and the treaty ports, and, for the first few years of the new system, they prospered.

Despite their shrinkage in numbers, the Americans left in China still played prominent roles. In Hong Kong, John Heard of A. Heard & Company was at age 36 considered an old China hand and one of the most respected members of the community. He belonged to all the top British clubs and was a renowned horseman whose stable frequently competed in the Happy Valley races. In Shanghai, Frederick Townsend Ward, a Salem, Massachusetts-born steamship officer, played a crucial role in ending the Taiping Rebellion.

By 1860, Western opinions about the Taiping had changed. Rumors seeped into Shanghai about Hong Xiuquan's increasing isolation and eccentricity, and new Taiping militancy was again threatening Shanghai and the nearby trading centers. On Hong's renewed invitation, Isaacher Roberts had visited him, hoping to return the Taiping leader to the narrow path of his brand of Protestantism. Hong, for his part,

also tried to convert the Baptist to the Taiping way. Neither succeeded, and meanwhile Western newspapers in Shanghai mocked Roberts as a Taiping dupe. Both the Qing and the foreign powers had decided it was time to bring an end to the Heavenly Kingdom of Great Peace.

In 1860, a consortium of Shanghai Chinese bankers and local officials hired Frederick Ward to form a mercenary army to fight the Taiping. The choice of the wiry, dark-haired Ward, who had little experience in China, was not an anomaly: He had participated in military operations in Central America, and was rumored to have trained the rebel army of the notorious filibuster William Walker in Nicaragua. With the aid of a few other American adventurers, Ward trained a force of 200 Filipinos and managed to capture an important Taiping town. Although he lost the town a month later, Ward managed to recruit thousands of Chinese soldiers, train them at his Songjiang base and inflict impressive defeats on the Taiping. His achievements with a Chinese army confounded

The race course at Happy Valley, ca. 1873

Frederick Townsend Ward's "Ever-Victorious Army"

the Westerners in Shanghai, because they did not believe the Chinese were mentally capable of adopting modern military techniques. The Chinese, however, were ecstatic; they gave him modern weapons and his army the honorific, the "Ever-Victorious Army." Shortly afterward, Ward married the daughter of a rich Shanghai Chinese.

Ward's troops were not the only forces fighting the Taiping; Chinese regular forces as well as British and French ships and soldiers also attacked the rebels. However, the disciplined Ever-Victorious Army was frequently at the forefront of these battles. Ward, who was granted the rank of general in the Chinese army, became famous for his prowess, bravery and custom of always having a cape over his shoulders and a Manila cigar in his mouth. In a September 1862 skirmish outside Ningbo, a stray bullet hit Ward in the stomach, and he died the next day. Ward was buried in Songjiang with full Chinese honors, and in 1877 the imperial government declared him an "immortal," the equivalent of a saint under the Confucian system, and constructed a temple over his tomb.

Ward was succeeded, first by, Henry Andrea Burgevine, his American second-in-command, and then by Major Charles Gordon, a British officer of the Royal Engineers. The Ever-Victorious Army continued its campaign as the spearhead of the Chinese army, which now had greatly improved weaponry, thanks in part to missionary school graduate Yung Wing. By the end of 1863, the Taiping's hold was broken, and their troops were in retreat. In mid-1864, Hong Xiuquan died of either illness or by his own hand. The Chinese troops breached the walls of Nanjing; those Taiping that did not commit suicide were slaughtered by the imperial troops.

With the Taiping threat finally abolished, and the American Civil War over, one would expect American trade to surge back to China. It did not. The American houses remaining in China had prospered during the war. The commission business—buying and selling for merchants and manufacturers in the United States and Britain—remained their mainstay, and they were also making tidy profits on the Chinese intercoastal trade. Russell & Company owned the controlling interest in the Shanghai Steam Navigation Company, which at its peak had 16 steamships plying the waters between the treaty ports. When the Hongkong and Shanghai Bank was founded in the mid-1860s, Albert Heard was on the first board of directors. Russell & Company was not at first convinced of the bank's prospects; in 1866, however, they changed their mind. W.H. Forbes, their managing partner in China, joined the board and served on it for decades, including one term as chairman in 1888 and 1889.

Nevertheless, the business climate in both China and the United States was changing, and the old ways of doing business were not bringing in the same rates of return as the boom days of the 1840s and 50s. Faster ships and new telegraph services

Russell & Company Headquarters, Canton, ca. 1870

This poster commemorates the May 10, 1869 completion of the first transcontinental railroad. Many Chinese contributed to the building of the railroads, as they paid Chinese shipowners for passage to America by entering into labor contracts, usually signing on as railway workers

greatly reduced the time it took goods and information to travel between the continents. To and from Europe, the Suez Canal eliminated the need to sail around Africa; crossing the Pacific Ocean, the Pacific Mail's fleet of steamships linked up with transcontinental trains in California. Manufacturers in the United States and Chinese comprador firms in Hong Kong and Shanghai discovered that they did not need trading firms as intermediaries—they began to sell directly to their customers. Long the mainstay of the China trade, the profits from exporting tea and cotton began to disappear as competitors with cheaper products arose in India, Sri Lanka and Japan.

Back in the States, money flowed, but not to China. After the Reconstruction, young men still headed West, but their journeys ended at the Pacific. Far more money could be made from investments in the American West—railways, mines, ranching—than in ventures in China or any other foreign country. Even the younger generations of the great New England and New York trading families followed this trend. The China trade stagnated due to lack of interest.

While the business community dwindled, diplomatic and missionary efforts increased. The United States government had to forge close ties with China to deal with the hot potato of Chinese immigration. Thousands of Chinese continued to stream into the United States every year; they were met by increasing anti-Chinese violence, particularly in the West, fanned by opportunistic politicians of both parties. Anson Burlingame, American ambassador to Beijing in the early 1860s, became such friends with Chinese officials that he was

Crew of the USS Ossipee, *1887. During the 19th century there was no segregation of naval men*

The steamer Suwonada *in Hong Kong Harbor*

THE CHINA TEA CLIPPERS

From 1845 to 1860, America ruled the seas between China and the West. They had the fastest, sleekest ships and could carry the most precious cargo—tea—to Europe and America far more rapidly than their British competition.

In previous decades, the bulk of the tea shipments had been carried west by the lumbering fleets of the East India Company. Due to the constant danger of attack from pirates and from Continental enemies (war was a perennial in 18th- and early 19th-century Europe), these boats traveled in massive convoys, so their speed was only as fast as the slowest ship. The American ships, on the other hand, traveled alone, and for them speed, maneuverability and shallow drafts were crucial. U.S. shipyards began to design ships to compete in the China trade.

In 1832, a Baltimore merchant built a ship named the *Ann McKim;* it was designed to look like a Baltimore clipper, a type of small sailing vessel used by privateers in the War of 1812, only larger and with three masts. Her prow was straight and her lines were narrow, perfect for cutting through waves at a high rate of speed; in comparison, the old East India Company ships were slow, waddling tubs. The *Ann McKim* could not carry as much cargo, but she made up for it with speed. Merchants realized that vast profits could be made if they could bring the year's crop of tea to Western markets before the competition.

In the early 1840s, a New York ship designer named John Willis Griffiths took the ideas of the *Ann McKim*—narrow lines, straight bow—and refined them into a larger, faster ship with more sail area built specifically for the China trade. His creation was the *Rainbow,* successfully launched in 1845 to the surprise of the dockyard *cognoscenti* who thought that she would surely sink. Instead, she made the trip to Canton in the record time of 92 days out and 88 days back, not only paying her construction cost but making her owners a 100 percent profit. Shortly thereafter, another New York dockyard launched the *Houqua,* commissioned by A.A. Low & Brothers in honor of their longtime trading partner in Canton. The *Houqua* and the *Rainbow* began the clipper ship revolution.

These advances came at a perfect time for American ship captains, because in the late 1840s the British government repealed the Navigation Laws; British ships lost the monopoly on carrying cargo between Britain and the colonies. Americans stole the tea trade from the British ships. The first to ply the China to Britain route was the *Oriental,* chartered in 1850 by Russell & Company to carry $48,000 worth of tea to London. She did this in the record time of 97 days. For the next 10 years, Americans controlled the shipment of tea between China and the West.

The 1850s saw the first of the great clipper races from Canton to London. As soon as the new crop of tea was stowed in the clipper's hold, the ship weighed anchor and headed to sea, flying across the waves under huge expanses of billowing sail. The ships sped at upward of 18 knots an hour until they reached the doldrums, patches of ocean where barely a breath of wind stirred the water. There they would have to wait for days or weeks until the weather turned and they could get under way again. The races ended in London or New York, where the ships often arrived within minutes of each other. The entire city would be agog with news of the race—the tea clippers were by far the elite of the shipping world—and the tea would be in the shops the following morning.

The greatest of all clipper ship designers was probably Donald McKay, for whom the American Club's McKay's Bar is named. In 1850 and 1851, he built the *Stag Hound* and the *Flying Fish,* two of the most famous of the "extreme" clipper ships, with more knife-like lines and a record amount of sails. The *Stag Hound* was the largest ship on the seas at the time; despite its size, it made the trip from Canton to New York in 85 days. The *Flying Fish* still holds the record of the fastest time of a sailing ship from New York to San Francisco via Cape Horn—89 days.

The era of American tea clippers ended around 1860, when the United States drifted out of China due to its own internal distractions and the British shipbuilders finally began to build their own clippers. The clipper era lasted another decade, with more great races and records broken—all by British boats—but the end was already near. The chugging of steamships was heard on the China coast.

In 1869, the Suez Canal was opened. Ungainly, smoke-puffing steamships could use the canal, cutting the time between London and Hong Kong to 40 days, while the glorious clipper ships still had to sail around the Cape of Good Hope. The lucrative cargoes went to steam, while the sailing ships lived out their days hauling wool from Australia.

By the end of the 1880s, clipper ships were anachronisms. Most were mothballed; a few were saved to use as training ships. Over the following decades, advances in technology made shipping faster and more economical, but it would never be more romantic.

~ANDREW COE

A Chinese view of American diplomats being transported up the Peiho, 1859

hired to be their diplomatic representative to the United States and Europe. On his much-publicized 1868 friendship tour of the United States, he signed a treaty guaranteeing that the Chinese would continue to be allowed to enter. Political pressure (and a touch of racism) persuaded the American presidents of the 1880s to rescind this agreement and sign bills excluding the vast majority of Chinese immigrants.

The other pressing diplomatic issue was extraterritorial rights in the treaty ports. The Americans had always affirmed that under the most-favored nation clauses of their treaties the foreign settlements were not British possessions but open to citizens of all the foreign powers. However, the lack of adequate consular representation had allowed Britain to become the primary leaseholder and then sub-lease the land to whomever it pleased, keeping the best locations for itself. In 1863, after much persuasion by Burlingame, the British agreed to allow their Shanghai district to become the International Settlement, incorporating the American Settlement immediately to the north. The French refused to join, moving their businesses and government offices to their own concession just to the west. For the next 90 years, this rather

jury-rigged arrangement was the basis for Shanghai's confusing patchwork of districts administered by separate and often conflicting government bodies. The principle of the International Settlement was also followed to a greater or lesser extent in the other treaty ports.

Those Americans that took fullest advantage of the new openings in China were not businessmen but missionaries. From their bases in the main treaty ports, they spread into China's interior. In 1889, there were nearly 500 American Protestant missionaries in China overseeing a pool of converts numbering 1,300, as well as 9,000 students in thriving mission schools. It was not known how many of these converts were "rice Christians," claiming belief in exchange for food, housing and education. Nevertheless, these figures finally began to satisfy the highly numbers-conscious mission boards back in the U.S. who had been bankrolling the missionaries for so many years with so little success. Success brought danger, however, as anti-Western feeling began to increase, particularly in the North. Miles from the nearest treaty port and nearly undefended, the missionaries were often the closest and easiest targets.

While God's work boomed, the old American trading firms began to disappear. Business conditions in China had changed, and Stateside financiers did not think that the companies' marginal returns made them worth propping up—their money could be better used elsewhere. In 1876, A. Heard & Company failed, and Albert Heard was forced to resign from the Hongkong and Shanghai Banking Corporation board. A decade later, it was followed by Olyphant & Company, whose China headquarters had been in Shanghai. Russell & Company managed to hang on until 1891. A few years earlier, W.H. Forbes had helped found the National Bank of China, which hoped to become the Chinese version of the Hongkong and Shanghai Banking Corporation. When one of Russell's Boston partners made a bad bet on silver futures, the Hongkong and Shanghai Banking Corporation delayed a bail-out, forcing the firm to sell its assets. The firm that had dominated American business in China for the better part of a century was no more.

Despite these failures, new American companies were moving into China. Some were run by entrepreneurs whose ambition outran their financial backing; in the 1860s and 1870s, they attempted to sell to the Chinese government, then in the throes of a great modernization campaign, telephone, telegraph and railway equipment. Almost every one of the plans fell through, because for every Chinese official pushing Western technology there were two against it. Other American firms decided they were going to succeed in doing what so many had failed at: selling Western products in a country with a population reckoned to approach the half billion mark, potentially the largest market on Earth.

A view of Hong Kong Harbor looking northwest from Causeway Bay, 1846

CHAPTER THREE

The China Market

Westerners have been chasing the dream of a vast and wildly profitable Chinese market for their goods at least since the arrival of the Portuguese in the 16th century. It drove—or was the excuse for—Western powers' expansionist policies in the Middle Kingdom from 1839 on. Unfortunately, until the late 19th century no one could figure out how to make the dream a reality. Then the new efficiencies of the Industrial Revolution forced Westerners to give it another try.

By the 1880s, businesses had realized that their domestic markets would never be able to consume all the products that their factories were producing ever faster and cheaper. Big businesses swallowed smaller businesses and formed trusts with competitors, so they could maintain (or increase) their level of profits. They also began to look abroad for virgin markets to open with new and aggressive business methods.

The 1870s saw the appearance of the first American companies specializing in the export of Western products into China. The old trading firms had sold cotton fabric—long the most important American export to China—but since the 1860s that trade was taken over by Hong Kong and Shanghai Chinese firms. This new breed of American trader finally found a market for manufactured goods such as clocks, soap and canned food, much of it sold in the fast-growing foreign communities. In the 1870s, Louis and Joseph Getz, two German émigrés, opened a store in San Francisco that sold canned foods and cured meat under the Getzbest label to Shanghai, Hong Kong and other Asian ports. Getz Brothers and the successors to the other American export traders, such as the China and Japan Trading Company and the American Trading Company, are still thriving today. These traders also began to build a market for American kerosene produced by the first great American conglomerate.

In 1859, oil was discovered in Titusville, Pennsylvania, and out of it a new era was born. Within two decades, the oil industry was controlled by John D. Rockefeller's Standard Oil Trust. Oil producers had developed new methods of refining crude oil cheaply and efficiently, and soon refineries were pumping out millions of gallons of fuel. The problem was, there was no domestic market for all that oil: Coal and wood were still the primary fuels and horses still the main means of transportation; over-production threatened to bust the industry. Standard Oil saw the vast potential of China, where they had been selling a few thousand gallons a year through the trading firms, and in 1882 they decided to develop the market.

William Libby, an executive with Standard Oil of New York (one of the Standard Oil octopus's tentacles), was sent to Asia to develop the market. The problem was most Chinese lit their houses with vegetable-oil lamps. Standard Oil responded by distributing millions of free tin lamps under the Mei Foo ("beautiful confidence") brand name; the lamps were stamped with the Chinese characters for "Burn Standard Oil Kerosene." To build their share, they undercut the price of vegetable oil by 50 percent and developed an efficient marketing and distribution system from their base in Shanghai and later in Hong Kong and the main treaty ports.

In a radical break from the past, the business was transacted without the help of compradors. Before they went East, the young Standard Oil managers and salesmen had to survive a training program more rigorous than American diplomats heading to China. They had to speak Chinese and live near their customers, usually far from the nearest

AN EIGHT-DAY BARROW TRIP

It was my summer vacation, and for weeks I had planned to cross the Shantung peninsula by wheelbarrow. I chose this as the most direct and most exciting way of reaching Chefoo. My decision stirred up quite a hornet's nest. The whole group of missionaries where I taught were up in arms. It wasn't safe. I couldn't go alone. One man even had the gall to announce that no single woman should be allowed to go on any trip without the consent of the married men. I merely smiled and went ahead with my preparations.

Finally the arrangements had been made. And then four days before I planned to leave, the mayor of Weihsien sent word that no foreigner could travel without a soldier escort. I sent word back that I was unafraid and didn't desire a soldier escort. For three days the road was kept hot with messengers.

"You must."

"No, thank you. Shantung is safe."

"Suppose something happens to you? My reputation is at stake. The guard will arrive."

"Your humble servant is grateful but would not put Your Honor to that expense," I countered, although I knew the expense would fall on my shoulders.

Suddenly, in desperation, I decided to pull out a day early, telling no one but the barrow men and Chang Dagwo, who always accompanied me. Fortunately the other members of the compound didn't know of my exchanges with the mayor.

At daybreak I was up to supervise the packing of the barrow. It was important that nothing be forgotten, for it was to be an eight-day trip, and there were no stores along the way where forgotten things might be purchased.

By six o'clock we pulled out of the yard and rolled down the road to the great gate of our walled compound. And there, just outside the gate, standing at ease, was my soldier escort, four of them. I looked quickly at Chang and then at the barrow men. Who had leaked the news of my early departure? But their faces were inscrutable. They were all staring straight ahead.

"Stop," I cried. "I'm getting off." After an earlier experience of jumping off a barrow and having the change of weight upset the load, I had learned always to announce my intention so that the men could adjust their shoulders to be in balance. It saved having to repack.

I slid slowly off and walked up to the soldiers. They sprang to attention. "Will you kindly return to Weihsien. Word has already been sent to the mayor that you are not to go." My tone was polite but stern.

For a moment they stood staring at me. Then the leader stepped forward and fell to his knees. Before I could stop him, he had kowtowed three times in the dust. "Please, Yuan Giao-shi, we are going home for the harvest. The road has many bandits. We're afraid to go alone. Please, let us go with you. The bandits won't dare touch us if we are with a foreigner."

Turning quickly to hide a smile, I returned to the barrow. And we had a four-soldier escort.

For the first eighteen or twenty *li,* I walked in the cool of the morning. Then, as the sun grew hotter, I crawled

---

treaty port. By the early 20th century, Standard Oil's employees had a far better grasp of China than most old China hands and were considered among the elite of the foreign community. Their Chinese retailers, mostly shop-owners, also thrived from the trade, often becoming the most respected businessmen in their towns. In 1890, over 10 million gallons of oil were sold in China, and the amount increased exponentially year by year.

Another budding industrial giant with an overproduction problem was the American Tobacco Company. In 1881, American Tobacco's founder, James B. Duke, oversaw the invention of a machine that could produce millions of cigarettes a day, far more than American smokers could ever consume. According to company myth, when executives asked him where they were going to sell all those cig-

arettes, he asked for the atlas, opened it to China and said, "That is where we are going to sell the cigarettes." Cigarette sales to China began in 1890; a decade later they were selling over one billion a year aided by a bold marketing campaign. Visitors to provincial China complained that upon entering towns, instead of seeing quaint, typical scenes, they were confronted by colorful posters promoting cigarettes on every vertical surface, including ancient temple walls. Marketing became even more aggressive after 1902, when Duke formed British-American Tobacco with a British rival. American cigarettes were now sold in the most far-flung parts of the empire, reaching the remote villages of Inner Mongolia, for example, by yak train.

American optimism about the China market was tempered by the threat of foreign competition, which backed its up on the load and stretched out to enjoy the landscape in comfort. A well-packed wheelbarrow allows a passenger to recline at ease on the bedding, with the food box for a pillow.

There was a peace and contentment in the leisurely meanderings of a barrow through the harvest landscape that train and auto riders never know. We passed threshing floors where grain was being winnowed, donkeys piled high with vegetables for the market, a bride and groom in their red chairs. The kaleidoscopic panorama of populous Shantung flowed before us.

At one place we met a band of ruffians that I took for the much-feared bandits. The four soldiers evidently thought the same, for they stepped up close beside me for protection—theirs, not mine. But the ruffians passed with only a few remarks. Chang Da-gwo explained that they were thieves whom the authorities had sent out to catch other thieves. If they didn't bring in someone, they were beaten. The other thieves usually paid well and went free, while some innocent man was brought in as a thief.

About an hour before dark we pulled into our first inn. It seemed that bandits worked in the early evening hours, or at least travelers thought they did. For always on the road we stopped before dark, but started long before there was even a sign of daylight.

When we entered, the innkeeper was quite upset. "But a woman! What will I do with a woman?" he kept repeating to the innyard in general.

Chang Da-gwo went scouting. When he returned he informed the harassed innkeeper, "There's a storeroom back in the corner of the yard. I'll make the *giao-shi*

comfortable there, where she will be alone."

"But there's no *kang*. Where will she sleep?"

"She has her own wooden-canvas bed. I'll set it up for her. Then the innkeeper can crowd more men on the *kang* in the main room," he added diplomatically.

All of this time the villagers had been gathering. Word had gone around that a foreign woman had arrived, so quickly men, women, and children crowded in. By the time I was settled in my little room, it was dark. But that didn't bother the women. They pushed in after me till the room was filled with blue-clad figures and the smell of garlic. The light of the single candle showed a sea of eager faces.

I was fairly used by then to their surprise over my white face, my large feet, my age, and my unmarried status. But that evening, after asking the usual questions, one woman came up close and peered long and hard into my face. Then she burst out, speaking as much to the roomful as to me, "And you are just like us!"

"Why, yes, of course," I answered with a few mental reservations.

"You are thirty and unmarried and just like us!"

While I was trying to figure out what was coming, she turned to the crowd and said, "We have been told a woman would go straight to hell if she didn't get a mother-in-law, and this *giao-shi* is thirty and still looks like us!"

What could one say to that?

~Marjorie Rankin Steurt,
Broken Bits of Old China

---

commercial enterprises with far more than business know-how. In the 1890s, the United States did not have the might or the desire to carve out an Asian colony (with the exception of some Pacific islands, and the Philippines); the European powers did. This had begun with the Russians, who since the 17th century had been pressing south into Manchuria from Far Eastern Siberia. In 1880, the French had occupied Hanoi, capital of the Chinese tributary state of Annam (now Vietnam). After sporadic fighting and the breakdown of negotiations, the French anchored off Fuzhou in 1884 and bombarded the Chinese fleet, devastating the antiquated ships and inflicting huge loss of life. Annam became part of French Indochina, and Britain seized the opportunity to declare Burma, another state in the Chinese imperial orbit, a protectorate.

Europe's main competitor was Japan, which until Commodore Perry's 1854 expedition had been a self-isolated feudal state. After the sweeping reforms of the Meiji Restoration began in 1868, Japan was rapidly developing into an industrialized power willing to compete on both commercial and political fronts. In 1894, Korea, another Chinese vassal state, was rocked by a rebellion that threatened the royal family. Both China and Japan raced to "protect" the royal family; Japan won and installed a puppet ruler as regent. Over the next months, the Japanese and Chinese engaged in a escalating series of battles that spilled over into China, culminating in a brilliant Japanese victory in Weihaiwei, an important port in Shandong Province. Once again, the Chinese were forced to sue for peace; the terms of the Treaty of Shimonoseki were the most onerous yet, with hundreds of millions of

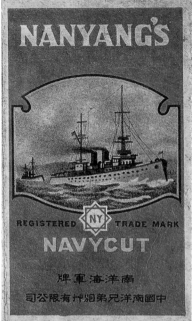

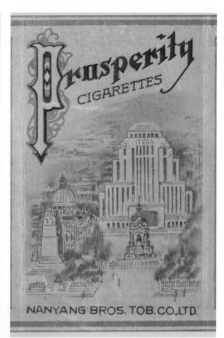

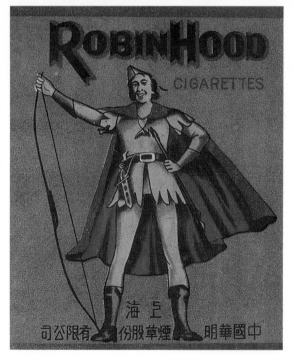

Chinese cigarettes manufactured by competitors of the British-American Tobacco Company

taels of silver in damages and numerous other humiliating concessions, including the ceding of Taiwan.

The Europeans saw China's weakness as an opportunity. When two of their missionaries were killed, the Germans used it as an excuse to occupy Qingdao, another Shandong port, and claim the surrounding countryside as their sphere of influence. The Russians strengthened their presence in Manchuria and occupied Port Arthur (now Lüshun), leading Britain to claim Weihaiwei just across the Gulf of Zhili. Britain also demanded and received a 99-year lease on the New Territories north of Kowloon. The French claimed special rights in the provinces nearest Vietnam, including Hainan Island. Even the Italians extracted a lease for territorial rights in and around Ningbo. As China was being carved up, the American businessmen could only watch and worry about lost opportunities in the opening of the vast China market.

Washington was also getting pressure from the missionary community to redefine its role in China. Anti-foreign feeling was increasing, and the missionaries were on the front lines of the Western incursion into China. Inflamed by virulent anti-Christian propaganda, mobs in Nanjing, Chengdu and in Fujian and Jiangsu provinces attacked mission buildings and threatened both missionaries and converts. American diplomats were not necessarily sympathetic; they blamed the missionaries for rashly moving into areas known to be hotbeds of nativism, such as Hunan Province, and then demanding military protection. Nevertheless, the diplomats convinced the reformists under Emperor Guangxu to accept full responsibility for protecting missions. The United States also sent two additional steamships to patrol the Yangtze River and the China coast.

In 1899, President McKinley's government finally announced its new China policy. The policy was designed to protect America's China interests and to foster the vision that the United States and China shared a "special relationship." This was based on the fact that the United States had never used force in its dealings with China. There was also thought to be some shared history—both nations had had to deal with European aggression. The racist anti-Chinese exclusionary laws from the 1880s on were not mentioned in discussions of this idealized relationship.

Formulated by Secretary of State John Hay, the Open Door Policy requested that Japan and the European powers respect China's government and territorial integrity and allow all the powers, including the United States, equal access to the facilities of the treaty ports. The other nations reluctantly agreed, largely because they realized that further annexations would bring them into military conflict with each other.

The Open Door Policy may have slowed imperialist designs on China, but events continued to steamroll ahead, pushing the Chinese government and Westerners into another bloody conflict. In September 1898, Cixi, the Dowager Empress, suddenly returned to Beijing and arrested Emperor Guangxu, her nephew, whom she had placed on the throne in 1875. At the same time there arose in Shandong Province a nativist militia force, largely poor peasants, who called themselves the Boxers United in Righteousness. Christian missions were their primary target, and they destroyed many mission buildings and killed several converts. They believed a new age would dawn in 1900, and in late spring of that year they began to move north and west toward Beijing, destroying on the way all symbols of the West from clocks to train lines and killing six Europeans.

The Western powers quickly reacted to the Boxer threat, especially after it became clear that they were supported by the Dowager Empress. In early June, the guard on Beijing's legation quarter was strengthened by an allied force of British, French, Russian, American, Italian and Japanese troops. Immediately thereafter, the Boxers cut the rail line between Beijing and the coast. Another international force was dispatched from allied warships in the Gulf of Zhili, but they were attacked and defeated by a Boxer army. The legations were now isolated, and the Dowager Empress ordered her troops to resist any foreign invasion. The Boxers swarmed through Beijing burning foreign churches, businesses and homes and killing Chinese converts.

After the allies seized the Dagu forts outside Tianjin, the Dowager Empress declared war on the foreigners and organized the Boxers into the imperial army. On June 20, all foreigners in Beijing assembled in the legation quarter hoping to be escorted to the coast. Instead, they heard the news that the German ambassador had been assassinated and

Cixi, the Dowager Empress (1834-1908)

that they were surrounded by Boxer militias bent on their extermination—an escape attempt would mean death. They were besieged. With no one but themselves to turn to, the foreign residents organized a highly effective defense. All non-combatants were moved to the British legation, whose fortifications were designed by F. D. Gamewell, an American Methodist minister. Despite near-constant attacks and extremely low food supplies, the 3,800 foreigners and Chinese converts besieged in the legation were relatively lucky. Only 75 foreigners were killed out of 800; casualty rates among the Chinese do not appear to have been recorded.

Those foreigners, mostly missionaries, who were trapped in the provinces at the outbreak of the Boxer Rebellion, were less fortunate. The worst massacres took place in Shanxi Province, just west of Beijing. There 172 foreigners were killed, including 32 American missionary men, women and children. On a lesser scale, these killings were replicated in Henan, Hebei, Manchuria and Sichuan.

News of the massacres and the siege in Beijing quickly spread to the Western Hemisphere. In the United States, the sensationalist newspapers of the day stirred up anti-Chinese feeling with grossly exaggerated accounts, frequently reporting a savage slaughter of all foreigners in the legation quarter. These reports were fleshed out with descriptions of grisly Chinese customs —torture, Satanism, etc.—that portrayed "John Chinaman" as lower and crueler than an animal. Anti-Chinese violence spread and even Chinese diplomats were insulted by American officials.

The pressure to act was enormous, but the allied forces had a number of obstacles to overcome before they could march on Beijing. First, they had to take Tianjin, with its large foreign community (among them a young Herbert Hoover, then working as a mining engineer), from a hard-fighting Chinese force. The allies were embarrassed that it took weeks for 10,000 of their troops to defeat 15,000 Chinese, now equipped with more modern weaponry, mostly Mauser rifles. By the time they finally captured the city, Tianjin was in ruins and aflame. The allied soldiers released tension by looting the city; the Russians were apparently the worst offenders, but the Americans had to admit that, yes, some of their troops took part as well.

The road to Beijing was now open to them, but the allies wasted precious days bickering over who would supply the heavy weapons for the expedition. Japan was naturally the nearest military power; however, the Westerners did not want to open the door for another Japanese adventure, such as what happened after the 1894 Sino-Japanese War. Eventually, they reached an agreement, and on August 4th a force of about 20,000, including 8,000 Japanese and 2,100 Americans of the Chinese Relief Expedition (mainly Marines and Army cavalry and infantry from the Philippines), set out for Beijing.

(above) Peking Legations. In July 1900 these foreign defenders found this old cannon which they put to use against the Boxers. Christened the "International" but often referred to as "Old Betsy," the gun was manned by British and American Legation Guards

The Boxers (right) dressed in brightly colored clothing and wore headbands and religious amulets to protect themselves from foreign bullets

United States Marines in Beijing

Progress was slow, the road hot in the summer sun and muddy when it rained. The troops were beset by frequent small-scale attacks and responded by shooting everything in sight, including helpless local peasants. *". . . But not by Americans,"* [italics theirs] claimed the official report. There were also many complaints about the order of march: The Japanese, the quickest, were first, followed by the Russians, who were considered the slowest. The Russians liked to stop and rest in every village they entered; thus the Americans, just behind, were forced to take their rest stops unprotected from the broiling sun.

Finally, on August 14th they reached the walls of Beijing. The allies attacked on a number of fronts. The Chinese were distracted by a premature assault; on their side, the Americans took the brunt of the attack, while the British entered through a gate and managed to reach the legation quarter with almost no opposition. In the middle of the afternoon a company of Sikh troops marched into the British legation grounds, where they were met by the foreign residents, weak from hunger but dressed in their best clothes (they had heard that help was finally near). A spectator described the scene as "like a garden party."

The Dowager Empress fled with her court to Xi'an, and the next days were spent mopping up Chinese resistance. Punitive

expeditions were also sent out into the country supposedly to erase any potential threat but mostly to find booty and supplies for the coming winter. The allies, now in control, divided the city up into sections, each patrolled by one of the foreign forces. Once again, looting was widespread; the Americans claimed that much of their booty was not stolen but bought from the British (presumably the looters). Some American missionaries, such as W.S. Ament, also participated in looting, justifying their actions by the greater good of supporting their missionary activities (in a series of satires, Mark Twain gave them a withering reply). The American forces requisitioned as their headquarters the Temple of Agriculture in the southern part of the Chinese City. On August 28th, after much discussion, the allies marched through the inner gates of the Forbidden City—where "the foot of the white man had never pressed"—and took possession of the center of the Chinese universe.

No more humiliating defeat could be imagined. On September 1st, the allies and the remnants of the imperial government signed the Boxer Protocol. Even for the then 60-year-long history of Western-Chinese treaties, the terms were unprecedented. The leading pro-Boxer officials would be executed, a monument would be erected to the Western dead, arms imports would be forbidden for two years and the Beijing legation quarter could have permanent guards and artillery emplacements for defense. Most damagingly, the Qing government would have to pay a massively-inflated indemnity of 450 million taels, equal to almost twice the yearly imperial income. They were given 39 years to pay up, with significant interest charges.

It took 18 months for the Dowager Empress to return to Beijing. In the meantime, Westerners roamed through the Forbidden City, marvelling at the treasures, poking through the imperial bedrooms and trying out the thrones. As soon as some semblance of peace was restored, President McKinley withdrew most American troops, needing them to quell opposition to the American takeover in the Philippines. At the same time, he also greatly increased the naval American

Two views of old Hong Kong, ca. 1868

Two views of Macau, ca. 1873

USS Charleston *off Hong Kong, June 22, 1898*

presence on the China coast; soon there were almost 50 U.S. Navy ships on patrol, mostly small gunboats, in addition to three battleships nearby in the Pacific.

When the Dowager Empress resumed residence in the Forbidden City, she was in the mood for compromise. She opened her doors to foreign ambassadors and initiated a series of reforms aimed at modernizing the imperial system and, she hoped, propping up the tottering Qing Dynasty. The old examination system was abolished; ministries were established to oversee commercial and industrial affairs; and foreign affairs were reorganized and professionalized. Despite these changes, it was probably too late—events had moved ahead.

Chinese opposition to the imperial system had finally begun to appear. Democratic and republican ideals filtered across from the United States. Sun Yat-sen had attended mission schools in Hawaii, while his backer Charlie Soong had trained to be a missionary at a college in North Carolina. However, the growing anti-Chinese sentiments and immigration restrictions in the United States soon made England, France and, later, Japan far more attractive for Chinese students. If not for racism, the United States' influ-

ence on Chinese history would have been far greater. One center of revolutionary activity was Hong Kong, where Sun Yat-sen was for a time a medical student at the University. In 1895, he had tried to topple Canton's government from here, and it remained a center of his Revolutionary Alliance through the 1911 revolution.

With the Open Door Policy now established, Washington attempted to use it as a lever to increase American influence and access to business opportunities. In return, a much more politically-astute Chinese foreign office tried to convince the United States to act as a mediator in disputes with foreign powers. The United States asked the allies to reduce the outrageously inflated Boxer indemnity; they refused, and instead Washington agreed to donate much of their money to subsidizing Chinese education. When the Russian and Japanese conflict over Manchuria came to war in 1904 (bringing the devastating defeat of the Russian navy), the subsequent peace treaty negotiations were held in Portsmouth, New Hampshire. The Chinese were thankful for American help; however, they would not agree to force the foreign powers to give up their exclusive rights to ports, mines and railway concessions. For that,

USS Olympia *firing a Washington's birthday salute, Hong Kong Harbor, 1898*

the Chinese said, the Americans would have to play a much more active role, perhaps backed by military might, in defending the integrity of Chinese territory.

In 1905, American interests hit a substantial roadblock: The first widespread Chinese protest against the United States. Chinese communities across the United States sent reports home of racist acts and humiliations, many inflicted by the Bureau of Immigration. To protest, the Shanghai Chamber of Commerce announced plans for a boycott of all American goods. The boycott began on July 20th and quickly spread to Canton, that long-time hotbed of anti-foreign feeling, and other coastal cities. In Shanghai, a Cantonese student committed suicide on the steps of the American consulate. Although the boycott faded after a few months (it lasted into early 1906 in Canton), it did catch President Theodore Roosevelt's attention. Unfortunately, his extended review of the Chinese exclusion laws led to no concrete changes.

The Chinese now decided to make a more direct appeal for American support. They were particularly worried about Manchuria, a booming industrial region, where, despite a war, the Russians and Japanese were now even more firmly ensconced. First, a Chinese delegation visited American financiers, including E.H. Harriman, to offer them the rights to build a railway in South Manchuria and enlist their support in an industrial development bank. Next, they went down to Washington to convince the Roosevelt administration to give them political and, perhaps, military backing. President Roosevelt, however, had little attachment to China and the Chinese; he backed Russian rights in Manchuria and would rather have Japan tied up in China than threatening the Philippines. Stalled, the plan collapsed after the 1908 death of the Dowager Empress and a purge of the Chinese foreign office.

Roosevelt was succeeded by the weighty William Howard Taft. (On an earlier visit to Hong Kong, Taft had needed a record eight porters to carry his sedan chair; not to lose face, the Governor of Hong Kong was carried by eight porters for the next few months.) Taft and his Secretary of State, Philander Knox, decided to embark on a much more ambitious China policy than their predecessors. Once again the goal was Manchuria, but this time the United States, not China, was the initiator. Knox enlisted a group of the most prestigious Wall Street financiers, including J.P. Morgan and National

BANDITRY

In Chinese literature there is no permanent definition
of a bandit or non-bandit. The connotation depends on
time, circumstance, and subjective point of view.

~Li Chien-Nung

A famous instance of banditry occurred in 1923, when there was really no central government, except in name. Nevertheless the Peking government was held responsible by the Westerners, who had to negotiate with someone, and in the end the twenty-five odd foreigners were rescued. The case was notorious because it was so bold, and because so many nationalities were involved. It was called after the railway station near which it took place, Linching, in Shantung, where some bandits derailed the Tientsin-Pukow Express, abducting certain passengers, who had been on their way to Shanghai on the Blue Express, the best train on the line.

Shantung was a particularly bandit-ridden province, full of ex-soldiers who had no chance of employment. In the various armies at that time, in more or less loose information in North China, there were reckoned to be something over a million men, but they had no zeal in suppressing bandits. Many of them had followed this occupation, and might well do so again; they were unpaid, wretchedly clothed, hungry, unprincipled, undisciplined. On the mountainous borders of Shantung, where if need arose they could slip over a safer frontier, bandits could operate almost with impunity.

Linching was an almost ideal place for an ambush; here a thousand-odd bandits tore up a length of track, and then waited for the Express which thundered along in the middle of the night and was derailed. The bandits hurried aboard and forced about two hundred passengers off the train, not giving them time to dress, though they were quick about collecting their valuables.

The foreigners included British, Americans, Danes, Italians, Germans, and French, some of them on their way around the world as part of a luxury trip; others were businessmen. Among the tourists was Miss Lucy Aldrich, whose sister married into the Rockefeller family. The bandits had no idea who she was, and as she did not prove a good walker and they felt in a hurry, they soon left her in a field. She made her way to safety; probably they never knew what a prize they had abandoned.

A friend of ours happened to be on the Blue Express that night, a businessman called Day, who afterwards told us a good deal about it. He was a good observer, being very calm and optimistic. He could not help being amused throughout by the bandits' naiveté and ignorance, even when he was distressed over what they were doing. He was upset at the plight of some of the women, who were pushed off the train in their nightgowns, barefoot, and made to walk over the rough fields, or mounted on donkeys, which they found almost as bad. Mr. Day was sure everyone would come out unscathed, but there were dangerous possibilities of accidents—the bandits were ingenuous, but they were also armed. One youthful bandit came up to him and took his watch, offering him at the same time another, very inferior one, which he had taken off someone else's wrist a few moments before. Another man approached him, his two hands cupped together and brimming over with rings, asking him to value them for him. The bandits took the whole situation as a perfectly normal thing, unlike their indignant and appalled captives.

The prisoners were taken to an old fort on the top of a mountain and held for several weeks, while negotiations went on between the bandits, the Chinese authorities, and the various consuls concerned. It was uncomfortable in the camp, and the captives were both hungry and bored. A kindly missionary contrived to send them all he had to give: some pork and a few copies of the New Testament, gifts which were rather ruefully commented upon by a Jewish reporter (who, however, gratefully sent the man of God a contribution for his mission, when the affair was over).

Colonel Aldrich's textbook, *Practical Chinese,* contains a number of phrases to be used in these contingencies, like: "The local militia's Adjutant General says, 'We have already ordered a battalion of cavalry from Pao-t'ou to take along two motor cars and go to the rescue. It will not be long before the kidnapped persons are out of danger . . . I hope that this matter may have a most satisfactory conclusion.'"

~Enid Saunders Candlin,
The Breach in the Wall: A Memoir of the Old China

INCIDENT OF THE BLUE EXPRESS

Daybreak revealed one of the strangest sights that these ancient hills had ever witnessed. The train passengers, each still accompanied by two individual captors, were strung out for a half mile up the side of the mountain, while to the rear there was another straggling line of bandits almost as long, sweating under the loot they had taken from the train, including our suitcases and even the precious mattresses from the sleeping berths. As the sun came up and it grew warmer and the climb more precipitous, the bandits would dump the mattresses on the ground and sit or lie on them.

All of the bandits had trinkets they had taken from the compartments, including tooth brushes and paste, safety razors and shaving cream, cameras and rolls of films, fountain pens, rings of keys, pocket knives, tins of talcum powder, and women's beauty accessories. One bandit had found a lady's brassière which he had tied about his waist; he was using the compartments to carry his valuables. Since most of the passengers were without shoes, the going was slow and hazardous and painful, as there was only a narrow rocky path leading to the summit of the mountain. Since Berube and I had our shoes we walked faster and soon were at the head of the long line. There I noticed a woman riding a donkey bareback and having considerable difficulty in staying on and keeping her silk nightgown from blowing away entirely in the gale. I searched my mind to think of something I could do to help her. Noticing a bandit carrying a lady's broad-brimmed straw hat which he had taken from the train, I asked him for it and pointed toward the woman on the donkey. He laughed and handed me the hat. I caught up with the donkey-rider, who was Miss Aldrich, and handed her the hat, but she soon threw it away, as it was impossible to keep it on and remain on the donkey at the same time. She needed other articles of attire more than the hat.

Our slow pace up the mountainside was suddenly accelerated by rifle shots fired from a considerable distance in the rear which zimmed over our heads and ricocheted off the rocks above us. The shots were fired by a contingent of militia which had been dispatched from a nearby town by the railway authorities. Our captors immediately returned the fire, while we dodged for protection behind the nearest rocks, but there was little actual danger, as both sides were firing wild.

At about 10 o'clock in the morning we reached the top of the mountain, on which was a crude fort with walls and rifle rests all about. We climbed through an opening and fell in a heap, completely exhausted and nearly famished. After resting a few minutes we went through the available baggage brought up by the bandits, and managed to find a few needed articles of clothing. Someone would yell, "Hey, there, give me my pants," and there would be an exchange, much to the amusement of the bandits. Several of the men sacrificed their pajama shirts for use as bandages for the bleeding feet and sprained ankles of the women.

But the strangest scene of all was enacted when Mademoiselle Schonberg caught up with her mistress and joyously restored to her the family jewels. With great presence of mind Miss Aldrich carefully inspected the surrounding terrain and when the bandits looked the other way, she concealed the purse under a large flat stone. Later she borrowed a pencil from a bandit chief and made a rough sketch of the place where she had concealed the purse. Carefully folding the little piece of paper, she placed it in the toe of her shoes. Weeks later, after the bandit affair had been liquidated, a Chinese clerk in the Socony office in Tsinanfu went to the district, found the purse and returned it intact to the owner.

~John B. Powell,
My Twenty-five Years in China

City Bank, in a project to purchase Manchuria's railways from the Russians and Japanese and hand them over to Chinese control. Unfortunately, he counted on the support of Britain and Germany, who decided that it was not in their interests: The plan would give too much power to the United States. Another political/industrial scheme slid off the tracks.

For foreign business interests, railways were the prime plum that China had to offer. After a slow start, Chinese railway construction had finally taken off in the 1880s.

The industry boomed after the Boxer Rebellion, but increasing nationalism led to questions about why foreigners were granted concessions to strategic and potentially-profitable parts of China's infrastructure. By this time the Chinese had the money to build their own railways (with foreign machinery and know-how). In 1905, the American China Development Company, which in 1898 had acquired the rights to build a line between Canton and Hankou, was forced to sell them back to the Chinese. For a time the imperial government was determined to nationalize all Chinese railways; soon, however, they realized they could not do it alone. When government officials decided to ask foreign bankers for a loan to complete the Canton-Hankou line, they sparked a series of nationalistic protests in early 1911 that fueled the movement for revolution.

In October 1911, an investigation by Qing authorities into an accidental explosion at a bomb-making factory of Sun Yat-sen's Revolutionary Alliance turned up name lists of Alliance members. Rather than risk capture, the revolutionaries decide to fight back. Although its main support was among students, the Revolutionary Alliance was also backed by workers, provincial assemblymen and soldiers in the reorganized Chinese army, many of whom had lost faith in the government over railway concessions to foreigners. Military units rebelled in Wuhan, then in Shaanxi and Hunan provinces, toppling the local governments; revolutionary alliances replaced the leaderships of Shanxi, Jiangxi and Yunnan. After a series of military defeats, the Qing gave in to demands for the formation of a constitutional monarchy with Yuan Shikai, the populist governor of Tianjin, as its premier. Sun Yat-sen, fund-raising in the United States, learned about the revolution on a train heading to Kansas City. He headed home via London and Paris, where he asked that European governments not give financial support to the Qing forces. The United States also remained studiously neutral, all the while hoping for a rebel victory.

Sun Yat-sen and his wife, Soong Qingling

Sun Yat-sen returned to China on December 25, 1911 and within days was elected provisional president of a Chinese republic by delegates from provincial assemblies. Yuan Shikai still had the trust and backing of the army, however. Within a month Sun had to resign, because neither Yuan nor the army threw their support behind him. Meanwhile, the Manchu were in retreat. Supporters of the child Emperor Puyi and his relatives finally negotiated an agreement giving the imperial family protection and right to occupy the Forbidden City; in return, on February 12, 1912, Puyi abdicated the Chinese throne, ending two millennia of imperial rule.

While the other foreign powers adopted a wait-and-see approach to the new regime, the United States was more enthusiastic. The missionaries were particularly zealous in their support, seeing it as a crusade of Christian rebels against the pagan Manchus. Many revolutionary leaders, including Sun Yat-sen, were the products of mission schools, and their

By 1913, the China market was still a myth, at least for United States business interests. They were a distant sixth in China investment after, in descending order, Great Britain, Russia, Germany, Japan and France; the American share of foreign investment was 3.1% compared to Britain's 37.7%. Out of China's 5,771 miles of rail line, they had only built 29 miles, all by the American China Development Company. Due to local Chinese and Japanese competition, the American share of the cotton trade was quickly shrinking (and would disappear after 1929). The only place where the United States had a real presence was in Shanghai real estate and in oil products and tobacco. The International Banking Corporation, founded by New York financiers, had 14 branches in China by 1914, but was relatively small compared to the British banks. American businessmen blamed their problems on foreign opposition—and the British stranglehold on financing—blocking them from real profits. However, Standard Oil and British-American Tobacco proved that with a determined effort and an imaginative approach you could succeed in China. The truth was that the United States business community was still not very interested in China investments.

For the Americans, the only growth industry was, once again, in the missions. In the late 19th century, a religious revival had again swept through the United States, burning with particular intensity in colleges and universities. Thousands of students pledged themselves to overseas missions, many of them in China. This time, however, the fire-

Two-year old Puyi, who became China's last Emperor

republican ideals were obviously influenced by their American curricula. Yuan Shikai also played to the missionary audience by asking Protestant churches to "pray for" China, a widely-publicized act that won praise from American Protestants ranging from William Jennings Bryan to Woodrow Wilson, the new president. The new republican government raised hope that the United States could finally reap the benefits of the "special relationship."

and-brimstone was more subdued than in previous eras; saving souls was still a priority, but less intensely. For many missionaries, it was increasingly important to bring to the Chinese the other fruits of Western civilization, including improved health care, modern education and more rights for women. The militant behavior of missionaries during the Boxer Rebellion and their subsequent condemnation also helped change many attitudes.

Between 1900 and 1914, the United States was awash with campaigns to find volunteers and raise money for China missions. Using language highly reminiscent of the promotion of the American West in the late 19th century, veteran missionaries wrote books and pamphlets describing the Chinese mission field as "virgin soil waiting to be plowed." Thousands of Protestant missionaries and millions of dollars poured into China. Hundreds of mission schools and hospitals and six Christian colleges were opened. In 1914, the Rockefeller Foundation acquired control of the Peking Union Medical Foundation and built it into perhaps the finest hospital in Asia. In retrospect, the era between 1903 and 1925 was the golden age of the Protestant mission movement.

"Merry Widows" of Fuzhou, staff of the Southside Foreign School, 1908

Missionaries even managed to succeed in the most virulently anti-foreign parts of China. Founded in memory of a Yale missionary beheaded in 1892, the Yale-in-China project estab-

lished itself in Changsha, the capital of Hunan Province. The mission followed the model of Dr. Peter Parker: They downplayed the evangelical side and emphasized the medical side. The clinic was run by Dr. Edward Hume, whose treatment of

JOSEPH WHITTLESEY NOBLE, PENNSYLVANIA DENTIST

In 1887, at the age of twenty-five, Dr. Joseph Whittlesey Noble set up a dental practice in Hong Kong. Times were hard and his partner, Herbert Poate, gave up and returned to his native England.

Noble's luck changed when a wealthy American took him on a trip to Japan aboard his yacht as his personal dentist. Shortly afterwards we find him in the Forbidden City, fixing the teeth of the Manchu imperial family. Noble was soon opening dental clinics all over Asia.

With Sir Patrick Manson, Sir James Cantlie and Sir Kai Ho Kai, Noble was one of the founders of the Hong Kong College of Medicine, where Dr. Sun Yat-sen, the first President of the Republic of China, was a student.

Sir Patrick had also established the Dairy Farm Company to provide Hong Kong's population with fresh milk. After he left Hong Kong, the Dairy Farm herd was decimated by attacks of bubonic plague and rinderpest. Dr. Noble acquired the company at a very distressed price.

Noble was one of those taipans who seems to have sat on the board of almost every major Hong Kong company. The list includes the Ice and Cold Storage Co., Hong Kong Hotel Co., Hong Kong Tramways, Hong Kong Electric Co., Green Island Cement and many others.

Like many successful businessmen, Noble had ambitions of becoming a press baron. His opportunity arose in 1907, when Alfred Cunningham, the brilliant founder of the *South China Morning Post,* went on vacation. Noble, who was on the board of the newspaper, staged a coup. He accused Cunningham of gross mismanagement and spending too much money on paper and ink. Cunningham was fired.

In 1911, Noble bought outright the *Hongkong Telegraph* which was later amalgamated with the *Morning Post.* He returned to Pennsylvania in 1925 and died in 1949.

Today Dr. Joseph Whittlesey Noble, taipan, educator, dairy farmer, imperial dentist and press baron, is best remembered as the owner of the first automobile in Hong Kong.

~ARTHUR HACKER

(top) Yale-in-China instructors in Victory Parade, 1918
(above) Yale-in-China Surgical Service, Hsiang Ya Hospital, September 1935

both rich and poor patients forged personal ties that allowed the program to weather China's turbulence. Yale-in-China built the clinic into a hospital and medical school and also established a secondary school that became known as one of the region's best. In 1919, the program hired as editor of its magazine a local student radical named Mao Zedong.

Not all missionaries were as savvy as Hume; many were young, naive and on their first trip outside the United States. They could not get over China's foreignness and, having little evangelical success, returned home as soon as their tours were up. One of the most frequent criticisms of foreign missionaries was that they did not have enough faith in Chinese converts to give them positions of authority. Notable exceptions were the Young Men's and Young Women's Christian Associations. Since the late 19th century, the YMCAs and YWCAs had concentrated on China's urban areas, constructing large buildings and offering a wide range of social, athletic and educational programs. Young urban Chinese, raised in a far different social and political setting than their parents, joined these organizations in droves. By the early 1920s, the Ys had over 50,000 members, and Chinese occupied a significant number of administrative positions.

The inroads American and British missionaries were making into China

Beginning chemistry class, Old Ginling missionary school, before 1919

American educators had a far greater impact than many missionaries. Old Ginling, 1919

during the early 20th century finally began to worry the Catholics. There had always been significantly more Catholic missionaries—the vast majority of them French—and Catholic converts in China (in 1914, there were estimated to be 1.4 million Catholics and a little over 250,000 Protestants). Despite much opposition from the French missionary establishment, in 1915 the Vatican decided the time had come to head off the

competition. The spearhead of the English-language Catholic mission movement was to be the Maryknoll Society (formally known as the Catholic Foreign Mission Society of America), based near Ossining, New York. Unfortunately, when they arrived in China in 1921, they found their main problem was dealing with the cultural barrier between themselves and the French, who distrusted these relative newcomers to the faith.

FOREIGN FLAGS FOR SALE

American officials did less flag selling than many others but were not entirely guiltless. More than thirty years ago a young American consul was given his first post at an unimportant port in South China. On the following Christmas he found several dozen live turkeys in his compound and his kitchen full of hams and cases of liquor. The houseboy, who had worked in the consulate for years, explained that these were Christmas presents from the "American subjects" living in the consular district. The fact that any Americans besides a few missionaries were under his protection was news to the consul, and he started an investigation which disclosed some interesting and profitable activities of his predecessor.

The latter had issued "certificates of good character" to hundreds of Chinese, affixing the consular seal to each and collecting the consular notarial fee. The certificates were good for only one year, and their renewal provided a neat little annual revenue in fees alone. Those were the days when American consuls got very small salaries or no salaries at all, and their principal compensation came from the fees they collected. Honest consuls, who were not unknown, had a hard time saving up enough money for the return fare when a change of administration would mean the appointment of a successor; but those who were adept at manipulating fees enjoyed a fair degree of prosperity. There was nothing technically illegal about issuing these certificates of good character, but the intent was to protect the holders from Chinese courts. Any Chinese official who glanced at the imposing consular seal would come to the conclusion that the holder of the document was some kind of American and would think twice before sending him to jail or ordering his head chopped off. . . .

ও

At frequent intervals some upcountry missionary would come to Shanghai to denounce the wickedness of the city as exemplified by the lives of the foreigners. I suppose all of us could qualify as horrible examples. About fifteen years ago one of these missionaries, after a careful but inexpert survey of the iniquities of the place, came to the conclusion that Gabriel would soon blow his horn if for no other reason than to bring destruction to the sinful foreigners of Shanghai. He said it was the most wicked city in the world, but there were some doubts as to his authority to express an opinion on this subject, for investigation

showed that he had never been to Port Said or Saigon and had passed through Nagasaki without becoming acquainted with its water-front dives. He deserted his post upcountry to come to Shanghai with this direful message and preached a good many sermons and passed out tracts.

The Chinese greatly enjoyed listening to a denunciation of sins of the foreigners, but their enjoyment palled when they learned that they were included. He finally set the day—a very inconvenient day—for it meant that the end of the world would come just when Shanghai people would be enjoying the spring races. He had gone too far. Shanghailanders surveyed themselves and their neighbors and came to the conclusion that the city was not so sinful as it had been painted. They felt about the same as New Yorkers felt a short time ago when the supposed wickedness of the place was assailed by a visiting governor. They were so far above the level of iniquity he had described that they felt positively virtuous. The community was pondering what to do about it when the problem was solved for them.

Some waggish newspapermen got together and issued an extra "doomsday" edition of a fake newspaper confirming the fact that the prophecy of the missionary had been fulfilled. Crowds at the race track were startled and then amused when newsboys offered them papers with a screaming banner headline announcing:

WORLD COMES TO AN END

The paper containing news dispatches from all the great capitals told of the event and in interviews told of the reactions of many famous men. The news editor, in a summary of these dispatches, noted that the world had apparently come to an end no earlier in Shanghai than in the home town of the apostle who had denounced its wickedness. The leading editorial was very philosophic in tone and came to the well-reasoned conclusion that it had not been such a bad world after all. There was also a pleasant little editorial note commending the always efficient Shanghai Municipal Police on how they had handled a very unusual situation. The sensational missionary soon went on home leave and never was heard of again in Shanghai.

~Carl Crow,
Foreign Devils in the Flowery Kingdom

American Catholics found they had more in common with fellow American missionaries, even though they were Protestant. The Maryknoll Fathers and other Catholic mission groups persisted, building missions throughout China, but they did not weaken the burgeoning Protestant presence.

That the missionaries succeeded in the years following the downfall of the Qing is an impressive achievement. Yuan Shikai's rule soon deteriorated into dictatorship; he was convinced (by an American advisor, among others) that a supreme authority was needed in China and began gathering the trappings of imperial power around him. Unfortunately, this effort took place concurrently with the first years of the Great War. The European powers were distracted at home, and the Japanese decided to fill the vacuum. In 1915, they promulgated their Twenty-One Demands, asking for greatly increased rights in North and Central China. Although he negotiated them down, Yuan was forced to submit. The subsequent massive protests and anti-Japanese boycott broke his government and weakened Beijing's authority over the provinces. Yuan died in early 1916, leaving China to a new class of ruler—warlords. For the next decade, China was broken into pieces, each part ruled by a local despot, usually an ex-army officer primarily concerned with profits and power.

In 1919, the Chinese received another blow. The Chinese delegation to the Versailles Peace Conference discovered that, in return for Japanese naval support, the British, French and Italians had signed a secret treaty with the Japanese giving them all Germany's rights in Shandong Province. In addition, the politicians who ran China's greatly weakened national government had also signed secret agreements with the Japanese with further concessions. When the news reached China, it sparked a student demonstration in Beijing on May 4, 1919. Thus began the May 4th Movement, consisting mainly of students, which was determined to build a new China without the impediments of the Confucian past or the hypocrisies of the West (as revealed in the brutalities of World War I and at the Versailles Conference). Many of these new energies were channeled into Sun Yat-sen's Guomindang or, later, into the Chinese Communist Party, which was formed in 1921 under direction of the Comintern (the international arm of the new Soviet Union).

United States Marines on a "jitney" in China, 1916

Miss Betty Guden, a graduate of Wellesley College, outfitted her rickshaw driver with a bicycle

In the postwar turmoil, the foreign populations thrived — except for the Germans, whose influence and numbers dropped dramatically. The center of foreign interests was Shanghai, the most modern city in China. By the 1920s, a line of modern office buildings was rising along the Bund, the stretch of Huangpu River waterfront that was the site of the first foreign settlement. These graceful colonial and Art Deco buildings housed the most important Shanghai institutions, including the Customs House, the Municipal Council, the Shanghai Club and the many of the major banks. Just across Suzhou Creek stood the American and Japanese consulates, the Hongkong and Shanghai Bank and the Astor House Hotel. To the west lay the race course—the center of the foreign community's social calendar—with its tennis courts and cricket field inside the oval of the track. Further west and to the northeast, wide avenues ran through miles of gardened suburbs with elegant European-style mansions hiding behind tall walls. Immediately south of the International

Settlement and east of the Chinese City lay the French Concession with its separate administration and police force.

Before World War I, life in Shanghai—at least for the more respectable part of the foreign community—was divided between business and social life. Work does not seem to have been that time-consuming—for many the work day ran from 10 A.M. to 3 P.M.—and life at home was largely run by servants. Foreigners had lots of time on their hands. The main recreations were sports, including rowing, golf and horseback riding, and drinking—rounds and rounds of whiskey sodas either at the club (the Shanghai Club claimed to have the longest bar in the world) or before dinner parties at home.

For the wives, the parties ended at ten, when all respectable women retired to bed. For the men, the socializing continued and often included excursions into Shanghai's demimonde. In the early 1900s, the city's fanciest brothel was American-owned: Gracie Gale's establishment at 52 Jiangxi

Road. Plushly decorated in Belle Epoque furnishings, her establishment sported a wide variety of imported talent, most, like Gale, natives of San Francisco's Barbary Coast. Gale's girls set the fashion standard for Shanghai's foreign women; during the day they paraded through Shanghai's streets in open carriages as a sort of moving advertisement. Respectable women were openly scandalized but secretly took notes on their outfits and passed the information on to their dressmakers. Gale's brothel began to decline in the 1920s, when a month with a recently arrived Russian mistress cost less than a night with one of her girls.

Foreigners usually had little, if any, contact with the Chinese community, except for servants and the occasional wealthy Chinese business partner they

Fuzhou races, 1910

might meet through work. Foreign social life was particularly segregated, not only from the Chinese but from their own countrymen. As in many British-dominated settings, people's lives were determined by an elaborate series of finely-tuned distinctions. For instance, a certain section of the Shanghai Club bar was reserved for the taipans, the leaders

of the business community. If a junior manager took a seat there, he risked not only a reprimand but expulsion from the club and loss of all his business contacts—his career in Shanghai would be over.

(continues on page 94)

"CRAZY" HARRY ABBOTT, AVIATOR

"Crazy" Harry Abbott, like his father Wayne Abbott, was an aviator. Wayne, a former circus bareback rider and balloonist, held the high altitude parachute jump record of 7,800 feet until 1919, when Harry beat his father's record with a jump of 8,300 feet.

Harry was also a circus performer and flying instructor. In 1922, he went to China where he spent the next couple of years training pilots and fighting as a mercenary in the air force of Sun Yat-sen. He rose to the rank of Lieutenant-Colonel, fought in three major battles and was wounded.

He resigned in 1924 and moved to Hong Kong. A year later he leased a flat area of land at Kai Tak, known as the Kowloon City Field, where Kai Tak International Airport is today.

Harry bought a damaged Curtiss JN-4C biplane and set about repairing it. A former high wire walker, Harry planned to put on a wing-walking act, but just as he stepped out on to the wing of his aircraft, the engine stalled. The plane crashed

on landing. He repaired it again and a few weeks later crashed it again.

Undeterred by these disasters, "Crazy" Harry bought a new plane and started a flying school. The official opening of the Abbott School of Aviation was designed to be a spectacular affair. Unfortunately everything went wrong. The lucky firecrackers tied to the tail of his plane were damp and refused to explode. Worse still, the parachute jump performed by his gallant mechanic, Reg Earnshaw, ended in disaster. Earnshaw completely missed the airport and fell into the harbor and drowned.

Harry ran out of money and moved to San Francisco where he started another flying school at Mill's Field, which later became the San Francisco International Airport. This time he was successful. In 1930, having made a fortune, Harry decided to build his own plane, the Abbott Baby. It crashed and Harry was killed. He was only twenty-nine.

~ARTHUR HACKER

DON'T DRINK THE WATER!

Among the characteristics of the foreign devil was an ability to keep sober under conditions that, to the outside observer, made that fact appear well-nigh incredible. It may as well be admitted that the foreigner on the China Coast drank a great deal. In no place in China in the early days was there any water that could be used for cooking or drinking. In Shanghai the muddy Whangpoo was settled by the use of alum and no amount of filtering or boiling would completely remove the alum taste. An infusion of whisky or gin not only made the water palatable but was thought by many of the doctors of that period to be efficacious in the destruction of germs. The same doctors thought malaria came from excretions from the soil and induced the municipal council to prohibit the laying of drains during the summer months. They were probably wrong about the efficacy of whisky and gin but their opinions were honest and they had many followers. To this day no one drinks water that has not been filtered and either boiled or distilled and how flat, tasteless and unsatisfying it is as a drink. And as no one can be sure that the water has been properly filtered and boiled it is generally looked on as a dangerous drink. In the course of years whisky may cause hardening of the arteries but it will not bring on an attack of typhoid. Wine and spirits of all kinds were always abundant on the China Coast for their importation did not have to await the development of cold storage. With a small import duty and no excise or license fees to pay, prices were cheaper than any other place in the world. Conditions are different now but a quarter of a century ago liquor was so cheap that there was an elaborately stocked sideboard in almost every home.

Thomas Cook, the pioneer travel agent, came to Shanghai in the early days of the settlement and was so shocked by the drinking habits of the foreigners that he spent all his time while in the port distributing tracts about the evils of hard drink. The temperance movement never languished for lack of human material. There was always at least one local resident who viewed the habits of his fellow townsmen with alarm. In 1911 it was Consul General Wilder who tried to get every young American to sign the pledge on his arrival. One Sunday the consul general fell in a faint while on his way home from church. A fellow parishioner rushed into a near-by bar and brought out a glass of brandy. Just as the stricken man was about to open his lips he closed them tight and whispered, "That's whisky. Take it away, I'd rather die than have a drop of alcohol pass my lips."

He was one of the very few foreigners who was so allergic to alcohol. The foreign devil drank, but in so far as that is possible, he drank wisely. The "double thrill" cocktails I see advertised in this morning's *New York Times,* and hasty gulping of drinks in order to down as many as possible before catching the subway, were not for him. Scotch was the favorite drink and when mixed with a liberal amount of soda or plain water it had an alcoholic content about equal to that of beer. Drinks were consumed in leisurely fashion and the question of who was likely to win the annual golf championship or how much money a Chinese general had received to call off his troops might be pretty thoroughly threshed out before the second round was ordered. There were probably few places in the world where the per-capita consumption of alcoholic drinks was greater than at the Shanghai Club during the tiffin hour nor few places that presented a more perfect picture of decorous conviviality.

The American Club was not quite so decorous for we will be noisy and boisterous—drinks or no drinks. It was not only the loud talk but the rattle of dice that made it a noisy place. As a means of encouraging though not forcing a "no treat" custom, members of the American Club always shook for drinks. After a man had had one drink, whether he had lost and paid for the round or had won and enjoyed a free drink, his obligations were washed out. He was free to stay or go just as he liked. . . .

✑

Most of the drunks were visitors. The only time the American Club became a bedlam was when the officers of the American Marines arrived and took advantage of their privilege as visitors to the club. But they were not the only newcomers who had to learn from experience the soundness of the advice:

Meantime, my friend, it would be no sin

To mix more water with your gin

I recall one very famous star of Hollywood and Broadway who came to Shanghai with a troupe of performers to give one of our very infrequent home-side shows. We all bought tickets and a packed house waited long for the show to open. It finally opened but didn't last long. The famous star had forgotten his lines. The pretty little ingénue staggered slightly as she entered. That was one time the show did not go on for the very good reason that the troupe had lingered too long at the Astor House bar. The curtain was rung down and the promoter of the enterprise sadly returned us our money.

–Carl Crow,
Foreign Devils in the Flowery Kingdom

Wartime Shipping Board poster by artist James Montgomery Flagg

Recruiting poster for the Navy by artist Howard Chandler Christy

After World War I, Shanghai regained the attention of both Europe and America—money and people returned. The 1920s also saw the arrival of White Russians fleeing the Soviet Union, the first of numerous waves of refugees from European conflicts. The diversification of the foreign population brought a more varied social life, with new restaurants, nightclubs, dance halls, movie houses and houses of ill repute. There had been a seamy side to Shanghai since the 1850s, but now the city began to acquire the cosmopolitan anything-goes character that achieved notoriety through numerous novels, plays and films (culminating, and perhaps ending, with Orson Welles's "Lady from Shanghai").

American businessmen had used Europe's distraction during the war to gain a firmer foothold in China. Corporate executives, merchants and bankers were joined by dozens of American professionals—lawyers, accountants, doctors and engineers—as well as teachers, shopkeepers, journalists and musicians (American jazz was the rage). During the early 1920s, the major American corporations represented in Shanghai—and in China as a whole—were Standard Oil of New York, British-American

Tobacco (based in London but run by American managers), American Express, Singer Sewing Machine, General Electric and the National Bank of New York (precursor to Citibank), which had bought out the International Bank of Commerce. There were also numerous small- and medium-sized import-export companies specializing in selling Chinese products to the United States and American products in China.

A sign of the American business community's prominence was the election of Stirling Fessenden, a native of Maine and a Shanghai lawyer since 1906, as head of the Shanghai Municipal Council. Fessenden reigned for a number of terms and became known as the "Lord Mayor of Shanghai." A canny political operator, he was often accused of using "American-style" election tactics, such as arm-twisting and ballot box-stuffing. (He was later forgiven for these tactics when he used them during the 1930s in political battles against the Japanese.) No major decision was made in the American community without the assent of Fessenden, his partner Major C.P. Holcomb and Standard Oil's V.G. Lyman, who were considered the top three Americans in Shanghai.

U.S. Consul-General McWade and wife with liveried palanquin bearers, Canton, 1902

A CURDLED ROMANCE

There is one classic and unexaggerated story of the curdled romance of a young American who was proprietor of his own business in Moukden. He had left a girl behind him in Iowa and the only hindrance to their marriage lay in the difficulty he had in saving enough money to set up a housekeeping establishment and meet the rather heavy cost of transportation. Finally his savings were augmented by drawing a lucky number in a sweepstake and he joyfully mailed a draft with a detailed letter of instructions. He had reserved passage on a specific steamer from Seattle and he would meet the steamer in Yokohama where they would be married and spend their honeymoon on the beautiful Inland Sea of Japan. As the steamer schedule did not allow time for any further correspondence, she was to cable him a single code word which would mean that she had received the letter and would be on the boat.

John received the cable and was in Yokohama for the arrival of the boat but there was no Mary among the passengers who crowded the rail. Her name was not on the passenger list and she sent him no message. Full of anxiety he sent her a cable and in reply received a message:

"Letter in Moukden."

The letter didn't arrive until several weeks later and read as follows:

Dear John:

I know you are going to be very disappointed and may be angry with me, but it can't be helped. I did intend to marry you like I said I would, but it was a long time ago and I never knew for sure whether you were going to be able to save up the money or not. After you went back to China the last time I began going with Sam and he wanted me to marry him and I told him I wouldn't but he kept asking me just the same and was jealous every time I got a letter from you.

When your letter came with the money in it and I sent you the message I told him about it and he felt awful bad. He said he didn't have nothing more to live for and talked about committing suicide. I felt very sorry for him.

Then he told me what a terrible place China was to live in and how the Chinese eat rats and kill all their girl babies and a lot of other things you never told me about. He said I would be lonesome there because I wouldn't know anyone but you, and I guess I would of been but I hadn't thought of it before. We've got the dandiest crowd here now and the boys have organized a string quartette and we have a dance at the Odd Fellows Hall every other Saturday night. The boys pay the rent for the hall and the girls bring the supper. It's lots of fun—more fun than when you were here because the boys hadn't started their orchestra.

Well, Sam and I talked it over a long time. I said I was sorry for you and he said I shouldn't be because you very probably had a Chinese girl, which I hadn't suspected you of after all the things you wrote me about how funny looking the Chinese girls are. I saw one of them in Des Moines, and how any white man would have anything to do with them I can't understand.

Sam said you had given me the money to do what I liked with and that if I would marry him he would pay it back to you so that you would have some money coming to you that you didn't expect. So that is what we did and Sam will begin paying the money back after the first of the year. There wasn't quite enough to pay on the rugs and the refrigerator. Sam says we ought to be awful grateful to you, and we are.

Yours sincerely,

Mary

(Mrs. Samuel H. Jones)

The last time I saw John in Moukden he was still a bachelor and the framed letter occupied a prominent position over his cocktail bar.

–Carl Crow,
Foreign Devils in the Flowery Kingdom

DRESS CODE

At the American Club the most troublesome controversy for years was over the rule requiring members and guests to wear coats in the public rooms. The Shanghai Club was adamant not only as to coats but also as to ties and though there may have been some who disliked the rule no one ever made an issue of it. Some rebellious members endorsed the rule insofar as it applied to coats and observed it meticulously but obeyed only the letter of the law regarding ties. The thinnest and narrowest possible ties encircled their collars but were never completely tied. Many of us carried ties in our pockets and completed our toilets as we went up the club steps. The only person I ever heard of who went into the club both coatless and tieless was a guest of mine, a United States Senator, and an old personal friend. There was nothing I could do about it because he was garbed that way when I picked him up at the jetty. But the only reason I didn't get a sharp letter from the committee was because I anticipated their censure and wrote a letter of explanation before they had time to write to me.

The controversy over coats in the American Club came up every summer, about the Fourth of July which was traditionally the first genuinely hot day of the year. The most ardent supporters of the coatless policy were newcomers experiencing the moist and depressing China Coast heat for the first time. As a member of the committee over a long period of years it was often my duty to defend the rule and attempt to bring the rebels into line. The stock argument was that, with the exception of coolies, all Chinese wore jackets even in the hottest weather. The club servants were required to wear jackets and tape their trousers at the ankles and therefore it was, to say the least, *infra dig* for club members to be dressed like beachcombers while the boys who served drinks and meals were dressed in the style appropriate to those who cater to the wants of gentlemen. The logical and inevitable rejoinder made by the rebels was that they had been served at many restaurants in America where the waiters had dinner jackets with black ties or even tail coats with white ties and the guests were dressed as they damn well pleased.

And so the argument raged over a period of years with one committee bending before the storm and relaxing the rule and succeeding committees enforcing it. The issue played a vital part in the club elections. On several occasions the controversy waxed so bitter that members openly threatened to resign from the club if the rule was enforced and the supporters of the rule said go ahead and resign and be damned to you. But no one ever did.

~Carl Crow,
Foreign Devils in the Flowery Kingdom

The American Club, Shanghai, ca. 1935

America's commercial interest in Shanghai was equalled or perhaps surpassed by the American missionary interest. American Protestant missionary groups were one of the largest landholders in the city, with property valued between $43 and $80 million (roughly half of the total American investment). Although many other foreign religious groups had establishments in Shanghai, they were far outnumbered by the Americans, who were supported by—and accused of being agents of—American corporations. (In the eyes of many foreign competitors, this missionary-business alliance was actually a front for the United States's plot to take over China—Standard Oil and YMCA worked hand-in-hand toward this goal, said a French newspaper.) The most important American group was the American Church Mission (Episcopal), followed by the Methodists, Presbyterians, the YMCA and YWCA, the Shanghai Mission to Rickshawmen and the Coolie Class and a number of ecumenical associations. The voice of the Protestant community was the *Chinese Recorder*, one of the most influential of Shanghai's many foreign newspapers.

A hallmark of Shanghai American life was its intense associational impulse, partly as a replication of British club life. Back in the States, business associations, fraternal lodges and the like were a hallowed feature of middle class life (as satirized in Sinclair Lewis's *Babbitt* and *Main Street*). Nearly every type of (reputable) business and leisure activity had its own club, from the Shanghai American Players (theater) to the American Women's Club to numerous sports clubs. The leading American club was the American Association of China, which in 1917 was supplanted by the founding of the American Club.

Shanghai's American Club, located at 33 Nanking Road, quickly became the center of the American community—its restaurant served steak and apple pie. In March 1925, the club moved to its 12-story brick building on Fuzhou Road. The upper floors were rented to an American university for their Shanghai campus, while downstairs contained the club facilities, including, of course, the bar, a dining room and a Chinese-style mah-jong room. At the opening ceremony, J. Harold Dollar (of the Dollar Shipping Lines) remarked that the building was a sign that the Americans were in Shanghai to stay.

One of the notable features of American clubs in Shanghai was that they allowed Chinese as members—with the exception of the American Club in its early days. The American University Club, the Union Club of China and the Shanghai Rotary Club were all American or American-dominated clubs that encouraged Chinese to join. This was in strong contrast to most of the French and British clubs, particularly the Shanghai Club, and it certainly strengthened American business and missionary ties with the Chinese community.

Perhaps the most bizarre outgrowth of Shanghai's club culture was the 1924 founding of the "Three K Party", the China branch of the Ku Klux Klan (then at the height of its popularity in the U.S.). Its leaders were Captain L.D. "Peg-leg" Kearny, a well-known local adventurer, and two Chinese who claimed American citizenship. The Three Ks' goals were fighting opium, arms-smuggling (strange—Kearny was an arms smuggler) and Bolshevism. They claimed 40,000

THE GRAND OLD MAN OF CHINA

It was not until a few years ago that the question of Chinese membership in the American Club was brought up, and for several years it was a matter the membership argued about without coming to any decision. We were afraid that once we let in Chinese members they might begin a process of absorption and we would in a few years find that it was not an American but a Chinese club. That was what had happened in Japan when the clubs organized by foreigners began to let in Japanese members. It wasn't very long before the Japanese had the upper hand and were dictating what foreigners should be allowed to join. That had also happened in several golf clubs in China to which Japanese had been elected.

The movement to let Chinese into the American Club was started with the high-principled idea that it was the right and proper thing to do, but I must admit that it never gathered much headway until it became a matter of expediency. Shrinking club revenues made it appear desirable to add new members and so I had the honor of proposing the Grand Old Man of China, Tang Shao Yi, as the first Chinese member. With his election the precedent had been created and the bars were down. But much to our surprise, and a little to our disappointment, there was no rush of Chinese candidates. Several of the leading Chinese joined, just to show their appreciation of the fact that they could, but seldom used the club. We never had more than a half-dozen Chinese who actually enjoyed the club and took part in its affairs. . . .

~Carl Crow,
Foreign Devils in the Flowery Kingdom

members in China and showed journalists filing cabinets supposedly filled with membership rosters. The newspapers, however, reported that the total membership most likely numbered three, and the resulting humiliation embarrassed the Three K Party into oblivion.

Despite Shanghai's gaiety and glamor, the more prescient foreigners realized that life there was a bit like dancing on the *Titanic* as it steamed toward the iceberg. In early 1925, Sun Yat-sen died of cancer. At the time, his Guomindang was allied with the Chinese Communists and, with Soviet support and arms, was planning to suppress China's warlords, starting in Canton. While Sun was dying, Chiang Kai-shek, the Guomindang's military leader, began a campaign against the warlords controlling Canton and the surrounding province. The Guomindang won decisive victories and seemed poised to extend their campaign across the rest of China. Nationalism was once again in the air, and this did not bode well for relations with the foreign community.

In May 1925, Japanese guards at a Shanghai textile mill killed a striking worker. A wave of protests followed, culminating in a May 30 student demonstration march on Nanjing Road, Shanghai's famous shopping street. Arrested protesters were taken to a police station, followed by an angry crowd. When the crowd did not obey a British police inspector's order to disperse, he ordered his Chinese and Sikh constables to fire, killing eleven Chinese. The May 30th Incident sparked another series of protests; a general strike began on June 1, followed by days of rioting and 10 more Chinese deaths. The Shanghai Volunteer Corps and foreign marines patrolled the streets, while Chinese students organized and left-wing groups received thousands of new members. Relations between the foreign community and the Chinese were never the same again.

Shanghai, home to by far the largest and most important foreign community, was also the model for the smaller treaty ports. Tianjin, Hankou, Canton, Xiamen and the other ports

View on the Praya, Hong Kong, ca. 1873

all had foreign neighborhoods, an active club life and, if possible, a race course. In few of them, however, could the foreign powers agree to form a united International Settlement. Tianjin had separately administered neighborhoods for British, Russians, Japanese, Belgians, French and Italians, while Canton had British and French settlements. The British dominated the business and social life in most ports; during World War I, however, the Americans began to gain ground in both business and club life. In Tianjin, the American Association of North China was founded in 1915, and Canton's American Association of South China was founded in 1921 by missionaries, bankers and the American consul.

As with Shanghai, the period between 1920 and 1925 was something of a golden era for the smaller treaty ports. Then they too were hit with repercussions from the May 30th Incident. Riots broke out in Jinjiang, Hankou and Jiujiang, with deaths and the burning of consulates. On June 23,

marchers in Canton were machine-gunned by British troops firing from their settlement on Shamian Island; 52 Chinese were killed and many more wounded. In response, the Chinese began a massive boycott against British goods that spread to Hong Kong and lasted 16 months.

In Shanghai and the other treaty ports, businessmen sent their home offices cables that went something like: "If we can make it through these next few months, we'll be all right. Once China gets back on its feet, the possibilities are limitless. . . ." Over the next dozen years, they would find themselves sending those cables again and again. Soon they began to realize that although there were huge opportunities in China, there were also risks that would not soon disappear. It became more and more obvious that they needed a base near China, but apart, where they could do business without the constant threat of chaos.

Pomp and circumstance: Foundation Stone Ceremony for the new Hongkong and Shanghai Bank Building, 1934. His Excellency the Governor Sir William Peel inspecting the Guard of Honor supplied by the South Wales Borderers. Note the Hong Kong Club in the distance in the left part of the photo

CHAPTER FOUR

An Island of Calm

During the first two decades of the 20th century, Hong Kong was a haven of tranquility amidst China's turbulence. Those more adventurous—and eager for profits—deprecated it as a sleepy colonial backwater, and many decamped for Shanghai. Robert Dollar of Dollar Steam Ship Lines described Hong Kong as, "very dull . . . and going backward."

Robert Dollar (left) and his wife, with Mr. H.F. Alexander

Until World War I, opium remained important to the Hong Kong economy; afterward the trade continued but with many more restrictions and less profit. Although many treaty ports were dominated by the British, they had heterogenous populations and an international atmosphere. Hong Kong, on the other hand, was a devout bastion of the British Empire.

Hong Kong did contain some substantial American businesses—in 1894, Standard Oil built a station at Lai Chi Kok in Kowloon—but U.S. investment was small compared with Shanghai and the other large treaty ports. After Standard Oil, the major American businesses included the Vacuum Oil Company, Singer Sewing Machine, and three banks: the International Banking Corporation, Asia Banking Corporation and American Express. Hong Kong was also home to several American-owned trading firms, shops and car dealerships, among them the Harper family's Ford franchise.

In the early 1920s, some members of the American business community in both Hong Kong and China accused the British of using Hong Kong law to force them out of China. Many American businesses had organized in Hong Kong to evade the 12.5% U.S. corporate income tax, but a new ordinance said that all Hong Kong corporations must have a majority of British directors. The threat that many companies would have to fire their executives caused a huge outcry in the American business and diplomatic community. After months of frantic diplomatic correspondence and numerous newspaper editorials, pressure from the U.S. business community convinced Congress to pass the China Trade Act. This reduced U.S. taxes on foreign profits, so Americans had less motivation to organize in Hong Kong. Those U.S. companies based in Hong Kong, however, had to abide by local rules.

In 1911, Hong Kong's American population numbered less than 300; by 1921, it had crept up to 470 (compared with over

3,000 Americans in Shanghai). Not all the American residents were representatives of major industrial enterprises: A 1905 investigation by the United States consul found 36 American women working as prostitutes, nearly all of them (including "Miss Cloudy Corbett") in brothels on Hollywood Road, Lyndhurst Terrace and Wyndham Street. (In Shanghai during these decades, "American girl" was synonymous with "prostitute.") Nevertheless, most Americans were employees of U.S. or British firms and their families; the American missionary presence was tiny compared with the rest of China.

View of Des Voeux Road, ca. 1930

American social life, particularly for the more respectable classes, took place in British institutions, mainly the Hong Kong Club, the Jockey Club and the Yacht Club. Yankees were excluded from the summit of power—the top business and political positions—but they were welcome to join the

supporting cast. Americans also took part in many volunteer organizations. In 1922, 72 Americans joined a special constabulary force to patrol the streets during a strike that started with Chinese seamen and spread to nearly every Chinese laborer and servant.

The principal channel for American patriotic fervor was the 4th of July celebrations (Thanksgiving was more private and usually celebrated at home). In the 1910s and early 1920s, these parties were usually held in the Grill Room of the Hong Kong Hotel, the colony's finest, on Pedder Street between Des Voeux and Queen's Roads. The 1922 observance had over 400 attendees at a luncheon capped by toasts from the Consul-General, businessmen and the Governor of Hong Kong. (The orations were always reprinted in the following day's *South China Morning Post* and usually followed the lines of: despite our

The Fanling Hunt, 1935

An American sailor, aboard the USS Houston *in Hong Kong Harbor, looks out on the HMS* Medway, *flanked by eight submarines, 1932; (opposite) a small junk in Hong Kong Harbor, 1933*

differences during the Revolution, our two nations have forged strong and long-lasting bonds, etc., etc.) Later in the afternoon, the festivities moved to a baseball game at Happy Valley between single and married men, which the singles won 10 to 3. The day culminated in a dinner-dance at the Repulse Bay Hotel.

Although they were comfortable in the British social institutions, by 1919 the leaders of Hong Kong's American community had decided that it was time they had a club of their own. This proposal was probably impelled by the example of their compatriots in China: Nearly every major treaty port had its own American club or association providing the community with a focus and a unified voice to promote American interests. A 1919 article in the *Hong Kong Telegraph* discussing the idea stated:

"From a business standpoint the Club could be utilised most advantageously for it could bring different matters to the notice of the Washington Government as the occasion necessitates. By having an organisation of this nature the Americans here could get into better co-operation with their own Government. They could get support from the various Chambers of Commerce from which bodies they get facilities, while a good many other American mercantile firms have their own rules and regulations. The influence which an American Club, if properly organised, could bring to bear on the U.S. Government would be beneficial for the trade of Hong Kong, which is, after all, a distributing centre. We depend and shall continue to depend upon America for a big share of her trade because conditions in Europe are not as yet normal. . . . As a rule American business houses in Hongkong are decidedly progressive. There is no reason that with a progressive element like this we should not have an American Club in Hongkong, which could serve a dual purpose—socially and commercially. Expectations are based for the fulfilment of this scheme on the younger generations who will come out when this trade is again in full swing."

If promoting business would be the primary function of the club, sport would be the second. The club would organize a baseball league and try to build interest in basket-

ball, two games "in which the Chinese have shown particular adaptability." (The Hong Kong Baseball Association, playing at the Happy Valley soccer field, thrived during the late 1920s and 30s. Their main opposition was the "Mixed" team made up of Chinese, Japanese and Filipino graduates of American universities, and they also competed against teams from whatever U.S. naval ship was in harbor.)

Despite this enthusiasm, the actual opening of Hong Kong's American Club was delayed until 1925. On July 6, seven members of the American

The Repulse Bay Hotel (top) overlooking Repulse Bay and beach (bottom), ca. 1930s

American missionaries playing baseball, Nanjing, ca. 1930s; (right) sailors on liberty in Hong Kong, ca. 1929

business community signed the memorandum of association that formally founded the club. The signatories were J.A. Shaw, C.L. Shank, Gordon Duclos, J. Oram Sheppard, H.A.R. Conant, C.H. Benson and H.H. Pethick. All but Shank (probably a trader) were executives with the most important American corporations in Hong Kong: Standard Oil of New York, Singer Sewing Machine, American Express and Pacific Mail Steam Ship.

For its quarters, the club rented an upper floor (perhaps the fourth) in the old Rutton Building at 7 Duddell Street. This small office building was built in 1923 by H. Ruttonjee & Company, the wine and spirits firm owned by the Bombay Parsee Ruttonjee family. The Rutton Building remained the American Club's home until 1931. In 1982, the building was demolished to make way for the Ruttonjee Centre.

July 1925 was an interesting time to found a club in Hong Kong. After the May 30th Incident and the June 23rd killings in Canton, anti-foreign strikes spread to the colony. Organized with the help of the Chinese Communist Party in Canton, the strikes halted all work in Hong Kong and encouraged a mass exodus of Chinese. Over 250,000 left for Canton, and all British goods were boycotted. Emergency committees had to be established to keep up food and water supplies and staff the hospitals. Many American men joined the volunteer patrols, while their wives and daughters filled other crisis positions. The social life of the foreign community ground to a halt, and the American Independence Day celebrations, including the reception and the married vs. single men baseball game, were canceled. The strike was

broken by the end of the month, but the boycott of British goods lasted until September 1926, severely hurting Hong Kong's economy. This was the year that the Royal Jockey Club opened its doors to Chinese members.

The Hong Kong American Club's first home, Rutton Building

COCKTAILS AT THE CLUB

The Columbia Country Club was at least two miles beyond the point where in 1917 Shanghai ended and the farmland began. For many years increasing numbers of Chinese had been moving into the city, the only place where they were safe from kidnapping, bandits and official squeeze. They were pushing into the foreign settlement, buying up real estate and either driving the foreigners into the new apartment buildings springing up or pushing them farther out into the country. As a consequence a moderately sized American community had built up around the club.

I discovered a difference in attitude of the Americans I had known of old, most of them from small communities, the majority from the South. Drinking had been looked at askance and the young ones were told off when they were hitting it up too heavily. But times had changed. I sat on the veranda with a group of old friends and acquaintances watching the sunset across the tennis courts. By the time the sun had died down tables overflowed the veranda onto the lawn and until after nine Chinese boys were rushing back and forth at full speed to the musical clink of ice-cubes in tall glasses.

I was put up for the American Club in the foreign business section. At noontime the bar was packed from twelve to one, and after lunch until two every chair and sofa in the library was filled with a sprawling figure fast asleep. Between seven and eight the bar came to life again, roared with talk and laughter for an hour or so, ceased and again went into a coma awaiting the following noon.

The viewpoint of the American in China had switched to almost the opposite from what it had been in pioneer days. This settled existence of a few rounds of drinks at noon, a few more rounds after the office, followed by a few more before dinner, added to the mixed array that always went with the almost nightly exchange of dinner parties, answered a question that had been stirring around in my mind since my return from the North. The Americans had been going through a minor evolution of casting off homesick small-town inhibitions. Gradually they had adapted themsleves to the drinking habits of the English.

Adapting the British sophisticated attitude towards drinking as a part of their daily routine, the Americans had developed, as a natural sequence, the British comfortable attitude towards life in general, the habit of "muddlin' through." Business ups and downs should be taken comfortably. If things were bad now, maskee—cheerio—sooner or later they would pick up. Time would see to that. One always "muddled through" somehow and if one had managed to get along all okay with the old tried and true methods, why bother oneself to go out of one's way trying to change things. As one of my fellows in business was wont to say when an argument arose, "Peace be with you, brother. Peace be with you."

This was one reason why, as far as I could see, the western foreigner was turning over gradually to the Chinese the running of his business, spending less time travelling and more at the office, acting chiefly as adviser and getting information second-hand by reading reports and writing letters instead of keeping up direct contacts.

This partly explained, too, the discussions over extra-territoriality at a time when bandits, communists and war lords had the country severed into bits, making central governmental control utterly impossible. "Muddlin' through."

–James Lafayette Hutchison,
China Hand

Shanghai Club, 1928

For the next dozen years, Hong Kong, and its American community, returned to its accustomed leisurely pace. During this era—the last in which British culture was unquestionably dominant—the American Club was a modest organization whose primary role was as a businessmen's luncheon club. The main annual events were the 4th of July lunchtime reception, usually hosted by the Consul-General and the club president, and the New Year's Eve dance. The membership remained small, and the officers were generally taken from the same group of businessmen. These included Gordon Duclos of Singer Sewing Machine, club president for the first two years; J. Oram Sheppard of Pacific Mail Steam Ship, a perennial club secretary and president in 1933; and Lambert Dunbar, a well-known flour merchant, racehorse owner and local investor.

In 1931, the American Club moved to the Chung Tin Building at the corner of Des Voeux Road and Ice House Street. The club probably financed the move by selling debentures—one of the few remaining mementoes of the pre-war club is a 1931 debentures book. Fifty of the US $50 debentures were purchased by Robert Dollar of the steamship line, and all debentures were signed by Lambert Dunbar, the club secretary.

The Chung Tin Building remained the club's home only until April 1, 1936, when it moved into the brand-new Hongkong and Shanghai Bank Building, at the time probably the most innovative structure in Asia. Designed by G.L. Wilson of the British firm of Palmer and Turner, the building replaced the elaborate neoclassical 1886 bank at the same site, which had become too small. The new Art Deco structure was the first to use a high-tensile steel structure and the first in Hong Kong to be fully air-conditioned. The second through seventh floors were rented as office space, reachable by separate elevators from the bank's. On the fifth floor, the American Club rented a comfortable space with an adjoining balcony that would be its home until 1969.

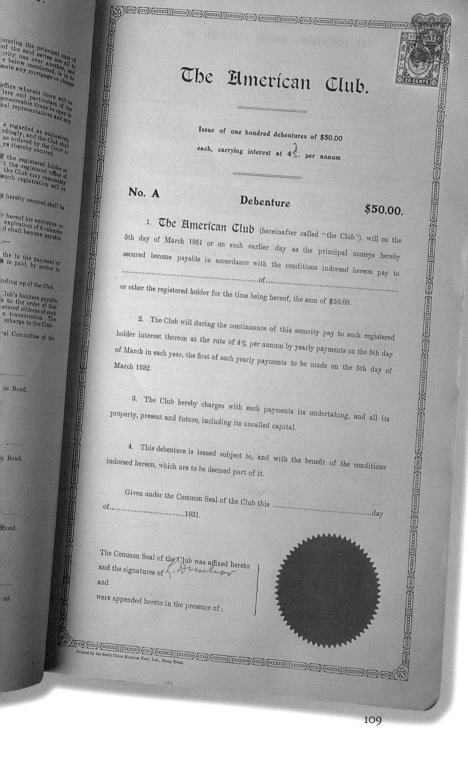

1931 debenture book, signed by then club secretary Lambert Dunbar

(above) The Foundation Stone ceremony on the site of the Hongkong and Shanghai Bank Building, October 17, 1934; (opposite) Hong Kong Harbor, ca. 1937. The USS Augusta *can be seen in the right center of the photo*

Every weekday lunch hour, the members would step out of the elevator into the small lobby and head straight to the bar. Its mahogany bar counter—much like the one in the club's present-day McKay's Bar—was the center of club members' orbit. The club decor was Somerset-Maugham-esque, with rattan furniture and white tablecloths, lacking only ceiling fans (not needed due to the air-conditioning). The members would seat themselves at a big round table and roll dice to see who paid for the drinks. Cocktails and beer were accompanied by all-American fare such as hamburgers, hot dogs and apple pie for dessert. After lunch, the members retired to the library for a post-prandial snooze before returning to work.

In the mid-1990s, only a few people remained who could remember the club during the 1930s. For George "Ronnie" Ross, the club was a regular luncheon spot; his Deacon & Company offices occupied the floor below. As a child, Phyllis Ross, daughter of (continues on page 114)

THE END OF AN ERA

The possibilities of a huge and profitable trade in China had intrigued American and other manufacturers for several generations but their hopes had never been fully realized. The period of Manchu rule was one of stagnation and of opposition to all foreign ideas and the use of foreign goods. The Revolution of 1911 and the establishment of the republic appeared to promise better things. Many times during the quarter of a century following this event we thought we saw prosperity just around the corner. We never turned the corner because a civil war or some political upheaval of one sort of another always intervened. I know that so far as I was personally concerned, every time I started to make a little money it appeared to be the signal for a Chinese warlord to ravage some part of the country, and start my Chinese accountants dipping their pens in the red-ink bottle. That had been the experience of all of my friends. But now the corner had definitely been turned. It was the opinion of all of us that there was a long period of prosperity ahead of us.

I had embodied some of these facts in a letter to a New Haven toothpaste manufacturer to accompany a proposal for his 1938 advertising. I could write to him with a good deal of confidence because his sales had been going up remarkably and I felt quite justified in suggesting that he should spend in 1938 about twice as much for advertising as he had spent in 1937.

I was finishing the final draft of the letter when the windowpanes in my office rattled and some of them broke, from the concussion of a huge bomb which Chinese aviators had dropped in an attempt to hit the Japanese flagship anchored about two hundred yards from the desk at which I was sitting. In quick succession we heard the deafening roar of two other bombs and then the vicious staccato of anti-aircraft guns.

It was in this way that the undeclared war came to me—as it came to thousands of other foreigners and to millions of Chinese who live in the colorful city of Shanghai. It marked the end of an era.

~Carl Crow,
Foreign Devils in the Flowery Kingdom

RISING CURTAIN

For several days there was telephone communication between Hong Kong and our hotel. I phoned the American Club one morning to ask a member of the American Consulate to take my movie films which were left there to some place for safekeeping.

"Oh, they are all right," he replied. "The Chinese looters won't touch those."

"That's not the point," I answered. "Those are historical documents, and valuable to our government, if nothing else. Can't you do something with them?"

No, he couldn't—and thus some of the most startling films of the Battle of Hong Kong were lost forever.

Another morning a rather muffled voice answered me. It was quite early in the morning, and it seemed a bit premature for too much liquor.

"Yes," said this friend. "I'm tight. So are the rest of us. A shell came directly through the club, in one side and out the other. And if you don't think we need a drink—lots of drinks—you're crazy!"

Why on earth the shell didn't explode as it passed through the room no military man can explain, for that is what usually happens when a shell hits hard surfaces, spraying the surroundings with shrapnel and slaughter. Five members of the American Club are living on borrowed time today, and any new and extra gray hairs they have now they earned in a legitimate manner!

The American Club was jammed with refugees by this time, sleeping on the floor, living on a minimum of water. The food which had been stored in the refrigerators was spoiling because the electric power was off. People had to climb up and down the long flights of stairs because the elevators were not running. There were no more air-raid sirens to disturb the citizens, because no provision had been made for auxiliary power to keep them going in case of destruction of the power house. Jap planes arrived at will, dived down as low as they wished, and let loose their darts of death. . . .

⌘

Late one night I called the American Club to report to one of the American Consulate staff who had asked that I let them know daily what was happening on our side of the island. Baron Guillaume had also requested me to ask the officials to get a military car to come for them at Repulse Bay, if there was any possible way to do so.

It was absolutely dark in the hotel, with the exception of pin-points of light from flashlights. The telephone system had now become a military line, and only a few people were supposed to use it.

There was a short distance between the wings, and Indian soldiers stood there, tall black shadows with their fixed guns. I had to be identified as I crossed the few feet. I stumbled up the stairs in smothering darkness, and into the small anteroom of the space which held the switchboard.

I took up the receiver and could hear Major Manners making a report to military headquarters, so I hung up. Later he told me I could not put a call through, but I managed to convince the Chinese telephone operator it was important.

I made my report to the Consulate and asked if they thought help was coming, because we were in a hopeless trap if it didn't. We had been told by British officers in the hotel that there weren't more than fifty or sixty Japs on our side of the island, but that didn't seem to add up correctly to some of us—there was too much firing, too many casualties, and I'd talked to too many of those boys who had slid down the hills for help and food.

"The Japs have landed a good-sized force at North Point," I was told. "The Japanese bombardment is gathering momentum; they are concentrating their heavy artillery against British positions on Mount Kellet and Mount Austin. One bomb crashed into the barracks on Austin and seemed to destroy it. We can see a steady stream of boats bringing Japanese troops and guns from Kowloon to the Taikoo shipyards on the island.

"We believe the Japs have a continuous line from the racecourse to Aberdeen, and are now half-way between Happy Valley and the center of the city. It seems evident that the island is being cut in half by a line of Jap soldiers extending clear across the peaks the length of the island, and we cannot see anything but surrender ahead. There is no help reaching Repulse Bay, according to our belief, for the troops are busy defending Hong Kong on this side and the naval base and Fort Stanley on yours. In fact, about all we can say to you is that we hope you can call us again tomorrow night, but in the meantime we all wish you good luck."

I hung up with a desperate feeling gripping my heart. Slowly the last words seeped deep into my mind: "We wish you good luck."

There was no doubt what was meant. The British were telling us differently, but the American observers, not swayed by wishful thinking or unbelief that this could happen to any part of the Empire, were facing the cold, stark truths. The Japs had landed a large force and were winning the battle.

What that American was saying to me was: "Good luck and goodbye. . . ."

ॐ

It was a tragic-looking harbor we crossed, with the masts of all the sunken and scuttled boats rising above the water like crosses marking the burial place of proud ships . . . and with the Rising Sun flag flying above all the craft still operating and on the piers. Here the Japanese navy were in charge, and they were a different type of men from the soldiers—more intelligent-looking, less brutal.

There were some gunboats in the harbor, and I counted twenty-six ships loaded to the waterline with booty that was being taken from Hong Kong. On the deck of one I could see hundreds of cars. Another was being loaded from a small boat with crates of American canned food. We had been given underground information that the British godowns had been opened, and an estimated hundred million dollars' worth of food, supplies, munitions, and guns,

all had been sent Japan-wards. I only hope the American submarine parts which had been held there for future action were destroyed before Nipponese occupation.

All the damage along the waterfront become more evident as we approached Hong Kong. The last week of the war had brought much additional shelling of the city. There was hardly a building which did not have open-mouthed holes, and the balcony had been ripped away from one which sided on the square. The modernistic Hong Kong and Shanghai Bank Building had gaping windows, with fluttering futile curtains in offices into which the Japanese had not yet moved. On the terrace of the American Club from which I had taken pictures, I saw a group of Japanese officers pointing things out to one another in their new domain.

~Gwen Dew, *Prisoner of the Japs*

A view from above the American Club balcony in the Hong Kong and Shanghai Bank Building, 1950

the Ford agency's Wallace Harper, would go to the club dining room—always open to women—for Saturday luncheons when it was customary for members to bring their families. The club was also the scene of many birthday parties and special children's events such as Halloween and Valentine's Day parties.

While Hong Kong life ticked along in its comfortable groove, events in the rest of China began to spiral ominously downward. In early 1927, the Guomindang's National Revolutionary Army was at the gates of Shanghai after a victorious year-long campaign that had captured most of the provinces between Shanghai and Canton. At this time,

THE CLUB SCENE OF SHANGHAI

The year was 1939 and the city was Shanghai, the most exotic and exciting city in China, if not in the world. Jewish refugees fleeing the Nazis were pouring in from Europe. The Japanese had been in China for almost ten years and their troops were slowly moving southward from Manchuria toward Shanghai. In Singapore the British were completing their sea-facing fortifications (who would have thought that the Japanese would come in by land?). And what was happening in the multinational city of Shanghai? Business as usual—and the club scene was swinging.

In that troubled year in Shanghai there were over two hundred active clubs besides the American Club. Every treaty port in China—and there were over forty of them—had its clubs, but none aspired to the variety and number of Shanghai's offerings. Alphabetically they ran from the Air Defense Club (after all there was a war coming . . . perhaps) to the Zero Club. And then there was the Amateur Dramatic Club, one of Shanghai's oldest; its club house was the Lyceum Theatre, which still stands today, and the bar in its Green Room was a popular daylight rendezvous not only for ADC members but also for Shanghai's sophisticated younger set.

As in China's other treaty ports, at the high end were the usual country clubs, three of them in fact, and clubs for the athletically oriented: a jockey club, a paper hunt club, a polo club, a yacht club, a swimming club and a swimming bath club, the Shanghai Football Club and its rival, the Shanghai Football Association or, even better, the Shanghai Rugby Union Football club, to say nothing of the cricket club; a gun club, a rifle club and a clay pigeon club; and of course a golf club and, for the younger set, even a junior golf club.

You could join the Shanghai Wheelers (a "social and racing cycle club"), lawn bowls or lawn tennis clubs; badminton or bowling clubs, the Shanghai Reel Club or the Shanghai Rowing Club, whose club house was on Suzhou Creek just behind the British Consulate General. The Union Church, just across the street, had its own clubs: the Union Church Badminton Club and the Union Church Tennis Club. Most surprising was perhaps the Ski and Winter Sports Club of China; one assumes their events were held elsewhere.

Outside the athletic sphere, most of the clubs were national in membership. Of the more than two hundred clubs in Shanghai in 1939, ninety were national in scope, representing

23 different countries. The city's large Russian émigré population was reflected in the eleven clubs and associations with the word Russia in the title. Some were philanthropic, such as the Russian Emigrants' Committee ("Administrative and Legal Assistance"), some social, such as the Russian Chess Club and the Russian Ex-Officers Club.

In both power and prestige in the International Settlement the British were the acknowledged elite. They controlled the most prestigious hongs (companies), such as Jardine, Matheson & Co., and Butterfield & Swire, and held the most important offices in the SMC, the Shanghai Municipal Council and the settlement's governing body. Their club was the Shanghai Club, whose stately club house was located at No. 3 The Bund, overlooking Shanghai's Huangpu River with its busy shipping lanes and off-loading facilities (consisting mostly of coolies' backs).

The club house, built in 1910 in the neo-classical style, was a massive white marble building with six Ionic columns which would have fitted well in with London's club scene. Its marble-floored lobby was an impressive 40 x 90 feet and was over 40 feet high, arched over by a barrel roof of frosted glass and encircled by an arcade on the mezzanine floor. Among the rooms on the upper floors were a card room, a writing room, dining rooms, a ballroom, and above that a number of bedrooms for resident members. All could be reached by twin elevators which ascended in the middle of the curving marble staircase. No expense was spared in making the club house an elegant but comfortable refuge for its privileged British members—male only, of course.

The club was most famous for its Long Bar, reputedly the longest in the world. There the taipans (big bosses) and griffins (junior officers and clerks) stood in exactly prescribed positions, by rank and as minutely calibrated as on a ruler. Up front near the window would be the leaders of the city's most powerful hongs and down in the shadows on the far end the newest, greenest griffin. God help the new boy in town who did not understand and observe the subtle gradations; the withering looks he received would soon have made his error clear, and if that did not work he would have been told off with chilly despatch. No one below the salt ever made that mistake a second time.

the Chinese Communist Party (CCP) was still part of the Guomindang alliance, even though rifts were rapidly developing between rightists and leftists. Communist agitators encouraged strikes and stirred up anti-foreign feeling in cities along the army's path.

When the army captured Nanjing in March, several foreigners were killed, including the American vice president of Nanjing University, and the American, British and Japanese consulates were looted. American and British warships shelled the city to clear an escape route for foreigners. Accusations about who was to blame for the killings flew between Communists and Chiang's supporters. Thousands

---

So select was membership that an anecdote is told that, in the days right after the Pearl Harbor attack, a young Brit was passing by the Club just as some incoming rounds were hitting uncomfortably close. For protection he sought to dart into the door of the club house only to be stopped short by a Colonel Blimp type who said, "Suh, you can not come in here, you are not a membah." Just then a round landed even closer. The club men mercifully decided to convene a quorum and quickly vote in their unfortunate compatriot—but only as a temporary member. The newest member then dived through the doorway as the third round landed just behind him.

In the French Concession there were two French clubs, but the acknowledged winner was the lovely and lively Cercle Sportif Français on Rue Cardinal Mercier. The word "sportif" in the title is perhaps misleading; although it did have a popular indoor swimming pool and a number of tennis courts, its focus was thoroughly social. It was also more egalitarian than its British and American counterparts. It did admit women, even if only forty at a time and with hundreds wait-listed, and, although late, it was the first to admit Chinese to its membership. Its spectacular white verandahed club house in Frenchtown's fashionable west end still dazzles us today.

The country clubs and golf clubs tended to straddle national lines; the Columbia Country Club, though theoretically American, was one of the most popular with Shanghailanders of all nationalities. Located in what was then the outskirts of the city, it had tennis courts, an arcaded outdoor swimming pool and an indoor squash court. The club house was in the Moorish/ Spanish Revival style, with a carriage portico in the front and a wide verandah in back for dining and dancing under the stars. Located conveniently nearby was a riding school run by former White Russian cavalry officers.

The Club is still there, now behind the garish portal of a pharmaceutical research and manufacturing facility. The once-lovely club house is now their offices, the squash court their bottling plant, and the green sward a truck parking lot. The swimming pool appears to be still in use, although swimmers must now share it with frogs and fish.

What then of the other clubs? The Shanghai Club ground floor, once the home of the Long Bar, is now a Kentucky Fried Chicken outlet and the upper floors are used by merchant seamen as a transient quarters and recreational facility;

once again the Club is a haven for foreigners. There are rumors that it will soon be renovated for use once again as a club facility for Shanghai's foreign businessmen.

The Japanese leased the Cercle Sportif Français and built above and behind it their Okura Garden Hotel, Shanghai's most luxurious. Although reconstruction took out the swimming pool and the billiards room, with the old green baize-covered pool tables, it managed to spare most of the function rooms, which still serve their original purpose. The bowling alley has become a café and the verandah, where one used to sit looking out over the lawns and tennis court, is now the hotel's entrance portico. One of the odd results of renovation work saw one of the two cupolas from the old roof moved into the garden; we wonder what became of the other one. The Japanese deserve praise for the masterful—and obviously very costly—renovation they did on the remainder of the building. Would that Shanghai's other fine old buildings were so fortunate.

As for the American Club, it is virtually unchanged except for a karaoke bar which long ago took over the bowling alley; however, that too has now closed and the building appears to be deserted. How it will be put to use is unclear, but since the building is municipally protected, it may survive the scourge of urban renewal.

What became then of the several hundred other clubs? Many had no facilities of their own or, in any event, none worth preserving. World War II closed them all down but in the post-war period some had a half-hearted revival, supported by the foreigners who stayed on, trying to restart their old business ventures and pick up the threads of their old, privileged lives. It was not to last.

In 1949 the communists marched into Shanghai and the resident foreigners soon found they no longer had a role to play in the new China. As they, one by one, closed their offices and departed, the club spirit and the club scene left with them. All the elegant old buildings gradually acquired new tenants and began their slow decline into disarray, drabness and decay. In today's new, vibrant and again foreigner-filled Shanghai, clubs are opening anew, but it will never be the same again. The old Shanghai, and the life there that made the club scene possible, is now no more than a distant memory.

~TESS JOHNSTON

of American refugees, mainly missionaries and employees of companies such as Standard Oil and British-American Tobacco, poured into Shanghai. Many missionaries refused to return to their isolated stations in the countryside, fearing that Chiang would encourage anti-foreign attacks on them.

In Shanghai, the CCP ordered a general strike beginning in early February. Over a half million workers left their jobs, power lines were cut and all strategic points seized. The city ground to a halt, and, although the CCP had ordered that foreigners not be harmed, many felt besieged. British troops took up positions in the International Settlement and in front of key businesses; barbed wire and sandbags were everywhere. The American community argued whether or not their military—at least 1,500 U.S. Marines were in town—should take part but generally were content to let the British lead the charge. If worse came to worse, they would escape to Manila on the waiting U.S. warships. Indeed, they were so little worried that hundreds of Americans attended a sumptuous Washington's Birthday dinner in the Majestic Hotel, as shells fell in other parts of the city.

While the CCP brought the city to its knees, Chiang Kai-shek was making other plans. For months he had been having secret meetings with the leading Chinese industrialists, represented by the Shanghai Chinese Chamber of Commerce, as well as with the Green Gang, the leading secret criminal organization, which was run by the Chinese chief of detectives of the French Concession police. From the industrialists he got money; from the gangsters, muscle. Early on the morning of April 12, the gangsters, backed by Nationalist troops loyal to Chiang, attacked the major union headquarters, killing dozens and arresting hundreds. The strike was broken, and so were the last remaining bonds between Chiang Kai-shek and the CCP.

After April 1927, the Nationalists and the Communists moved in distinctly different directions. It took some months for the Communist leadership, both in Wuhan, their stronghold, and Moscow, to realize that their partnership with the Guomindang was finally over. Finally, Stalin removed most of the CCP leadership and gave orders to start the revolution, with attempts in Hunan, Nanchang

The HMS Grimsby, *British sloop at Hong Kong in the 1930s. Among the other destroyers in the background are HMS* Dainty *and HMS* Diamond

*White Russian
émigrés,
Shanghai,
late 1920s*

and Canton—all failures. The Hunan action, called the Autumn Harvest Uprising, was led by Mao Zedong, ex-editor with the Yale-in-China program. For his failure, the Soviet-led leadership demoted him; with the remnants of his revolutionary army, he retreated to the mountains on the border between Jiangxi and Fujian provinces. Here he developed a rural-based revolutionary strategy that was eventually to bring him conquest of China.

Meanwhile, Chiang Kai-shek's Guomindang regime began to show a new, authoritarian aspect. Shanghai industrialists had bankrolled his takeover of the city; now Chiang began to force them to make even greater "loans" to his government. Sometimes this was out-and-out extortion: Green Gang members would kidnap the industrialists' sons until the money was paid. The gang also took over the largest labor unions and was given the opium concession, which operated under the name of the Guomindang's "Opium Suppression Bureau."

In December 1927, Chiang married Soong Meiling, the youngest of the famous Soong sisters, a graduate of Wellesley College and a YWCA worker. The foreign community, particularly the Americans, felt that this Christian, albeit bigamous (he already had a wife), union was a good omen for the future, and a 1928 treaty with the United States recognized Chiang's rule as the *de facto* government of China. American support of

Chiang was tempered by the stiff taxes he imposed on imported alcohol and tobacco and his increasing efforts to control the press and foreign-run schools for Chinese. The foreigners immediately invoked the extraterritoriality clauses of their treaties but eventually were forced to meet him halfway (British-American Tobacco negotiated a lower tax on their cigarettes, for example).

Between 1927 and 1937, Shanghai acquired its reputation as the Babylon of the Far East. On the one hand, it was China's most modern city, a hotbed of artistic ferment, with young Chinese social reformers and writers dressed in the latest European fashions dancing to American jazz and experimenting with sexual liberation and new literary styles. For those living in staid old Hong Kong, said Phyllis Ross, "Shanghai was where you went for fun," the scene of many weekend trips.

Beneath that glittering façade, however, Shanghai was one of the world's most vice-ridden cities. The Green Gang leader Du Yuesheng cruised Shanghai's streets in his armored limousine ferrying between opium dens, casinos and, in his guise as a respected businessman, meetings with Western dignitaries. No matter how bad things got, there was money to be made in Shanghai—at least for the first five years. After 1932, however, Shanghainese knew that they were dancing on the edge of the volcano.

A SHANGHAI BROTHEL

I asked her to tell me how many girls—Americans—she had used in her career as a brothel-keeper. She said that they numbered about two hundred. I asked her to tell me how she managed to find so many girls willing to take up such a life and she responded that the girls were not always willing, but that ways and means were found to persuade them.

Apparently the best way, the one most practiced, is to debauch the girl first. During her visits to the States she was in constant communication with agents who had likely prospects in mind. Very often the girls are already semi-prostitutes; that is, they are employed or living with their families and choose to gain money for themselves by discreet prostitution. She told me that in such cases, when the girls are successful and are at the same time seeking adventure, the task of persuading them to take the long journey to China is not difficult. They are given money for their expenses and are trusted to start the voyage. Often they start with no intention of keeping their end of the bargain when they reach Shanghai, but, since they are never able to think very clearly, they fall easy victims to the agents that meet them when they arrive at the port.

She told me that there are agents, acquainted with houses of prostitution in San Francisco, who watch for likely young girls who have been lured by drink and drugs into the profession there. The voyage to China is suggested and a settlement is made with the brothel-keeper who has control over the girl. She may be taken out by an agent or travel with another girl who has also chosen the Shanghai assignment.

"A great many of my girls," said Gracie Hale, "have left theatrical companies to come to my house. I once arranged, during my visit to California, for a theatrical tour of the Orient by a company that was formed for the very purpose of replenishing my supply of girls. Several of them had fallen ill. Two had died. And because of some trouble regarding money I had to drive two out of the house. They were cheating me. I do not know what became of them.

"I took fifty thousand dollars in cash with me to America. I invest most of my money there, because I intend to return some day and live there the rest of my life. But an agent, who had some experience with theatrical matters, proposed this stroke of business. Another procurer had marked out five girls for me—striking blondes—who had earned money as 'party girls,' or 'call girls.' A telephone call would bring them to the place where a party was going on," she explained. "They were also trying to commercialize their good looks by getting work on the burlesque stage and that sort of thing.

"There were ten girls in the company. At San Francisco they signed contracts to sing and dance during the tour. Each one was given a generous salary and a promise of transportation. My money paid their advances. Some sort of musical show was bought and a rehearsal was held, just to assure the girls that all was well. They were very enthusiastic. I had not seen the girls, because it is necessary for me to accept the recommendations of the agents, the procurers. But I attended this rehearsal and was pleased by their gayety and appearance.

"I went aboard the ship with them, but I did not introduce myself, of course. They were very gay during the voyage. When pay day came I handed over the cash for their salaries to the agent. The little love affairs that they had aboard the ship were not encouraged, of course. The manager of the troupe, my agent, was very strict and scolded them when they flirted. But, despite this, it was true that the darlings did not spend much time in their own cabins.

"They started their tour, played a few times here and there, and then arrived in Shanghai. There the enterprise fell to pieces—that is, the theatrical enterprise. The girls were destitute. They picked up a little money by prostitution in the second-class hotel where they were being kept by my agent. He abandoned them, at my direction. I came to their rescue, bought them clothes and liquor, and then brought them here. They were pleased by the stories told to them by the other American girls and I was very soon on my feet again. They were willing to work, especially under the easy conditions which I require. One or two of them determined to save their money and return to America, but the mere accumulation of money keeps them here. They have good bank acccounts and they have earned a great deal for me. They will never leave me until I am quite ready to replace them."

–Hendrik De Leeuw,
Cities of Sin

THE LIGHTS OF SHANGHAI

Shanghai was deliriously gay.

The disquieting, nerve-racking, sobering years of civil strife, of anti-foreign uprisings and demonstrations in and about Shanghai were ended. The barbed-wire entanglements were down. Martial law and the curfew were off. Grim tanks of war no longer paraded the streets. The threat of a Sovietized China was dismissed. Everyone heaved a deep thankful sigh. Chinese and foreigners alike—together—celebrated. Shanghai had passed through another of her "ten thousand deaths"; had awakened to new life. New life: an expression which Chiang Kai-shek was to make famous as the name of his inspiring, regenerative "New Life Movement."

Business, which had been at a standstill during the uncertain years of Communist invasion, broke, like a long restrained tide, into an exciting boom.

The luxurious Cathay Hotel, built at the cost of five million (Shanghai) dollars by Sir Victor Sassoon of the wealthy Sassoon family of Bombay and London, opened in a blaze of sophisticated splendor, with a gala dinner.

In our party were a number of Chinese girls. We of the European world wore trailing French creations which bared our backs. But the women of the Orient wore clinging, seductive gowns which were made high in the neck and long in the sleeve, but whose scant skirts were cut with tantalizing slits up either side. Mildly shocking slits which extended from the ankle hem to the knee. And their gowns of shimmering flowered silks, of gold and silver brocades, were enhanced by diamonds, jade, and pearls.

When I first arrived in Shanghai, Chinese girls were not seen at the night clubs and hotels. The only Chinese woman I knew who danced was Princess Der Ling, who, as Mrs. Thaddeus White, moved much in foreign circles in Peking and in Shanghai; she had been reared in Paris, had grown up in Europe, had been lady-in-waiting to the Empress Dowager in Peking, and was in reality a Manchu. A new era in the social life in Shanghai began when the late Mrs. Edwin S. Cunningham, wife of the American Consul General, invited a few of the wives of distinguished Chinese to her famous curry tiffin parties, and asked them to stay on for mah-jongg. She added their names to her dinner-party list. In her boudoir over fragrant jasmine tea, candied ginger and almond cookies, I met many of the high-class younger women, informally; came to know and to like them. They were eager for life, and, with the poise and grace which characterizes everything they do, surprised Shanghai by their mastery of modern dancing; with the ease with which they fell into sophisticated foreign social life; with their ability to converse with foreign diplomats in French and English. They were utterly charming, those innately well bred Chinese girls. I liked them so much, delighted in their friendship. . . .

ɔ

There were colored lights glowing red, green, gold, blue—dancing neon lights—lights sparkling like jewels; lights chasing up and down the sides of high buildings, to the tops of towers, far out over the sidewalks. Picturesque Chinese characters, sacred through the ages, enlarged to gigantic proportions, gleamed flamelike against a midnight sky; action lights, fascinated the Chinese even as the spectacular signs of Broadway thrill the man from out of town: Manhattan lights —set down in the mystery, the glamour of the Far East.

~ Edna Lee Booker,
News Is My Job: A Correspondent in War Torn China

Early in 1928, Chiang sent his forces north to wrest Beijing from the warlord Zhang Zuolin. Instead, they encountered Japanese troops in the Shandong town of Jinan, and the meeting suddenly deteriorated into a bloody, atrocity-filled battle. Chiang's troops were forced to withdraw by the arrival of Japanese reinforcements and decided to head west to avoid any further confrontation. The Nationalists' next target was Tianjin, but before they could attack, the Japanese convinced Zhang to retreat to Mukden, where they guaranteed him protection. Just before he arrived, rogue Japanese officers blew up the train, killing Zhang in the hope that it would give Japan the chance to seize all of Manchuria. Japan's government refused to take the opportunity, however, and Yan Xishan, a Guomindang-allied warlord, occupied Beijing. Chiang made his capital in Nanjing, farther from the powerful Japanese military machine.

After the Jinan battle, the mutual perceptions of the Japanese and the Guomindang regime hardened. Many Japanese felt that China's glory was past, and that Japan would now play the dominant role in Asia. State-supported Japanese industries would reorganize the faltering economies of their neighbors in Korea and China, and if they ran into opposition, they would be protected by the well-armed, modern and aggressive Japanese military. Jinan had shown the importance of troops for protecting Japanese interests. The effects of the following year's stock market crash devastated the market for Japanese goods in the United States, giving added urgency to Japan's plans for China. The drums for war were beating, and many Japanese army officers could not wait.

The years between 1928 and 1932 were profitable for China's Western business community. Although China's economy reeled from the 1929 stock market crash, foreign businesses were still doing well, particularly those selling war matériel and oil to Nationalists, warlords and even the Japanese. The crash also led to the devaluation of silver, to which the Chinese dollar was more or less pegged, so all traders selling Chinese goods abroad prospered despite new protectionist tariffs in the United States and Europe. Shanghai was still a hotbed of labor activity—strikes at General Edison, British-American Tobacco and many other firms slowed production—but the Guomindang was rapidly improving its control of unions, particularly after 1930. Many American businessmen who had lost their stateside jobs moved to China, where the frontier

The Japanese battleship Mutsu *leaving Hong Kong, April 14, 1928*

Chinese Nationalist soldiers in action against the Japanese in Shanghai, 1932

mentality still reigned and a smart Westerner could still make a quick buck. For China's millions of poor, however, the world-wide Depression made them only poorer.

In September 1931, Japanese army officers in Manchuria decided to incite a confrontation with the Nationalists. They blew up a stretch of railway outside Mukden and, claiming it was the act of Chinese army saboteurs, attacked the Chinese army barracks in Mukden. At the same time, the Japanese army commander in Korea sent his troops to cross the Yalu River into China. The Nationalists were no match for this force, and Chiang Kai-shek ordered his forces to withdraw. By early 1932, the Japanese controlled Manchuria, which they renamed Manchukuo, a puppet state nominally ruled by Puyi, the last Emperor of China.

The seizure of Manchuria inflamed Chinese feeling against the Japanese. That sentiment soon encompassed all foreigners, and another round of boycotts began in the treaty ports. By the end of January, Shanghai was in another state of emergency, with foreign troops patrolling the concessions. A minor skirmish between Japanese and Guomindang troops was followed by a full-scale battle, with Japanese

troops attacking and planes dropping bombs on a Chinese district.

Fierce fighting between Japanese and Chinese forces continued for weeks. All trade stopped; foreign warehouses were destroyed; and patrols of Japanese volunteers accosted Westerners, including some prominent taipans, and killed Chinese. Western nationals were given instructions on their evacuation routes. The district north of Suzhou Creek was burned, and corpses piled up in the streets. According to Ernest Hauser, the rats there were "fat and sleek," while the dogs, "still as bony as they used to be," had greatly multiplied. In early March, reinforcements brought the number of Japanese troops to 90,000, and the Nationalists, realizing that victory was impossible, withdrew from the city. Japan unilaterally declared a truce, and after months of negotiations, Shanghai became a "neutral" zone—with a greatly increased Japanese military garrison.

The battle for Shanghai was a blow from which the city never really recovered. Shipping had stopped, orders had been canceled, and even a year later trade was half of pre-battle levels. Many foreigners left the city; they were replaced by others, but the community was never the same.

For those who stayed, each firecracker now sounded like a gunshot, and they never lost their sense of unease. Not only were there more Japanese soldiers, Japanese businesses

A FOOL'S PARADISE

I was marched to the American Club just next door. The Japs had wasted no time in taking over, the first sign of good sense they had shown as yet. It was a fine building filled with happy memories for me. As we went in I saw soldiers leaving with arms loaded with books. I felt like yelling a protest. The club had one of the best libraries in the Orient, and it seemed a sacrilege to see these books carried away by ignorant Japanese soldiers. Following the Nazi example, they burned all the books —including works of Lafcadio Hearn, who wrote so beautifully of the culture of Japan and the beauty of their poetry.

We walked by the big room where Americans had met nearly every afternoon to comfort each other in their homesicknesses. No matter how each of us claimed to love the Orient, down deep we were homesick and our almost daily meeting around the famous American Club table was a pretty clear indication of that. I caught a glimpse of that table as I passed the open door of the club room. I had sat there and swapped yarns with friends for twenty years. I had listened to red-headed H. R. Knickerbocker's tales of Germany there and had talked with Jimmy Young of INS about the mysteries of the Orient. I had learned to respect the brilliance and courage of J. B. Powell there and I had succumbed to the charm of the late Douglas Fairbanks at that table. I had met Ronald Colman and Roy Chapman Andrews there, and Somerset Maugham. Old shipmates, like Mark Hanna and Floyd Gibbons, had sat with me there and we had told pleasant lies and had laughed and sown the seeds of everlasting friendship around the old mahogany table. Now a group of Jap officers sat around it.

It was noon. No one at the club seemed to know what to do with me, either. Obviously they were awaiting orders from higher echelons. Finally those orders came and we all went back to the cars and headed for the oddly named Broadway Mansions, a fine sixteen-story apartment hotel. They took me to the fifth floor but they didn't question me. I was treated as a naval officer and quite satisfied with my lot. Of course I was living in a fool's paradise, but I didn't know it then.

~Quentin Reynolds,
Officially Dead: The Story of Commander C.D. Smith

were more aggressive—they paid Chinese workers in notes issued by their own banks, forcing them to buy in Japanese stores—and Japanese clamored for more representation in local government.

In mid-1932, the economy was whacked by the sudden increase in the world price of silver. Commodity prices plummeted, bank credit disappeared, and dozens of Shanghai industries went bust. All the big foreign players, such as Standard Oil (now operating as Standard-Vacuum Oil) remained in China, although with far less enthusiasm.

Japan's aggression was now the main problem. In early 1933, the Japanese army had pushed the Nationalists south of the Great Wall and forced the Guomindang to sign another humiliating treaty. Unfortunately, Chiang Kai-shek believed that the Communists rather than the Japanese were the main enemy. He had the majority of the Communist army blockaded in Jiangxi Province and was planning an offensive, when the Communists broke out of the encirclement and began their famous Long March to safety. For more than a year, the Communist army and leadership, including Mao, Lin Biao and Zhou Enlai, were constantly on the move, harassed by the Nationalists and suffering disease, exhaustion and, for many, death. Those who survived ended up in Yan'an in Shaanxi Province, far from the bulk of the Nationalist army.

In 1936, Chiang sent the army of his warlord ally Zhang Xueliang to roust the Communists. After his troops were defeated in some minor battles, Zhang began to wonder if the Japanese were not the real enemy—Japanese troops were again pushing south from Manchukuo and putting down strikes in Qingdao. When Chiang flew up to Xi'an, Shaanxi's capital, to test Zhang's loyalty, Zhang placed him under arrest and called for a national conference on China's salvation.

This act threw the country into chaos. Rumors flew that Chiang had been killed, and foreign businessmen, who saw no hope in a China without Chiang, again began to make plans to leave. The Nationalist leadership and Zhou Enlai flew to Xi'an to negotiate, not just for Chiang but, it seemed, for China's future. After two weeks, it became clear that, for both the Communists and the Guomindang, Chiang was the most powerful personality in China (even Stalin still believed Chiang could be redeemed). Zhang finally released Chiang with his verbal commitment to reassess the Japanese danger, and the leader flew home on Christmas Day, 1936. Zhang was arrested on Chiang's orders, and the Nationalist troops ended the offensive against the Communists in Shaanxi. China would now unite against the Japanese.

It was probably too late. Although there were many moderates in the Japanese government, their army was belligerent and not in their control. In July 1937, a violent clash between Chinese and Japanese troops at the Marco Polo Bridge just west of Beijing led to a full-scale battle. Chiang Kai-shek tried to divert them by attacking Japanese positions in Shanghai. Rumors flew through the city, and tens of thousands of Chinese crowded into the International Settlement hoping to avoid the fighting.

On August 12th, the phones at the Japanese consulate and the major Japanese businesses went dead; two days later four Chinese Air Force planes, American-built Northrops, appeared over the city. The poorly-trained pilots had been dispatched by Claire Chennault, an ex-United States Air Force officer who had been hired to organize the Chinese Air Force. The Rev. Frank Rawlinson, the editor of the *Chinese Recorder* and one of the most prominent missionaries in China, stepped out of his car to look and was killed by a stray machine gun bullet.

GENERAL CHENNAULT

We went to call upon General Chennault. His room had a collegiate atmosphere, with flags and trophies. We were given cups of coffee—a great luxury. General Chennault, looking like a footballer, somwhat tired afer a victorious match, sat at a table behind a sign on which his name, perhaps rather unnecessarily, was printed in large letters. No other individual has done more for China in her fight against Japan. Before the attack on Pearl Harbour, his group of American volunteer pilots, the Flying Tigers, had written a wonderful little page of history. Now he is Chief of the U.S. Army Air Force in China: without his contribution, events in the Eastern theatre might have taken a very different course. His task has never been easy; he is always short of aircraft, supplies and co-operation; yet the personal effect he produces is one of wealth and magnanimity. Come what may, he maintains an unruffled calm and creates confidence in others. Formerly a renowned fighter pilot, the inventor of tactics that revolutionised aerial warfare, he knows every aspect of flying from personal experience. After the last war he organised commercial air circuses that toured America. For five years he was Chief Instructor of the Chinese Air Force Cadet School. At his desk he now deals simultaneously with Washington and Chungking, as he directs the manifold policies and tendencies of this vast organisation.

With the passage of years, he has become a little deaf; his mouth is

tight-bitten and turns down at the corners. His complexion, yellow, as if stained by walnut juice, is pitted with deep crevices, and the skin around the jaw and neck is as wrinkled as the poor quality windbreaker that he wears, with the Flying Tiger painted crudely on the pocket. His black shaggy hair is beginning to be peppered with grey. Yet there is much about him that refuses to grow up. His shyness and utter simplicity are boyish qualities; his Red Indian eyes have a schoolroom mischief in them; and it is only when members of his staff come in that one has a glimpse of the power he wields so quietly. He reads their suggestions. "No—that leaves a loophole—phrase that sentence differently, more emphatically. No, you didn't quite get my thought there." He starts to write. Much of his work is now largely a matter of literary composition. The free and easy side of American army life is here exemplified. Perhaps Americans take all generals as a sort of joke—a joke particularly enjoyed by generals —and doubtless are right in doing so. "Hey, General," said his secretary. "Hadn't you better put your blouse on?"

"Where's the general's blouse? Anyone seen a General's blouse? The General's lost his blouse!" At last someone stretched out an arm.

"Here'y'are, General!" And with a wry smile and a shake of the head, the General changed his tunic.

–Cecil Beaton,
Chinese Diary & Album

General Chennault

BATTLE OF POOTUNG PT.
SHANGHAI 1937

A United States cruiser off Shanghai, during the Japanese attacks of October and November 1937

"When [the planes] were over the Nanking Road intersection," said journalist Ernest Hauser, "two black dots appeared below one of the planes."

"Bombs."

"The taipans stood on the rooftops of their white office buildings and watched the two dots grow bigger. Death had come to the Settlement, and the taipans were there, with binoculars, to watch their city die."

The bombs had been meant for the Japanese warships in the harbor. Instead, they exploded at the corner of the Bund and Nanjing Road, Shanghai's busiest intersection, and in front of the Cathay Hotel. Hundreds were killed, including one American. Another bomb landed on the Great World amusement center, killing over one thousand. For the first time, foreigners were evacuated from Shanghai. Americans, mainly women and children, grabbed a few

(below) The Bund, Shanghai, during bombings by the Japanese in 1937

Survivors of the Panay *on board the USS* Oahu, *Shanghai*

basic belongings, and departed on the *President Taft*. This exodus marked the beginning of the end for the treaty port system; Westerners would never again have privileged legal status in China. That night, Japanese warships began to shell the city, beginning a bloody three-month battle.

The Chinese fought bravely, but the Japanese had the advantage: tanks, warships and fleets of planes raining bombs down on the city. After suffering casualties of nearly 60 percent of their forces, in mid-November the Chinese retreated west toward Nanjing. As the Japanese approached, the Guomindang warlord fled the city, leaving it open to the invaders. The Nanjing American community, including the U.S. Consul, and many Chinese employees of Standard Oil, were evacuated onto the USS *Panay*, a Navy gunboat, and two Standard Oil ships, which headed upriver and anchored. A spy sent word to the Japanese; two planes bombed and strafed the ships, sinking them with many casualties.

The *Panay* incident was a minor sideshow to the "Rape of Nanjing," which was notable not only for its utter brutality and destruction, but for the fact that newsreel cameramen were able to capture some of the atrocities. Many of the dead and wounded were carried to American missionary hospitals, where the doctors photographed the victims and sent reports via the U.S. consular network. When photographs of Chinese dead appeared in newspapers and the newsreels played in the cinemas, the American public was shocked. The Japan-

ese were condemned as savage animals. Over the next few years, when any hope of conciliation between the United States and Japan was raised, it was squashed by memories of Nanjing.

In Shanghai, the treaty port system nominally continued, although under *de facto* Japanese control. All land north of Suzhou Creek was now Japanese, and anybody passing into this zone had to pay a "toll" and bow to Japanese troops. In the Chinese district, robbers openly roamed the streets, and gambling and opium dens owned by either the Japanese army or their Chinese gangsters proliferated (before, most gambling had been confined to the International Settlement). In late 1938, the American community was shocked by the hold-up of a dozen prominent citizens by pistol-packing bandits just outside the Columbia Country Club in the western suburbs of the Settlement. Factories were dismantled and their machinery was sent back to Japan; statues were torn from their pedestals and melted down for the metal. For the first two years of the occupation, Westerners watched in dismay from the International Settlement but, surprisingly, they stayed—they had seen too much chaos over the preceding years to immediately flee.

After the capture of Shanghai, Hong Kong became China's main trading port and the principal conduit of equipment and ammunition to the Nationalist army. For about a year, foreign dealers in trucks, airplanes and other matériel made a huge profit as supplies poured through the colony. The Japanese capture of Canton and the surrounding Pearl River region in October 1938 ended the boom and cut off Hong Kong from its inland trading routes. Tens of thousands of Chinese refugees streamed south to the colony. Hong Kong was now isolated, and Japanese troops lay just over the border of the New Territories.

At the end of 1938, China was divided into three sections. The Japanese controlled most of the coast, including all the important ports, as well as the rich industries and mineral resources of Manchukuo. The Nationalists retained inland Southwestern China, which they ruled from Chongqing.

CAPTAIN MUSICK AND MYRTLE (THE HONG KONG CLIPPER)

Captain Edwin Musick, Pan Am's chief pilot in the first years of trans-Pacific flight, was a man of few words. In April 1935, while high over the Pacific, on the historic first Clipper proving flight from the U. S. mainland to Hawaii, Musick was making another routine radio report. But the public relations department back in San Francisco wanted some eloquent copy to fill the evening editions. Overnight, Musick had become an American hero—and Pan Am wanted to cash in on his popularity. "Send something about the sunset over the Pacific," he was instructed. In his characteristically laconic manner Musick radioed back, "Sunset: 6:39 GMT."

Relatively little is known about Ed Musick's early years as a pilot. He flew as an exhibition pilot, Daredevil Musick, and then for the U. S. Marines in World War I as an instructor. There are rumors that in the 1920s he flew alcohol for a bootlegger. Not atypical for an adventurous young pilot in the lean years, perhaps, but his real fame was yet to come. Musick had already gained a reputation as a serious and professional pilot when he joined Pan American Airways in 1927. Quickly rising to the top, Ed Musick became Pan American's chief pilot with the coveted title, Master of Ocean Flying Boats, graduating at the top of his training class. He was hand-picked to set up the trans-ocean flying school and to select and train the best available pilots for the airline. Musick's next task was to test the first of the new trans-ocean flying boats coming off the line at the Sikorsky plant in Bridgeport, Connecticut. The key to trans-ocean flying was to be a completely new aircraft with unprecedented range, speed and load-carrying capacity. When Musick saw Sikorsky's gleaming silver, four-engined design he knew he had a winner. She was a beauty and could she perform. "Boy! Has she got stuff!" Mu-

sick yelled in a rare burst of enthusiasm when he firewalled the throttles on the first test flight. The S-42 broke eight world records for speed and distance during her flight testing. The plane became the workhorse of the Pan American fleet. Even when the newer, larger Clippers became available, the S-42 was used for all the long-range proving flights to establish the new Pacific routes. When Captain Musick brought the S-42 to San Francisco for the first trans-Pacific flight in 1935, banner headlines read:

GIANT SILVER CLIPPER SHIP ARRIVES FOR TRANS-PACIFIC SERVICE!

The public was enthralled and thousands turned out to witness the arrival and several weeks later the departure of the *Pan American Clipper* on the first proving flight to Hawaii. The date was April 16, 1935. History was being made and Captain Musick was the hero of the day.

The fabulous Clipper flying boats of Pan American Airways System operated in the Pacific from 1935 to 1941. During that brief period before World War II, the Clippers carried the rich and famous, movie stars and statesmen—and even a few ordinary citizens as well—on a pioneering route from North America to the Orient via Hawaii, Midway, Wake, Guam and Manila. Pan Am called their flying boats "Clippers," and gave each one an individual name much like the seagoing Clipper ships of another era.

In the trans-Pacific service there were three classes of flying boats: the Sikorsky S-42, the Martin M-130 and the Boeing 314. Each was progressively larger, more luxurious and more capable than its predecessor. Although the fares were usually far beyond the reach of the average American, the Pan American

Clippers nevertheless captured the imagination of the American public. These flying boats were the technological wonder of the age. In their time they were the largest passenger planes built, symbolizing the promising new capabilities of American aviation. They contained features one would find on the finest ocean liners, including comfortable lounge chairs and settees, upper and lower berths, a dining lounge, private dressing rooms and lavatories —a degree of luxury and style no longer found on commercial flights. Dinner was served by uniformed stewards, on tables set with white linen tablecloths, fine china and silverware. The name *China Clipper* came to evoke a sense of adventure, romance and the spell of distant, exotic lands—the lure of the mysterious Orient.

Of the ten Sikorsky S-42s built, one became particularly well known in the Far East. She was the *Hong Kong Clipper*, affectionately nicknamed *Myrtle*, assigned to the Manila-to-Hong Kong leg of the trans-Pacific route in 1937 and then again in 1941. Captain Musick himself was at the controls on many of the earlier flights, majestically circling the harbor and alighting near the seaplane mooring area at Kai Tak—he could make every landing look beautiful and he was known to enjoy flying into Hong Kong.

Both Musick and the *Myrtle* met with untimely ends. Musick, ever the perfectionist, was surveying a new route to New Zealand aboard another S-42, the *Samoan Clipper*, He and his crew of six embarked on the final leg from Pago Pago, Samoa at dawn, January 11, 1938. Two hours into the flight Musick radioed that he was turning back due to an oil leak in the number four engine. A little less than an hour later he reported that he was going to jettison fuel to lighten the heavy aircraft prior to landing. A few minutes later he indicated that more fuel was being dumped —and then no further word. From the few traces of wreckage that were eventually found it was theorized that while venting fuel a spark had ignited the gasoline vapor which had accumulated in the wing and the Clipper and her crew disappeared in a single blinding flash. It was a tragic loss for aviation and the first crash of a Pan American Clipper at sea.

The *Hong Kong Clipper* was a victim of war. She was anchored in the flying boat moorage area just off Kai Tak prepared for the scheduled flight to Manila on the morning of Monday, December 8, 1941. *Myrtle*, always a sweet flying ship, was preflighted and ready for her twelfth shuttle flight. Passengers had assembled at their various hotels and embarkation points. Captain Fred Ralph had heard rumors of war. In fact, he had orders to fly *Myrtle* not to Manila, which was under attack, but to a lake near Kunming and presumed safety in the interior of China until contingency plans could be made. As Ralph and his crew stood on the tarmac discussing the situation, he noticed formations of aircraft approaching Kai Tak from the north. Ralph and his crew ran for cover as the bombs started falling. Ralph could see *Myrtle* riding at anchor still untouched. He prayed. Then the Japanese planes came in to strafe. Bullets and cannon shells splintered against concrete and buildings and ricocheted everywhere. He could see splashes in the water all around *Myrtle* as the Japanese pilots tried their best to destroy the big flying boat. Six passes he counted with no results— but on the seventh pass they finally found their mark. *Myrtle* was set afire and burned and sank at her moorings, too late for that last flight to safety.

The Clipper era ended with the advent of war in the Pacific. By 1945, landplane development and the worldwide development of new airports left the prewar flying boats in an uncompetitive position. Their age of luxurious, glamorous and adventurous travel had lasted only six short years.

~ CLIFF DUNNAWAY

Captain Musick (second from left) with crew and Clipper passengers on one of the early trips to Hong Kong

Their main supply route was the Burma Road, a rough track carved out with British help from the jungles and mountains between Kunming and Mandalay. The Communist section was the smallest, a portion of Northwestern China to the west of Yan'an. These boundaries would more or less stand until mid-1944.

For Westerners in China, the great question was who would protect them in the event of war. It soon became evident that it would not be Britain, and this became crystal-clear after the outbreak of the European war in September 1939. The only other choice was the United States, but there the voices for isolation were louder than the interventionists. F.D. Roosevelt slowly cut off Japanese access to military equipment but, unless there was some blatant Japanese aggression against American soil, he could do no more. The U.S. Navy did have ships stationed along the China Coast, but their tonnage was dwarfed by the Japanese. If they did not leave, Westerners realized, they would be engulfed by the coming conflict.

Americans began to leave China in 1939. After Shanghai, most of them lived in Tianjin, Canton and the lesser treaty ports. The more optimistic moved only as far as Hong Kong, hoping the storm would quickly pass, but the rest sailed for Manila or the United States. From Hong Kong, the main exodus came in the July of 1940, when the British government ordered the evacuation of British women and children to Australia, and the U.S. consulate advised Americans to return home. The Hong Kong American Club's 4th of July party was cancelled and the money given to a war preparation fund. By early 1941, the only Americans left in China were the consulate staff, essential employees of major businesses, a few missionaries, the curious and the foolhardy.

Most of 1941 was spent in tense waiting. Conflicts continued between Communists and Nationalists; Chiang's troops decimated Mao's New Fourth Army, which had remained in Jiangxi Province. The Communist-Nationalist alliance against the Japanese, weak from the start, was now almost non-existent. At the same time, the Japanese were subjecting the Nationalist base of Chongqing to constant bombardment. After much negotiation, President Roosevelt allowed the Nationalists to buy 100 new fighter planes and hire dozens of American pilots "on leave" from the U.S. military. These

The U.S. Embassy in Nanjing guarded by Japanese sentries, ca. 1938

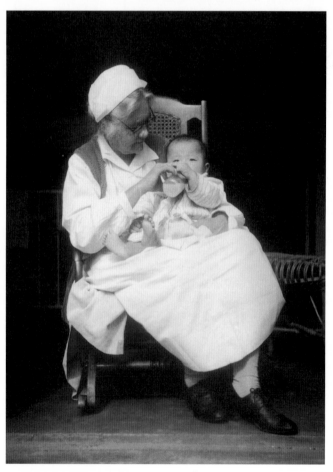

Iva Hynds, who, despite her 67 years, remained at her post in the University Hospital, Nanjing, when the Chinese staff of doctors and nurses departed before the fall of the city

BEFORE THE FALL

I hardly knew where to turn that first day. I went to the lobby of the Hong Kong Hotel and found it filled with a nervous milling crowd. Connecting it with the Gloucester Hotel was an arcade, and hundreds of Chinese had already moved into this with their mothers, fathers, children, grandparents, and rice bowls. Many did not move out until the war ended, except as the sanitation squad ousted them for a few hours each morning to disinfect and clean the place. These two hotels were supposed to be among the most strongly constructed buildings in Hong Kong, and thus were considered as safe as an air-raid shelter.

In fact, one of the directors of the Gloucester Building told me that after its construction the directors in England had demanded an explanation of the great cost. An inquiry followed, during which it was discovered that seventy times more steel had been used in it than had been specified!

Later I went to the American Club, and here was gathered a rather sick-looking group of people. They all sat looking into space, thinking of their families at home and what it means to be completely cut off from America when war crashes down. Some of them looked rather green, and I wondered what color fear is when it comes to the surface of the skin. I even wondered what shade my skin had turned. But by the next day every American around the club had jumped into some sort of war work, and from then on did everything he could to be of service in the defense of the city.

The terrace of the American Club became my watching-post. The club was in the Shanghai and Hong Kong Bank Building, the city's finest and highest, a smart modernistic-looking edifice facing the waterfront, but separated from it by a block of green park. The terrace ran on three sides, so from it one could look across the water toward Kowloon, up and down the harbor, down on the city, and up toward the Peak. From here I took my first pictures of the Japanese planes coming over, and of the white puffs of anti-aircraft fire, which always seemed just to miss. We never saw the British fire bring down a plane, although several hits were reported. There were no British planes to send up....

✑

The Hong Kong and Shanghai Bank Building, in which the American Club was located, was hit five times this day by shells. It was not much damaged, although the impacts swayed the edifice like a rocking cradle. Inside, the relief workers went on with their tasks, shifting their supplies out of danger even as the shelling was going on. The outside of the building was pockmarked, but it takes more than that to stop sturdy hearts.

I had been on the streets taking shots of the Chinese vanishing into the air-raid tunnels, and when I reached the bank building I had to slide in past a guard at the back entrance. He shook his head disapprovingly at my being out during an air raid, but let me in nevertheless.

The elevators had stopped running, so I started to climb up the back fire-emergency stairs. Ordinarily no one would ever use these, and it was only because of this unusual situation that I did.

As I reached the floor on which some of the American government offices were located, I smelled smoke. Naturally I tried to locate it, wondering if a shell had set fire to something. There was a small terrace outside a window on the stairway, and there an American government man was burning great stacks of official papers, emptying baskets on to the blaze.

Suddenly I realized what this meant. The American government expected that Hong Kong was going to fall!

I became sure of it when the official turned to me, saying: "Please don't tell anyone you happened to see this. It might start a panic."

–Gwen Dew, *Prisoner of the Japs*

became the core of the Flying Tigers and its offspring (Civil Air Transport and Air America), a force of American aviators that flew combat missions in East Asia for the next 30 years.

War between Japan and the Western Allies finally came to China on December 8, 1941. In Shanghai, it was over in a matter of hours. Japanese warships shelled whatever British or American naval vessel put up a resistance. The Japanese army arrested those Westerners they considered dangerous, confining them in the Bridge House Gaol—a name that became synonymous with cruelty and torture—while the rest were detained at their homes. Those Americans living in the Shanghai American Club were given an hour to leave, and the premises were taken over for Japanese offices. In other Chinese cities, such as Beijing, already under complete Japanese control, American civilians were permitted more freedom, sometimes waiting months or years (early 1943 in Beijing) until being forced into internment camps. American soldiers and sailors were immediately sent to prisoner-of-war camps.

The capture of Hong Kong was longer and bloodier. On the night of December 7th, Hong Kong's elite, including Madame Sun Yat-sen and Madame H.H. Kung, gathered for a dance to raise money for Allied War Relief. In the middle of a number, T.B. Wilson of American President Lines stopped the music and announced that all men on active duty should report to their stations at once. The Japanese had crossed the border of the New Territories. Within a few hours, Japanese planes had destroyed what little air defenses the colony had. Hong Kongers were trapped; they knew that eventually they would be overrun.

Over the next few days, the Hongkong and Shanghai Bank building became a center of activity. As the tallest building in the colony, it was the frequent target of Japanese guns. One of the floors held the American consulate, where employees burned secret documents. In the American Club, the members constructed a secret compartment in which they hid the two original debenture books, a ship model, a copy of the Gilbert Stuart portrait of Washington and photographs of Presidents Coolidge, Hoover and Roosevelt. These treasures were re-discovered in 1962 by Gordon Vaughn. Other members, including Faye Booth of American President Lines, decided to prevent the capture of the club's ample supply of liquor by drinking as much of it as possible, all the while conscientiously signing chits for their consumption. Gwen Dew, an American journalist, called the club early one morning and the phone was answered by an obviously drunk American:

"'Yes,' said this friend. 'I'm tight. So are the rest of us. A shell came directly through the club, in one side and out the other. And if you don't think we need a drink—lots of drinks—you're crazy.'"

When Faye Booth returned to Hong Kong after the war, the (same) "bar boy" presented him with the chits.

The main defense force consisted of British and Canadian troops supplemented by the Hong Kong Volunteers, which

Officers and men of the USS Tulsa, *Hong Kong, August 7, 1941*

included a number of Americans. They were woefully out-manned and out-gunned, but London, perhaps stupidly, ordered them to fight to the very last, and they did. After Kowloon was captured, smoke rose from dozens of burning godowns and explosions wracked the Standard Oil depot, which had been set alight by its managers. Refugees crammed into the American Club, from the balcony of which they could watch Japanese dive-bombers obliterate Hong Kong's stately buildings. Finally, on Christmas Day 1941, the British surrendered.

The Japanese already had detailed plans for the "Captured Territory of Hong Kong." Enemy troops, including American Club member Bill Anderson and a handful of other fellow countrymen, were interned in various POW camps, the largest

A NARROW ESCAPE

I was standing on the roof of the American Club, about ten blocks distant, watching the fights between Chinese and Japanese planes when the bombs struck the plaza. The explosion shook the entire city. I hurried to the scene, and for the first time in my extensive coverage of battles, I actually saw human blood running in the gutters. When I got home late that night after covering the story, my shoes, socks, and trousers were caked with blood. I assisted the police and Red Cross in removing numerous charred bodies from motorcars which had been caught as the drivers of the cars moved around the circular island where the traffic signals were located. One car, a Ford, attracted my particular attention, as it was standing within twenty feet of the yawning crater in the asphalt where the bombs had fallen. There were three charred bodies in the car, two in the front and one in the rear. The driver, or rather his charred skeleton, sat perfectly erect with the blackened bones of his hands still grasping the wheel. When the bodies were removed from the car, the driver's license, upon which the owner of the car was sitting and which had thus escaped incineration, established his identity as a well known American businessman in Shanghai. The other figures in the car were his wife and the Chinese chauffeur. . . .

૯෨

Immediately after the publication of the "black-list" the municipal police stationed guards at all of the newspaper offices, and in my case sent a plain-clothes Chinese detective to sit in my front office and accompany me as I walked home in the evenings. Several days later, in the afternoon, as I was walking toward the American Club where I had resided for several years, I was struck on my back below my shoulder by an object which I thought was a piece of wood about a foot and a half long and about two inches in diameter. I was nearly knocked down by the blow, and, thinking a piece of timber had fallen from a scaffolding where carpenters were making repairs, I glanced upward, but saw nothing. I then looked at the object which had glanced off my back against the wall of the building and was still rolling along the sidewalk a few feet from where I was standing. Noticing that it was wrapped in a newspaper, and not suspecting its nature, I reached down and picked it up. As my fingers closed on the missile I realized that it was a "potato-masher" type of hand-grenade used by both Japanese and Chinese armies. I resisted the impulse to drop it, as I noticed that the cord which released the mechanism had only been pulled part way out; had I thrown it down the shock might have caused it to explode. It was nothing short of a miracle that it had failed to explode when it glanced off my shoulder and struck the building.

By this time my bodyguard, who was walking several feet behind me on the crowded sidewalk, came running up and I showed him the hand-grenade. He immediately drew his revolver and glanced around at the crowd which had began to assemble. I told him to go to the corner and summon a policeman, in the meantime carefully placing the explosive on the sidewalk and motioning the people to keep away from it. Soon a Chinese policeman hurried up and after I had explained the incident he, with what seemed to me a singular lack of imagination, also picked up the grenade and carried it, held at arm's length in front of him, with my bodyguard walking ahead to clear the way, to the central police station, where it was immersed in a bucket of water. Examination showed it to be a live bomb, but the man who tossed it had been apparently in too great a hurry as he failed to pull the firing pin out sufficiently to cause the grenade to explode. It was suggested in some quarters that the intention might have been only to frighten me and cause me to discontinue my critical editorial policy regarding the activities of the Japanese and their puppets. The police, however, discounted this suggestion.

A few days after the attack on me a man having close connections with both the Japanese and the Nanking puppets called on me and suggested that I "sell" the *China Weekly Review*. I indignantly rejected the offer.

~John B. Powell,
My Twenty-five Years in China

of which was in Shamshuipo. After a period of confusion, the majority of enemy (i.e. British, American, Canadian, Russian and Dutch) civilians were sent to Stanley Prison, now converted into an enormous internment camp. The noted journalist Joseph Alsop, bumped from the last flight out of Hong Kong by Madame H.H. Kung's dog, had the foresight to tear down one of the American Club's heavy brown curtains to use as his prison blanket.

Not all Westerners lived in the camps. Foreign bankers were kept under arrest in one of the seediest Chinese hotels; every day they were marched to their offices to liquidate their business and open the safe deposit boxes under the eyes of Japanese officials, some of whom had attended school in the United States. Those who could escaped, making the dangerous trek west through enemy territory to Chongqing, the capital of Free China, which was rapidly becoming an American military base. Portuguese, French and nationals of neutral nations were allowed to remain at large; many moved to Macau where they lived hungry but relatively free.

A British Army base, Stanley Fort became home to 3,500 prisoners of both sexes and all ages. Most of the 350 Americans were crowded into an apartment building, with dozens occupying spaces meant for a small family and as many as 82 sharing one toilet. An old recreation building was home to 50 American men and became the new "American Club," with a kitchen run by "Pop" Gingles (owner of the post-World War II bar of the same name).

Marines guarding a Standard Oil fire in Tianjin, China, December 25, 1927

Japanese troops in Canton

Japanese troops marching through the streets of Kowloon, December 28, 1941

Bankers being marched to their offices during the early months of the Japanese Occupation, Hong Kong

BY RIGHT OF CONQUEST

The area that was to become our home, called Camp Stanley, was on a rocky peninsula, ending in a high cliffed promontory. Just beyond us was Fort Stanley, which had been the original reason for erecting any buildings here. Then houses had been built; later the British had erected a modern jail, a college and school had been developed, and apartment houses for the wardens and minor Indian civil servants had been added. Adjoining us, but on the mainland, was the small Chinese fishing village called Stanley. The section was hilly, and the climbing was precipitous—hard on weakened legs and hearts.

In one section the British had built seven apartments to house 260 Indian civil servants. The Japanese now herded 780 Britishers there, most from the finest section of Hong Kong, the Peak. I think they took particular glee in putting those who had lived in the best surroundings into the worst now. This was the least desirable section, because it was low and without a breeze. Parts of it had been badly blasted away and could not be repaired. The toilet facilities were extremely inadequate, perhaps even for the Indians before, so it was not a pleasant situation now.

On the top of the one steep hill was St. Stephen's College, of which the classrooms were turned into dormitories. As many as twenty men lived in one room, sleeping on the floor, or on improvised beds made out of doors or boxes, or whatever the owner's ingenuity created. In another building the British police were placed.

Three small bungalows nearby held 45 to 50 people apiece. Two of my good friends, Lucile Eichenbaum and Margaret Jay, lived on the open porch of one, and were al-

Stanley during World War II, *watercolor by Hong Kong and Shanghai Bank staff member I.H.C. Higet during his internment in Stanley Prisoner of War Camp. Owing to scant resources, the artist used both sides of the paper*

ways being rained on, blown out by small typhoons, or frozen. Someone finally built a low wall for them out of remains of other buildings, and this formed some sort of protection.

On an opposite hill was the group of buildings which housed most of the British and Americans. These were apartment buildings, and every single room, from kitchens to entry halls, was occupied. In fact it was considered quite a prize if you got a servant's room, because these were so tiny it was impossible to put more than two in them. Imagine an existence where a room six by seven feet is considered the choicest place!

In the living-rooms of most of the apartments eight or ten people lived, men and women thrown together, often with three or four children. As many as 82 used one toilet in these quarters.

Only a comparatively small number of internees had brought army cots, because no one had any warning or any idea of the treatment to be accorded them, but the Japanese never recognized the need of furnishing sleeping equipment for their prisoners. Seventy-five per cent slept on the floor, on narrow army cots, or on beds made of slabs of wood raised from the floor by blocks of stones taken from blasted buildings. Everyone tried to get his body away from the floor at night, if possible, because of the scorpions which infested the camp.

Between the two hills was what we called "the American Club." It had been a recreation building and club, and 50 American men were billeted there. They had the best place in camp, because their rooms were more fully equipped, the building was in better repair, and there was a complete kitchen in running order when they moved in. Food-

preparation was immediately taken over by Gingles, an ex-navy man who had had restaurants in Hong Kong for years. Because food was his hobby and he was cooking for such a small number, he could get better results with the rice, and pull tricks with the small amounts of extras that were issued.

Next to this was the Dutch building, similar to the American and British apartments, but not quite so crowded.

In all there were more than 3,000 British, 70 Dutch, and 350 Americans. There was no place to cook for the large number of people when they were herded into camp, so emergency kitchens were set up with no help from the Japs, created out of rubble by the internees. The Americans got busy at once and constructed stone ranges, makeshift utensils, and a huge boiling pan for rice. From this place were served 257 people twice a day for the next half-year.

The British weren't quite so quick to adapt themselves to circumstances as the Americans, for they still felt: "This can't happen to us," and "They can't do this to us." Of course the Japs weren't supposed to treat prisoners of war in this manner, but they were doing so, and there was no redress but to make the best of it. For three months the British internees from the Indian quarters climbed almost half a mile to the British apartments to get their pails of food, and then finally managed to erect a kitchen in their own quarter.

One Englishman remarked to an American: "You are lucky to have so many of your working classes here to build things," and was amazed to find that the men indicated were bankers, brokers, and executives of our biggest firms.

~Gwen Dew,
Prisoner of the Japs

The Japanese warders gave food grudgingly; the daily rations were two bowls of rice and some watery gravy. The internees considered themselves lucky if they received some stringy buffalo meat or rotting fish heads. Many Chinese friends and ex-employees risked their lives to send parcels of food and medicine into the camp, but they were not enough to avert nutrition problems and disease—a number of internees died, mainly the very old and very young. In the hot summer sun, prisoners stripped down to the tattered bare essentials. This did not spark a wave of immorality sweeping the camp, as some expected. The "rice diet" took the edge off desire.

When the prisoners asked the Japanese authorities for reading material—boredom was one of the camp's greatest miseries —they sent in the library from the American Club. (The club itself, along with the entire Hongkong Bank Building, had been taken over by the Japanese command.) The books passed from hand to hand, wearing down to near-illegibility from overuse, and became one of the great escapes from their terrible situation. At war's end, the books were returned to the club, and, the story goes, only four volumes were found missing.

In occupied China, the Japanese also ran POW camps containing hundreds of U.S. sailors and soldiers. Shanghai had the largest civilian internment camps—over 1,000 Americans were held there—but there were also camps in Qingdao,

PRISONER OF WAR

In Hong Kong, I had word from Colonel Chennault to wait at the airport until I could get on one of the Chinese aircraft that were still flying between Hong Kong and Chungking by night. These flights continued to be made for three nights. However, I had no priority or special recognition signal to give the China Aviation officials at the airport. So I waited there with the rest of the mob who were trying desperately to flee the island until, on the third night, I was told I would be put on the very last flight to Chungking. And so it seemed, until, at the very last instant, I was informed by the unfriendly officials that I would not be allowed aboard the flight. I complained bitterly, and the level of my bitterness increased when I was informed by a fellow traveler that I had been bumped from my seat in favor of Mme. H.H. Kung's very large, well-fed dog. . . .

స

The British resistance on Hong Kong was brief, and when the city was surrendered on Christmas Day 1941, only a few days after the Japanese attack, I reported again to Colonel Condon. This time he told me that my only course was to forget that I was a member of the AVG—fortunately, I had traveled in civilian clothes—and to pretend that I had never left my old trade as a newspaperman. He warned, prophetically, that Japanese military internment would be a very hard business indeed, but that civilian internment would be less hard and might even offer opportunities for escape. And, finally, he believed the Japanese might well end up exchanging many of the civilian internees because of the burden they would impose.

As it turned out, this was an incomparably brave and, in many ways, magnanimous thing for Mid to do since I was, in fact, a U.S. military officer and, therefore, in no way eligible for the kind of treatment he proposed. I should not have been able to masquerade as a civilian prisoner at all had Mid not, in effect, ordered me to do so. What is more, I now ran the risk, as a military man out of uniform, of being considered a spy. This did not occur to me at the time, although I am sure Mid was aware of it and chose not to tell me for fear I might give away the game. As it was, I had little trouble slipping calmly back into my former role of newspaperman, and without a uniform I am sure I looked less like a soldier to the Japanese than the great majority of other foreign male civilians then milling about in occupied Hong Kong.

Once this decision had been taken, Mid Condon and I proceeded to the old Gloucester Hotel in Hong Kong, where almost all the English and Americans in the colony had gathered. I had a fair number of second-rate sapphires purchased in Burma, and I wanted to get them sewn into the collar of my coat. Mid suggested to me that his marvelously beautiful Eurasian mistress, being convent-trained, would be able to do the job for me. She was staying also at the Gloucester, and so later on that evening I felt my way through endless unlit corridors until I reached her room. The room was lit by one candle, by the light of which Mid's mistress appeared even more beautiful than I had remembered her being (I think she eventually established a close connection with one of the higher Japanese administrators of Hong Kong). With her in the room was her sixteen-year-old sister, who was also a startling beauty. I explained to this unlikely pair what I needed; Mid's mistress explained that she had forgotten how to sew but that her sister, who was fresh out of the convent, would certainly remember. And so, in these odd circumstances, the job of hiding my jewels began.

The ensuing scene illustrates how so many of the dramas in my life have turned into comedies. Here, in the flickering candlelight, were two dazzlingly beautiful girls helping a soon-to-be prisoner of war sew jewels into the collar of his tweed jacket. Although the windows were closed to keep out smoke from the flaming city, one could hear the heavy beat of Japanese military bands as they led the victorious Japanese forces into the city (the majority had landed by sea, on the backside of Hong Kong island). A more dramatic scene would be hard to imagine. My sapphires glowed in the dim light as the lovely sister bent intently to her work. The comic touch was added by Mid Condon's mistress, who, throughout the operation, kept scratching herself and saying repeatedly, "Goddamn that Mid! He's given me scabies [an unpleasant skin rash caused by mites] he caught on maneuvers. Goddamn that Condon. I wish I'd never met him! Goddamn these scabies he gave me!"

After my sapphires had been sewed safely into my coat collar, I thanked the ladies most warmly for their kindness and departed. The next morning, I went to the American Club in the Hong Kong and Shanghai Bank building, the place of temporary internment earmarked by the Japanese for the small number of Americans then in Hong Kong. Unlike the others, I occupied myself, in the days before the Japanese gave us our orders, with borrowing all the cash I could and with buying all the food supplies I could for what was bound to be a lengthy internment. By the end of my time in the American Club, I had accumulated a considerable store of very cheap food. But I had not solved the problem of carrying it, nor had I done anything about bedding, which I was sure the Japanese would not provide.

Solving the bedding problem was the purpose of my last foray into the city streets. For one Hong Kong dollar (then U.S. 25 cents), I managed to buy a coolie's carrying pole, two bamboo woven baskets, and the means of attaching the baskets to the ends of the pole. The next day, the Japanese ordered us all to the parade ground just above the city center. As we left the American Club that morning, I solved my future bedding problems by pulling down from one of the club's high dining-room windows a very heavy brown, ribbed, silk-interlined curtain. Hence, I appeared at the parade ground, which was the assembly point for Westerners who were going into internment, with my coolie's carrying pole over my shoulder and, balanced on each end, my baskets full of provisions and bedding.

The sight of me so encumbered caused one of the great English traders of Hong Kong, locally called "taipans"—I think the man may have been the head of Butterfield and Swire—to reproach me with an air of haughty rebuke. Our Japanese captors had already informed us that we would be marched down the city's main thoroughfare, Queen's Road, to our next place of internment. This order was not without symbolic purpose, for the Chinese had been commanded to gather in mobs on either side of the road purely for the purpose of spectacle. The white rulers of the colony would be thus be marched off to jail in humiliating and public defeat.

For the great taipan, this feudal ceremony was tantamount to walking naked down Queen's Road, and he was in a furious commotion. "Young man," he said icily, "you're not going to walk down Queen's Road with a coolie's carrying pole and those two baskets of stuff, are you?" I replied that I thought I would. "But don't you see," he said, "we'll all lose face." Thereupon, I'm afraid I turned on the taipan and said, rather rudely, that if he reflected carefully upon it, the events of the past weeks had not left the foreign community in Hong Kong with enough face to be worth conserving anyway. At this, the taipan turned bright red and stalked away, and that was the end of our conversation.

~Joseph Alsop,
"I've Seen the Best of It," Memoirs

Weixian, Beijing, Hankou, Yangzhou, Canton and Xiamen. Conditions in these camps paralleled Stanley: overcrowding, malnutrition, boredom and maltreatment by Japanese and Chinese collaborator guards.

Of all the internees, perhaps those kept at Pudong Camp, Shanghai's largest, were the most resourceful. The camp was home to dozens of the finest American university professors in China, and they banded together to form Pudong University, offering over a hundred courses from 80 instructors. The curriculum ranged from courses in 11 different languages to instruction in algebra, abnormal psychology and yoga. The course in Chinese culture was the most popular, followed by Russian, due to the many Russians in Shanghai. The camp also had a library of 11,000 books, because most of the prisoners had managed to carry three or four volumes into the camp.

Needing slave labor to keep their war machine running, in 1942 the Japanese shipped thousands of male prisoners, almost all POWs, to Japan. In April, the *Lisbon Maru* sailed from Hong Kong with almost 2,000 prisoners aboard, including a number of Americans. The boat was torpedoed by an American submarine (a number of Japanese ships carrying POWs went down this way), and the Japanese crew abandoned ship, leaving the prisoners to die below decks. Amazingly, over 700 survived, only to be shipped to slave labor camps in Japan for the length of the war.

In 1942 and 1943, hundreds of Americans and other foreigners managed to leave the internment camps for home. The United States and Japan agreed on an exchange of civilian prisoners, including their consulate staffs, journalists and businessmen. After months or years of prison and, for some, torture, Americans were placed on the *Asama Maru* and *Conte Verde,* which sailed west, while the *Gripsholm* sailed east from New York with a ship full of Japanese. In Mozambique or in the Indian port of Goa, both Portuguese colonies, the exchange was made, and a couple of weeks later the ex-prisoners sailed into New York and freedom. A number of them wrote articles and books about their experiences, reminding Americans of their imprisoned countrymen and of the depredations wrought on China by the Japanese.

By mid-1942, it was obvious that the war in China would be won only with American help. The British had lost "impregnable" Singapore, the Burma Road was cut and now they were fighting for their very survival in Europe. Their commitment to fighting the war in East Asia was necessarily reduced. The commander of the American war effort in China was *(continues on page 142)*

A poster issued during the Occupation urging local citizens of Hong Kong to utilize radio calisthenics programs. Note the old Hong Kong and Shanghai Bank Building

SATURDAY NIGHT FEVER

The United States Army Observer Group, code name the Dixie Mission, was sent on a secret mission approved by US President Franklin D. Roosevelt and dispatched under overall command of General Joseph Stilwell from the China-Burma-India Theater of War, in Chongqing. The mission was sent in two groups of nine. The first, which included John Colling, arrived in Yan'an on July 22, 1944; the second arrived on August 7, 1944.

The Dixie Mission's objectives were to establish liaison with the Chinese Communists; to save downed B-29 crews who were bombing Tokyo and Manchuria from bases in Chengdu; and to determine the effectiveness of the Communists as a fighting force to help in a US invasion of Shandong peninsula, China, preparatory to what was then the intended full-scale Allied invasion of Japan after Germany's surrender.

On August 6, 1945 an atomic bomb was dropped on Hiroshima. On August 8, the Soviet Union declared war on Japan and Russian armies stormed into Manchuria. On August 9, another atomic bomb was dropped on Nagasaki. On August 10, Japan made a tentative offer of surrender. On August 14, US Army General Henry H. Arnold launched a thousand-plane raid on the Japanese mainland. The planes were still aloft when Emperor Hirohito announced Japan's unconditional surrender. The Dixie Mission was formally recalled on August 16, 1945.

☙

In our leisure time, sports were a high priority. We played American softball, ping pong, volleyball, and basketball. Zhou En-lai, a good outfielder who liked baseball tremendously, would play whenever time permitted. Further entertainment included movies which were brought up with the supply flights from Chongqing. The usual GI fare, which included the introduction of Mickey Mouse (better known in Chinese as 'Mickey Lau Shu') was the first opportunity many of the peasant people had to see the silver screen.

In confusion over what the screen was, many of the peasants when they first saw it would come up, touch the screen and look behind to see if it was real.

Yenan's 'Pear Orchard' featured Saturday night dancing and entertainment. Everyone was invited, including the members of the Japanese Emancipation League (JEL) who readily mingled with the Chinese men and women. This was the center of all relaxation and small talk. It was here, between dances and presentations, that we heard most clearly about the Communist dream.

Local musicians, although in short supply, usually played Chinese stringed instruments. Music that rasped and spluttered out of an old phonograph machine included 'Yankee Doodle Dandy' and American folk music. We danced the foxtrot and other Western ballroom styles, but most frequently swayed to the 'yang ke', or rice sprout dance, which closely resembled a conga.

Theater was an important propaganda tool of the Communists, and the most memorable events in the Pear Orchard were the folk drama adaptations. Young soldiers would comb the countryside for authentic songs and dances, which contained political messages and resistance propaganda, which they would then take back to Yenan to rework into skits. Themes included tilling the soil and hiding Chinese soldiers from the Japanese. Taxes were either paid in kind, or with paper currency, which was illustrated in the play with a paper drawing and an actual piece of millet.

The leaders moved easily among their people, and danced often and with anyone who asked. Accompanying these leaders, on and off the dance floor, were their wives —all of whom were important. Prior to Yenan, Zhou Su-fei (Madam Ma Hai-de) and Jiang Qing (Madam Mao Ze-dong) were movie actresses. Kang Ke-ching (Madam Zhu De) was a peasant guerrilla fighter. And Deng Ying-chao (Madam Zhou En-lai), an educated Hunanese, was a national leader of women's organizations.

–John Colling,
Spirit of Yenan

"Saturday Night Fever" in the Pear Orchard, Yan'an's local weekly disco

AN ATTACK ON OCCUPIED HONG KONG

The Flying Tigers—officially the American Volunteer Group or AVG—brought the first bitter taste of defeat to the Japanese in the skies over Burma and China during the desperate days of 1941. The China Air Task Force (CATF), successor to the AVG, was activated on July 4, 1942. The CATF was an interim organization consisting of a few more men and planes to hold the line against the Japanese until a full-fledged American Air Force could be organized. The CATF was always fighting the odds—ill-supplied and outnumbered—but upon its activation the United States became officially and irrevocably involved in the air war in China which had been raging since 1937.

The commanding officer of the CATF was Brigadier General Claire L. Chennault—"Old Leatherface" he was called—the no-nonsense, tough-as-nails, former commander of the AVG. Chennault had been in China as early as 1937, observing at first hand Japanese tactics and aircraft in the skies over Shanghai and other beleaguered Chinese cities. He was a tactical genius and a superb leader who instilled a fierce loyalty in those who served under him. He taught his men how to beat the Japanese by using unorthodox tactics—how to capitalize on the strengths of the outnumbered American planes and exploit the weaknesses of the Japanese. He taught them to choose the time and place to fight—never to fight on the enemy's terms.

By 1942 there were only a few hundred Americans fighting in China and the CATF had only fifty-one fighters (mostly P-40s from the AVG), seven B-25 medium bombers and ten P-43s borrowed from the Chinese. By early 1943 the assets of the CATF had increased to about 170 aircraft—still far short of the hundreds of aircraft available to the Japanese.

Colonel Robert L. Scott was one of those Americans who just couldn't wait to get into the fight. He had been flying transports—"delivery wagons" he called them—over the Hump between India and China in 1942 but that hadn't offered him the excitement he craved—and he was tired of being a sitting duck for Japanese fighters. Landing in Guilin following another routine Hump flight, Scott begged a single war-weary P-40 from Chennault so that he could fly a few fighter missions himself out of Assam, India. Scott used the plane to fly dangerous, one-plane missions, bombing and strafing ground troops. Between sorties while re-arming and re-fueling he would have ground crews repaint the prominent propeller spinner of the P-40 in a different color—first white, then blue, red and so on. Scott would then hit the ground formations from a different direction each time, leading the beleaguered Japanese to report that they were being attacked by several different squadrons of aircraft! Little did they know that Scott's was the only P-40 operating out of Assam at the time. Scott became known as the One-Man Air Force.

At 34 years of age Scott was considered too old to be a fighter pilot but he refused to let that stand in his way. He was

Colonel Robert L. Scott, Jr., first commander of the 23rd Fighter Group, China Air Task Force, with armorers on the wing of his P-40 prior to his last combat mission, January 1, 1943, Kunming, China

such a natural fighter pilot that his talents immediately became apparent to Chennault who facilitated Scott's permanent transfer out of transports and into the CATF. Scott served as commander of Chennault's fighter force from July 1, 1942 to January 9, 1943, earning twelve confirmed aerial victories.

The CATF deployed its meager resources with such efficiency and ferocity that the Japanese again thought they were up against a much larger force. Scott described the first bombing mission against Hong Kong in his classic book *God is My Copilot*. The mission for that day, 25 October 1942, consisted of a flight of ten B-25 bombers with an escort of seven P-40s led by Scott. They would hit the docks at Kowloon; the shipping crowded in and around Victoria Harbor and the dry docks on Hong Kong Island. The group staged out of Kunming to Kwelin (Guilin) where they were serviced and re-fueled for the attack. The formation approached Hong Kong from the west near Macau, the bombers at 17,000 feet and the fighters providing top cover at 20,000 feet. "We came across the Great West Channel, passed north of Stonecutters Island and came to our turning point seven miles north of Kowloon. The bombers were turning south now for the bombing run. This was the crucial moment." When Scott saw dust trails far below at Kai Tak he knew that the Japanese fighters were rising to the attack. The familiar black and white puffs of anti-aircraft fire began to dot the sky, the concussions rocking the aircraft as the gunners sought the range and altitude of the Americans. Scott watched with fascination as the strings of yellow bombs

fell from the B-25s toward the targets below and erupted in explosions which sent up clouds of smoke. But "where were the enemy fighters?" he wondered. He hadn't long to wait as the interceptors from Kai Tak, after their long steep climb, reached the level of the bombers now running for home. Scott called out, "Bandits ahead—Zeros! At eleven o'clock." As the ensuing battle raged above the harbor the sky was torn by tracers, fire and explosions and the swirling shapes of planes in the confusion of aerial combat. A number of planes were seen to fall into the harbor. In minutes, however, the sky was clear of planes with only the criss-crossing paths of vapor and smoke to mark the battle. Scott's plane had not been hit and he had shot down four of the enemy! In the exuberance of victory he "looped above Victoria Harbor and dove straight for the Peninsula Hotel" where he knew the high-ranking Japanese staff officers were billeted. "My tracers ripped into the shining, plate glass of the penthouses at the top level and I saw the broken windows cascade like snow to the streets many floors below." Scott made two more passes at the hotel but the final one ended abruptly as he was out of ammunition. Then he flew "right into the smoke and through it right down to treetop levels . . . headed northwest to get out of Japanese territory sooner, and went as fast as I could for Guilin."

That mission was the first of many. The CATF and its successor, the United States 14th Air Force, virtually eliminated the Japanese from the skies over China in the succeeding months. Robert Scott left China in 1943 with twelve enemy planes to his credit. Looking back on his China experience, Scott treasures, more than any medal, award or victory, the honest and heartfelt gratitude expressed to him by the Chinese people. Scott and his compatriots from the American Volunteer Group, the China Air Task Force and the 14th Air Force are still fondly remembered in China today.

~ CLIFF DUNNAWAY

USNR Lts. James S. Swope and Charles R. Stimson study reconnaissance photographs of Hong Kong on board the USS Hornet. *The carrier's planes hit Hong Kong on January 16, 1945. Stimson, in the background, was one of the war's leading "aces," with 16 "kills" in F4F and F6F aircraft*

John Colling, later an American Club member, and Kachin scouts in Burma

General "Vinegar Joe" Stilwell, who had to contend with Claire Chennault and Chiang Kai-shek (who he called "Peanut" behind his back) over strategy. Chennault, who favored air power over ground troops, began construction on a line of air bases across Free China. Meanwhile, Nationalist (and Communist) troops harassed the Japanese, keeping them diverted from the Americans who were beginning to fight their way back across the Pacific.

Back in the United States, Roosevelt had finally committed himself to the Chinese cause. He now convinced the Allies to abolish the extraterritoriality system—the treaty ports, along with Taiwan and Manchukuo, were now officially Chinese (or would be after the Japanese were ousted)—and tried to convince the British to give up their colony of Hong Kong. The British, of course, refused, and the debate raged in secret diplomatic channels for the duration of the war.

In June 1944, the first B-29 bombers took off from Free China and bombed strategic targets in Japan and its occupied territories. The Japanese struck back, massively, racing south from the Yangtze Valley and west from Canton and threatening Chongqing. Chennault's beloved air bases were heavily damaged. Chiang Kai-shek's retreating troops were robbed and killed by Chinese peasants. The Nationalist Army had been supported by a brutal campaign of forced conscription and punitive taxes, even during famine, and now their victims were taking revenge. President Roosevelt began to lose faith in the Nationalist leader. He decided to send a team, called the Dixie Mission, to Yan'an to re-establish ties with the Communists.

One of those sent to Yan'an was John Colling, an OSS officer who was the son of an American army officer in Tianjin (and later became a Hong Kong American Club member). After the intrigue and corruption of Chongqing, he was

Mao Zedong and Patrick J. Hurley at the start of the 1945 Chongqing coalition talks

greatly impressed by the honesty, devotion and enthusiasm he found in the Communist base camp. With very poor weaponry, they were adept at constructing homemade guns and bombs, and when that ran out they used axes, hoes and their fists against the enemy. The Americans filled their free hours in Yan'an with games, frequently baseball with Zhou Enlai playing an enthusiastic outfield.

The Dixie Mission returned to the United States in 1945; they wanted to report that the Communists were dedicated, passionate and had won the support of millions of Chinese. They would conquer China, some mission members felt. Unfortunately, Washington was not ready to hear this. They were snubbed by both the political and military establishment, and their participation in the Dixie Mission made them targets for the anti-communist witchhunts of the early Cold War era.

In the closing months of the war, the United States had decided to hold its nose and continue to back Chiang. Back-ing the Communists was too dangerous politically, both at home and with the (non-Soviet) allies, and Chiang was the only alternative. The Allies cut him out of the negotiations at Yalta, where the shape of the immediate post-war world was decided. The Soviet Union would be given the Sakhalin and Kuril Islands and numerous rights in Manchuria and the neighboring northern China provinces. Chiang could not protest, because he was even losing support in his own party, and without American supplies his regime would collapse.

Although the Japanese were slowly being pushed back, in mid-1945 most military experts thought the war would last at least another 18 months. Then, on August 6 the Ameri-cans dropped an atomic bomb on Hiroshima. Two days later the Soviet Union invaded Manchukuo. On August 9, the U.S. unleashed another atomic bomb on Nagasaki. Five days later, the Japanese surrendered. After eight years of war, no one knew what peace would look like.

FLYING WITH "C-NAK"

In its time it was the epitome of wild adventure—flying by the seat of the pants in the early airliners over some of the roughest and most unforgiving terrain in the world to serve the teeming cities of China. It was the China National Aviation Corporation (CNAC), founded in 1929 by the Curtiss-Wright Aeronautical Corporation of Buffalo, New York in partnership with the Chinese Government, and subsequently absorbed by the Pan American Airways System in 1933. CNAC faced monumental difficulties in bringing aviation to China in the early 1930s in an environment of war, revolution, and economic and social chaos. The insiders called it "C-NAK." Most of the pilots were Americans.

Royal Leonard was one of those Americans. Drawn inexorably to the Orient in the wild days of the 1930s, once he saw China he never wanted to go home again. He didn't look the part of a swashbuckling, do-or-die airman, but once you flew with Roy you knew he had that special touch—and probably a guardian angel working overtime as well. Roy was an unassuming sort, medium height, brown hair, thin, matter-of-fact and invariably good tempered. Although born in Wisconsin, he grew up in Waco, Texas. As an Army Air Corps flight cadet in 1925 he was a student of Claire Chennault, following which he was both a barnstormer and an airline pilot. That was all before he was bitten by the China bug.

He went to China in 1935 and spent the next six years as the personal pilot for the Young Marshal, Chang Hsueh-liang, and the Generalissimo and Madam Chiang Kai-shek.

He came to know China so well, it has been said, that from the wilds of Outer Mongolia to the coastal cities of Shanghai and Hong Kong he knew virtually every airway and landing field by heart. The Generalissimo trusted Roy to fly military leaders and diplomats from every nation over every part of China. He made some of the first flights into Tibet in 1936 flying a Boeing 247. He was always ready and willing to take on seemingly impossible flights in extremely inclement weather. But that was all part of the Royal Leonard legend. To him it was all business-as-usual. Nothing was impossible.

Roy was flying DC-2s out of Hong Kong's Kai Tak aerodrome in early 1941, facing more than the usual difficulties of distance, terrain and weather. Japanese troops were massing near the China-Hong Kong border and all flights to mainland destinations had to fly directly over the hostile guns of the Japanese, who were not above taking a few pot-shots at a lone airliner. Two unarmed CNAC planes had already been shot down. Consequently all flying was done at night and the worse the weather, the better. One typical DC-2 flight left Hong Kong at 4:30 A.M. in a high wind. The aircraft was loaded with freight, and eight sleepy passengers bound for destinations in China. Roy flew the plane alone—no co-pilot, radio operator or stewardess. The passengers were each given a rough, brown blanket and a brown, paper bag for throwing up and told to strap themselves in tightly. The plane's cabin was neither heated nor pressurized and the flight would be very cold and very rough indeed and much of it would be at

CNAC DC-2 arriving in Yunnan, China, 1940. It was in planes like this that Roy Leonard made his reputation

high altitude. Immediately after takeoff the plane began spiraling upwards to gain as much altitude as possible. At about 14,000 feet with all lights extinguished it crossed the Japanese lines, brightly lit, far below. Then the weather closed in.

Gusting winds, rain and hail beat against the metal fuselage with the sound of a thousand tin drums; the temperature both outside and inside was below freezing and the passengers hid beneath their blankets—some wailing and vomiting and some suffering and praying silently. Roy opened his side window a crack and judged the air speed that way because all the instruments were frozen! He knew that if the speed dropped below 63 miles per hour the plane would stall and go into a spin—but there was no cause for anxiety—he'd often done it that way! One needed to have confidence in a pilot who took these conditions in his stride.

The storm lasted for over an hour, after which conditions eased. The rest of the flight would be easy. He landed at Chongqing at 10 A.M. The gravel runway, under water during the wet season, was on a narrow island in the middle of the Yangtze River. Here he off-loaded some passengers, took on a few more and topped up the tanks with fuel. Taking off from Chongqing, the plane flew low, along the narrow winding valleys, far beneath the towering mountain peaks, seeking to avoid patrolling Japanese fighters. At times he was bucking 60 mile-per-hour headwinds that made the plane seem to stand still in mid-air. Then he climbed level with the ridge lines, popping up to peer over and then quickly dropping back down. "Want to see how things are at Kunming," he said.

When he was satisfied he flew straight in under a smokey sky, thankfully clear of Japanese bombers. The daily bombing was already finished and the ground crews had already scurried about to clean up the field, fill in the bomb craters and get ready to receive the next CNAC flight. After refueling and exchanging passengers he was off again, flying at 13,000 feet over the tortuous switchbacks of the Burma Road. He needed the extra altitude on this leg because the treacherous and unpredictable down-draughts could plunge the plane thousands of feet in mere seconds. He arrived at Lashio after 10 P.M. on a gravel runway illuminated by a row of flickering flare pots. Sixteen hours and 1,494 miles—that was the weekly Hong Kong to Lashio run. For Royal Leonard and the other pilots of CNAC it was just routine. But it's been noted that the passengers had a tendency to clap, with tears in their eyes, after every safe landing.

There has never been anything else quite like CNAC in the history of civil aviation. CNAC pilots flew by compass, seat-of-the-pants experience—and sheer guts. For their troubles, they earned $100 a month plus $10 for each extra hour above the mandatory 85. They were a different breed of men—immensely proud and in love with their type of flying. They were the best of men and machines against the elements, the enemy and the fates.

~Cliff Dunnaway

Sailors aboard the USS Missouri *look on as Japanese Foreign Minister Shigemitsu and Allied officers complete the ceremonies of Japan's surrender, Tokyo Bay, September 2, 1945*

CHAPTER FIVE

In a Red Shadow

Although the Japanese emperor formally surrendered on August 14, the war did not end at the same time across China. In some areas the fighting never stopped—the guns were simply turned on different enemies.

In Hong Kong, what remained of the British colonial government—weakened by four-and-a-half years of internment—took control of the city until the British fleet could steam into harbor on August 30 and accept surrender of the Japanese commander . The British had angrily refused Roosevelt's suggestion that they return the colony to China and had demanded their navy's right to be the first into Hong Kong. Chiang Kai-shek protested, but Roosevelt acquiesced.

Hong Kong was a mess. A State Department envoy cabled: "In general conditions very difficult." It suffered more from the effects of looting than from the 1941 fighting and the 31 American air raids during the war. The non-interned population had stripped nearly every building of wooden window frames and floor boards to use as fuel for heat and cooking. Although there was power, there were no replacement lightbulbs, so most streets were black at night. Far more serious were the food and housing shortages.

Chinese-style food supplies were barely adequate for the population, and the rice shortage was constant. Of Western food, there was almost none, except for whatever the fleet bought and a few cans left over from 1941 that shop-owners priced at astronomical levels. It took many months for the situation to ease, helped by large shipments of American rice and other staples (including tinned butter and powdered ice cream) sent by the United Nations Relief and Rehabilitation Administration (UNRRA), which was also active throughout China.

The housing shortage would last for years. The internees at Stanley had to stay in the camp, because there was no room for them in town. Many of their homes, including nearly all the houses up on the Peak, were empty shells, and the three best hotels were requisitioned by the military government. Even though tens of thousands of Chinese had been exiled into China by the Japanese, the destruction of buildings was so great that those remaining had to live ten or more to an apartment. British authorities took immediate measures to slow the flow of refugees returning to the colony.

Although they were stuck ten miles out of town, with transport almost non-existent, the Stanley internees immediately began to pick up the pieces of their lives, including their old occupations. John Stenerssen, a Norwegian national employed by American Express, had dropped 50 pounds in weight and and lost everything he possessed, except shorts and a shirt (he had no shoes). Nevertheless, he returned to his old office and re-assembled what was left of his Chinese staff, who during the war had kept him alive with food parcels. Most of the office furniture was gone, but the staff had hidden the business records and office machines in their homes.

The military government refused to give him permission to live in town, so he simply moved into his old office and, along with the staffs of Chase and City Bank, prepared to resume American banking in Hong Kong. On September 16, American Express re-opened from 11 A.M. to 1 P.M., allowing old depositors to withdraw nominal amounts from their accounts. "Everything running smoothly," he wrote back to the main office in New York. He also asked for a vacation, a parcel of food and cigarettes and the last few months of *Time, Life* and *Reader's Digest,* because he had not heard any news of the outside world for four years.

(opposite) Sailors at the foot of one of Hong Kong's "ladder streets" pause to count their foreign currency, 1953

Life member Arlando "Sonny" de Sales, who had spent most of the war in Macau, returned to Hong Kong in October and found that the family villa had been used as a Japanese officers' quarters. It was now administered by the British Custodian of Enemy Property and would not be returned to the family for months. In any case, many of their possessions were gone, either stolen by the Japanese or "borrowed" by the British (his mother found some of her furniture in the Officers' Mess). It would take months to put their lives together, and some of the pieces would never be found.

At the end of September, U.S. Naval Task Force 74 (part of the Seventh Fleet) arrived in Hong Kong. From that point on, the U.S. Navy was almost a constant presence in Hong Kong harbor, becoming a source of elation and anxiety among the locals. On the one hand, these ships were part of the great military machine that had freed them, bringing Japan to its knees. On the other hand, the presence ashore of hundreds of American sailors with U.S. dollars in their pockets caused prices in the delicate Hong Kong economy to skyrocket.

British naval officers, aware of some of the Anglo-American tensions over the colony's ownership, were heard to wonder what the Americans were doing in Hong Kong, fearing the ships presaged some dastardly maneuver to hand the colony to the Chinese. When the massive USS *Los Angeles* arrived in town a few weeks later, these mutterings increased: The huge battleship dwarfed the British navy, causing them to lose face. The Chinese were far more impressed by the Americans than anything British, and American officers were deluged with invitations from the local business community. At the higher levels of government, however, relations between British and American officials remained cordial and open.

(Still, American officials could not help gloating at their navy's size, for example on the 1946 arrival of two U.S. aircraft carriers: "Both carriers were in fighting trim, with decks filled with planes, and presented a most impressive appearance as they towered over every other ship in the harbor, including the battleship *Duke of York*.")

Hong Kong's American community took many months to revive. Aside from State Department officials and other government employees, the only American citizens in town were of Chinese or Portuguese origin who had managed to escape the camps (the rest had left on the repatriation boats). After four and a half years of occupation, almost all traces of the American Club (except for the club treasures secreted in the wall) had been erased from the Hongkong Bank Building, which had been the headquarters of the Japanese occupation. Nevertheless, American authorities began to lobby for the club's revival. In late 1945, George Hopper, the new American Consul-General, reported back to Washington:

"Plans are now being made to re-open the American Club of Hong Kong and to enlist a number of American Naval officers who will be given the privileges of this Club, thereby having some place to go ashore for the purpose of meeting their British colleagues."

According to Ronnie Ross (no relation to former General Manager Dick Ross), who had spent the last years of the war in a Japanese labor camp and was now back at his offices in the Hongkong Bank Building, the club's re-open-

Traders in their sampans cluster about the USS Princeton *to sell souvenirs to sailors*

U.S. sailors sightseeing, Shanghai, late 1940s

ing was gradual. At first, the only reason to visit the premises was less-than-glorious but essential: "It had the only functioning loo in the building." Over months, furniture was found and the bar and kitchen were restocked, and eventually the American Club was fully up and running. None of this could have been done without the help of the Hongkong and Shanghai Bank, which extended highly favorable loans to return their tenant to operation. According to Phyllis Ross, "We all said, thank goodness there's finally someplace we can go and get together."

By mid-1946 George Hopper could tell Washington:

"The reorganization of the American Club of Hong Kong, which has included a goodly number of Britishers, has provided a forum where men may foregather for lunch and for discussion of their business affairs. This Club was known throughout the Far East before the war for its excellent cuisine and bar, and the cordial atmosphere and informality that marked its management. As more new members are admitted to the Club its facilities have expanded until now the Club may be considered to be 'out of the woods' financially, although last fall it appeared that the heavy losses in equipment and lack of ready assets might have prevented its reorganization."

The Club's revival was not hurt by the fact that the United States was by far the most important foreign power in the Far East. American corporations—American Presidents Lines, U.S. Lines, City Bank, Chase, American Express, Pan Am, Kodak, NCR, Getz Brothers and Connell Brothers (another trading firm)—followed the military into Hong Kong, and the first thing their managers did on arrival was join the American Club.

Men outnumbered women by a ten to one margin in this migration, and the lack of companionship soon became a problem. By unwritten law, local Chinese girls were unacceptable as wives or girlfriends (at least girlfriends that could be presented on social occasions), leaving only the single expatriate women working as teachers or as nurses at Queen Mary Hospital.

On the other hand, for single American women such as Phyllis Ross, "It was lovely." As a teenager in the late 1940s, "I felt as if I was the pampered debutante of the time."

The American Club quickly became the center of the community in a way that it had not been before the war. Many of the Americans in Hong Kong were new arrivals, so they did not have strong ties to the British community, and in the post-war city, still rebuilding, there were very few alternatives.

"The American Club was very much home for us Americans," said Jerry O'Donnell, who came over in 1947 for Pan Am. "We had lunch there every day, because there were virtually no restaurants and only four decent hotels. We started lunch in the bar with liar's dice, and it never cost more than 50 cents U.S. or $3 Hong Kong for salad, soup, main course and dessert."

By 1948, Hong Kong had returned to its business-like but leisurely pace. While still suggesting that Britain return the colony to China, the United States had reduced the urgency of its request. Over the border in China, the Japanese surrender had not brought order but chaos and more war. It soon became apparent that the United States would need the British colony for something more than trade.

Back in 1945, the prospect of peace had revitalized the old Nationalist-Communist animosity. Once again, the first question was, to whom would the Japanese surrender in China? The United States was determined it would be to the Guomindang, the only government of China they recognized. At the same time, they attempted to forge a rapprochement between Mao and Chiang Kai-shek, flying Mao to Chongqing with the American ambassador as his escort.

While negotiations dragged on for almost two months, everybody jockeyed for position. Just before the surrender, the Communists had launched a massive attack on Japanese positions. When the Communist commander refused Chiang's order to desist, Chiang directed the Japanese troops to defend their positions. Battles raged through September as the Japanese and their Chinese collaborators ousted the Communists from many parts of Central China.

To Our Lady Patrons

AN INVITATION TO AN ECONOMICAL SAFEGUARD
To our lady patrons who are planning a journey, may we recommend that you change the cash you planned to carry with you into convenient, dependable
AMERICAN EXPRESS TRAVELLERS CHEQUES
When you carry these Cheques, you are a guest of the international travel organization behind them, and may use for your mail and cable headquarters the American Express offices in the principal cities of the world. Wherever you may go, its experienced travel staffs are ready to aid you.
These cheques are spendable everywhere and if lost or stolen, a refund is made.
Issued in denominations of
US $ 10, 20, 50 & 100 and
£ 2, 5 & 10.
also in Italian Lira and in Registered Marks for use in Germany and on German ships.
The AMERICAN EXPRESS CO. Inc.
4 Des Voeux Road, C.

American Express advertisement from the South China Morning Post, *ca. 1946*

The People's Militia preferred sabotage and surprise when fighting the Japanese. Despite their limited arms and ammunition, it is estimated that the Communist armies and People's Militia killed 350,000 Japanese from 1937 to 1945

Although officially uninvolved in the Nationalist-Communist conflict, the United States remained firmly on the side of the Guomindang. They flew Nationalist officials to Shanghai, Beijing and other cities to receive the Japanese surrender and supplied over 50,000 U.S. Marines to occupy the cities until the Nationalist troops arrived. Most of the Nationalist soldiers were ferried north by U.S. ships embarking from southern ports, principally Hong Kong, and by military and Civil Air Transport planes. (The presence of unruly Nationalist soldiers in the colony caused many problems— the local Chinese supported the Nationalists in confrontations with British police—and local authorities breathed a huge sigh of relief when the last one left.)

As the Japanese departed, the Nationalist, Communist and Soviet armies raced to grab all the plums they could. The Nationalists occupied the principal cities, the rail lines and the coast; quasi-governmental Nationalist business co-operatives took over the largest Japanese industries, providing an important source of income—and graft. The Soviet Army quickly swept through much of Manchuria. They

had agreed to withdraw by late November but delayed their departure so the Communists could occupy their positions and also so they could dismantle much of the equipment in Japanese factories and ship it back to the Soviet Union. When the Communists moved in, they miraculously found themselves in possession of the weaponry of 700,000 Japanese troops.

General George C. Marshall arrived in China at the end of 1945 with the mission of ending the conflict. Within weeks, the two sides had signed an agreement resolving all their differences. Unfortunately, neither side convinced all the factions within their own parties. Beginning in Manchuria and spreading south, a series of clashes between Communist and Nationalist forces increased in intensity through 1946. In November, Chiang Kai-shek told Marshall that the Guomindang had given up all hope of peaceful co-existence with the Communists. They would exterminate Mao's army and were confident they had the strength to succeed.

In this atmosphere of chaos and impending violence, the American business and missionary community returned to

(top) U.S. Navy Avenger over Beijing during show of strength flights, September 4, 1945; (above) General and Mrs. Chiang Kai-shek, back in China, return from a visit to a temple built in memory of Sun Yat-sen, May 17, 1946

American mission college glee club, 1947

*Runaway inflation—Shanghai telephone company
employees receive their pay in bales of notes, June 1948*

Shanghai, Tianjin and other Chinese cities. By mid-1946, 115 American businesses, both new and old, had opened offices in Shanghai. The head of the China-America Chamber of Commerce stated: "Despite extremely difficult conditions, American enterprise and ingenuity and the acute need in China for all types of American merchandise have resulted in a substantial volume of business. Some members of the Council have reported that the volume of their business has far exceeded their expectations and prospects for future business are good."

The businessmen were joined by missionaries, doctors and educators who re-opened schools, hospitals, churches and YMCAs in all their old haunts. Although they were citizens of the new dominant foreign power in China, the situation was very different than the prewar days. All extraterritorial rights had disappeared; the streets had been re-named in Chinese; and the local governments and police forces were stridently pro-Chinese. Most foreign clubs were forced to alter their rules and admit Chinese (except the Shanghai Club, which only went so far as to admit women to the party for the Royal Wedding). Americans were tolerated, but it was the Nationalist Chinese who ruled.

Unfortunately, they did not rule very well. Almost as soon as the Japanese surrendered, inflation began to spiral out of control. By September 1946, prices had risen almost 15-fold, while wages lagged far behind. Shanghai and other industrial centers were hit by waves of strikes; unemployment soared; and every effort by the Guomindang government to fix the economy failed miserably. In mid-1948, inflation reached a rate rivalled only by the economic collapse of Weimar Germany: One U.S. dollar was worth 12 million yuan. There were no large denomination bills, so you received your Chinese currency in stacks of bills, roughly at the rate of three pounds of yuan for every dollar.

"You had to carry a whole suitcase of currency to go have lunch," said John Shoemaker, then a CNAC pilot based in Shanghai.

In retrospect, Chiang Kai-shek's government probably would have collapsed of its own accord if the Communists had not beaten them to it.

With U.S. dollars in hand, Americans were more or less protected from inflation. Trying to do business in a system in which corruption was endemic, on the other hand, was a lesson in frustration. Millions of dollars worth of food and supplies poured into China from the UNRRA, which became known as "U Never Really Receive Anything!" Government-connected middlemen diverted the aid, and it soon found its way into marketplaces and shops at inflated prices.

American businessmen found that they were closed out of all major business projects. For example, American automobile dealers could not receive licenses to import new

American cars and trucks; meanwhile the streets of Shanghai were filled with brand-new Chryslers, Dodges and Fords being driven by rich Chinese. They discovered that all the most lucrative business deals were reserved for those with connections to the Chiang, Soong or Kung families. Everybody else might as well go home, and many Americans did, mainly shopkeepers and small traders, including numerous old China hands. The bigger American companies managed to succeed, particularly the oil companies, because their product was in chronically short supply. Still, they had to fight through bales of red tape (including new rules that all business with the government must be conducted in Chinese) and pay out huge amounts in graft to get the mandatory business licenses.

Despite these problems, Shanghai was a boom town, at least for 1946 and most of 1947. The hothouse economy was propped up by the UNRRA and the money of thousands of wealthy Chinese pouring into the city from the war-ravaged

PACIFIC DESTINIES: TRAVELS OF THE WONG FAMILY

The American presence in China has always been small compared to the Chinese presence in the United States. Since the 1850s, millions of Chinese have made the trip across the Pacific, at first in the holds of sailing ships and now in the comfort of airplanes. They have had a greater influence on their home country than the thousands of Americans who have lived and worked in China. Through sending home money, goods and information—and often returning themselves—they profoundly changed China's vision of the outer world and in many instances (the life of Sun Yat-sen, for example) altered that nation's destiny.

This exchange of people and ideas is illustrated by the family of Dr. Andrew Wong, past president of the American Club. The home of his ancestors was a village named Toisan in Guangdong Province not far from Canton. In the 1880s, his grandfather decided to try his luck in the New World, embarking on a boat from Canton bound for British Columbia. He settled in Victoria, B.C. and opened a match factory there. In 1896, Dr. Wong's father was born, but the idyll did not last long.

A smallpox epidemic hit the West Coast. The Chinese were blamed, and they were sent to internment camps. During the family's incarceration, the match factory burned down, leaving the family broke. When his father was four, they had to return to China.

Growing up in Toisan, Dr. Wong's father was always the smartest boy. As was customary in China, the village decided to help him; they pooled their money to pay for his education. He was sent back to Victoria, where he attended high school. From there, he managed to be accepted to the University of Minnesota. The only problem was, he was poor.

In Minneapolis, he was semi-adopted by the city's small Chinatown. In return for tutoring the restaurant and laundry workers in English, they fed him and paid him so he could afford his tuition and lodging. He studied dentistry and in his spare time raised money for Dr. Sun Yat-sen's revolutionary movement.

Around 1920, he had the good fortune to meet the leader himself. Dr. Sun Yat-sen gave him the honorific name "Ming San" meaning "doctor" with the characters reversed. When Dr. Wong Ming San received his degree, he decided to return to China, where he aspired to do great things. He had a letter of recommendation from Sun Yat-sen's son and hoped it would open doors to business or politics. When he returned to Canton, however, he discovered that the letter did not impress the city's leaders. He went back to dentistry, bringing modern American techniques to a country desperately in need of Western medicine.

The career of Toisan's favorite son prospered; his Canton practice included notable patients such as Madame Chiang Kai-shek. After World War II, which the family spent in Macau, Dr. Wong Ming San moved to Hong Kong at his wife's behest and became known as one of China's two most accomplished dental surgeons.

In 1951, the emigration resumed with the next generation. Following in his father's footsteps, Andrew Wong traveled to Canada to continue his education. This route took him to Albert College and Queen's College, both in Ontario, and then on to McGill University in Montreal. In 1967, Dr. Wong, now a neurosurgeon, accepted a teaching position at Stanford and he taught and practiced in the Bay Area for the next 15 years.

Dr. Wong and his family returned to Hong Kong at his wife's behest in 1982 and quickly established himself as one of the territory's pre-eminent neurosurgeons. In the years since, his children have also made the trip to the New World and back, becoming the fourth generation of Wongs to seek betterment across the Pacific and in the process serving both their adopted countries and the homeland of their ancestors.

~ANDREW COE

INTO RED AREAS

It was four o'clock in the afternoon, and already the light was turning gray. We knew we would have to hurry to make the thirty miles to Potow, first Communist city on the other side of the lines, before dark. Hastily we threw our cargo of iron cots and medicine boxes aboard the trucks and started out. As we wheeled through the gates of Tsanghsien's walls, a Kuomintang sentry at a barbed-wire barricade signaled us to a halt.

"You know me," said Barkley, smiling down at the sentry who came up to the cab of the truck, gun in hand. "I've been here before."

The sentry nodded.

"Who's that one," he said, jerking his head at me.

"UNRRA, too," said Barkley.

I sat silently in the cab, pretending I did not understand Chinese and trying hard to look like an international relief worker.

Having scrutinized me with casual curiosity, the sentry tapped our medicine boxes once or twice, then drew aside the barricade and motioned us out onto the North China Plain.

Drawing away from the city walls, we crossed the Grand Canal and entered no man's land. Our road was an undulating cart track where we plowed along jerkily, now rising even with the fields, now falling abruptly where metal-wheeled carts had dug deep ruts. On all sides of us, the fields rolled away, flatly, looking bare, brown and decayed in the gloomy winter light.

We went on for ten miles—fifteen—twenty—but there was not a sign of a Communist, not a soldier, not a gun.

Dusk came. The countryside grew gray, the wind cold. The air was boisterous with a leashed-in kind of wildness. The noises of the sky and land were humming as if at any moment they would break into a violent, uncontrollable roar. The wind whistled past our topless truck with crazy laughter; the dust infiltrated around the flanks of our wind-shield in a dirty cloud and we lurched, rolled and plunged across the plain which fled away everywhere with harsh, monotonous flatness.

We wished the Communists would pick us up quickly. We did not want to be shot at in the dark. We examined the plain to the limits of the horizon, but saw nothing.

It seemed as if the Kuomintang army might have rushed in here and taken all the outposts by surprise.

Turning from the fields, I bent down and lit a cigarette. Suddenly, below me, along the road on the right, there was a kind of stir, then a click, as of snapped rifle bolts, and at last —a terrifying shout. I jumped as if struck, Barkley slammed down on the brakes, and a dozen armed men sprang onto the truck as if they would tear us from our seats. We came to a grinding halt.

Unconsciously, I put up my arms to ward off blows, but that was not the intention of our boarding party.

"We've been expecting you," said one of the men; "we'll take you into Potow."

The militiamen—for that is who the boarders turned out to be—clambered aboard, some standing on the running boards, others lying flat on the hood of the radiator, and we went forward once more. A sharp crack rent the air and a bullet sang overhead like a bird. Our guards jumped from the truck; again we slammed to a halt. As more bullets whistled by, our guards ran forward, rifles in hand, bodies bent close to the ground, and mouths wide open, howling indistinguishable words. Passwords, we guessed, for the firing ceased, our companions returned to the truck and we went on again.

Coming once more to the Grand Canal, we halted at a bridge while a wooden gate was swung back and then crossed the river and entered Potow, first Communist-held stronghold on the destroyed Tientsin-Pukow Railway.

-Jack Belden,
China Shakes the World

north. Underneath the glitter, however, the poor were becoming poorer—hunger riots broke out in early 1947. Chiang Kai-shek's stern, Soviet-educated son, Chiang Ching-kuo, attempted to crack down on crime and corruption, but the problems were too deeply-rooted. His heavy-handed actions exacerbated tensions, and the middle class joined workers and students in massive demonstrations. By early 1948, the civil war had cut off the supply of raw materials to Shanghai's factories. Living off graft and foreign aid, the city could only wait until the inevitable revolution arrived at its gates. Once again, the Westerners made evacuation plans.

In mid-1947, the Communists slowed their retreat and began to counter-attack. By early 1948, the Nationalists barely held onto the cities and main rail lines of North China; in the countryside, the Communists held sway. In Nationalist territories, the government was also facing severe threats from the local citizenry, which had tired of the "Southerners'" corrupt, incompetent and often brutal rule. Beijing police machine-gunned a demonstration of student refugees from Manchuria, killing 14 and drawing an inevitable comparison between the Nationalists and the foreigners who had massacred Chinese in decades past.

Only United States aid—loans, armaments, training and transportation—kept the Guomindang alive. After the collapse of the Marshall peace effort, the American government lost all contact with the Communist side (leaving only a handful of journalists, such as Jack Belden, to report from within Communist territory). They decided to back the Nationalists for better or worse, and it soon turned out to be the latter. With no information from the enemy, they had no gauge of the Communists' strength, support and goals; they had no idea, at least in 1946, that their side would lose. As the main backer of the Nationalists, the United States was quickly tarred by the sins of its client. Chinese walls were soon splashed with "Yankee Go Home!", and anti-foreign mobs attacked American citizens.

General Ma, Governor of Ningxia Province, introduces General and Mrs. Claire Chennault to leaders of Muslim Chinese Nationalist forces, May 2, 1949

The Communists turned from guerrilla warfare to open battle in 1948. Seeing the writing on the wall, Chiang made plans to retreat to Taiwan, beginning with a brutal repression of Taiwanese politicians and intellectuals. Beijing and Tianjin fell in January 1949, and the Nationalist armies began to collapse. In April, Nanjing, Hangzhou and Wuhan surrendered with few shots fired, followed in May by the West's major foothold in China, Shanghai. The Nationalists ran, and the Communists ran after them, capturing China in record time (only the Southwest held out, Chongqing until November). On October 1, 1949, Mao Zedong stood atop the Gate of Heavenly Peace in Beijing and declared the founding of the People's Republic of China.

In Shanghai, the revolution came as a belated denouement. By the third week of May, flashes of guns could be seen on the horizon, and on May 24 the bulk of a Nationalist army arrived in the city, camping out in many major buildings and setting up guns on the Bund. The high-ranking Nationalist officials, meanwhile, had vanished. Shang-

hainese appeared on the streets not in their accustomed urban finery but in the heavy blue-cloth gowns of coolies. Everybody knew the end was near.

On the night of May 25, the Nationalist soldiers decamped, and the next morning the Red Army marched into town, poorly armed and shabbily dressed—looking like the peasant farmers that they largely were. The only bangs were provided by Nationalist soldiers taking pot-shots at the Communists to cover their retreat. Almost all trade and communication stopped, and no foreign ships or aircraft were allowed to land at the city. What was left of the foreign community—many had left in the previous months—could only sit around their offices and watch the Communist soldiers traipse in and out marveling at the modern appurtenances.

This new Shanghai was going to be very different. Prostitutes were rounded up and sent to school to learn honest trades; gambling disappeared; and foreign food and liquor vanished from local shops. The newspapers and radio were full of Shanghainese "confessions" of crimes against the proletariat, and spies and informers made open conversation impossible. To add to the air of uncertainty, every now and then a Nationalist plane would appear over the city to drop

*A parade celebrating the new Communist government proceeds down Seward
Street in Shanghai, November 1949*

Crowds fight to board a boat leaving Shanghai during the Communist takeover, November 11, 1949

a few bombs. The foreigners wanted to leave; the Communists could not understand why, and put huge bureaucratic obstacles in their way.

Finally, on September 24, 1,000 foreigners, the bulk of the remaining expatriate community, boarded the American liner *General Gordon* to set sail for San Francisco via Hong Kong. For most, this was the last time they would set foot in China. Many had now been twice burned; they had lost it all in 1941 and now were losing it all again in 1949. For the White Russians in Shanghai, including the Zigal family, now of Hong Kong, who had owned Shanghai's General Motors dealership, this was the third flight into exile—the first was the 1918 Russian Revolution. If they ever returned to do business in China, they would always have an eye on the way out.

Those Americans who stayed in China after the Communist takeover were almost all missionaries (including doctors and educators). They were uneasy about the future —the Communists associated them, often mistakenly, with the Guomindang—but they saw no cause for immediate alarm. The new PRC government had enough trouble building a Communist state out of the chaos that was China and did not think a few thousand Americans were any particular danger. Despite the U.S. support of the Guomindang and Washington's refusal to recognize the PRC, the United

Nanjing Safety Zone Committee at their headquarters, 1937

States was not overtly threatening to the new regime—Truman's China policy was "disengagement." That uneasy peace ended on June 25, 1950, when North Korean troops invaded South Korea.

At the head of a United Nations army, the U.S. leaped to South Korea's aid. Intense U.N. bombing of North Korea was followed by General MacArthur's brilliant September 15 landing behind enemy lines at Inchon. Their supply lines cut off, the North Korean army was soon in retreat, and by mid-October MacArthur's forces were approaching the Yalu River on the Chinese border. Mao decided to send Chinese troops into the war—Japan's actions in 1931 had already shown him that Korea was crucial to China's defense—and MacArthur's troops were met by a withering counter-attack by Chinese "volunteers." China and the United States were at war.

The Korean War dragged on until the July 1953 truce that divided North and South Korea into their present boundaries. The war also froze the United States and China into the mutually antagonistic positions they would hold for over two

The Yale-in-China staff's farewell dinner before evacuation, 1948

DEATH KNELL OF IMPERIALISM

On the evening of April 20, within a few hours of Mao Tze-tung's order, the People's Liberation Army began to cross the Yangtze River. Landing operations proceeded along a 350-mile front from Kiukiang in the west to Kiangyin in the east. The Yangtze in this section of China is sometimes two miles wide and it is deep enough to allow the passage of ocean-going steamers and warships of nearly every size and description. To negotiate this formidable water barrier, the Communists had only wooden boats, junks, and rafts. Everything they would need in South China, including artillery, ammunition, provisions and supplies of all kinds had to be ferried over the river by these primitive means. To halt the Yangtze crossing, the Kuomintang had a navy and an air force. Outwardly, the odds appeared in favor of Chiang Kai-shek.

But there was almost no resistance to the crossing. The Chinese navy, which had been partially equipped and trained by the United States, showed little stomach for a fight. The air force, which had also been furnished to Chiang by the United States and which might conceivably have turned the crossing into a holocaust, seldom appeared to give battle to the Communists.

The Kuomintang had deployed nearly half a million troops to man the Yangtze, but their fighting power was not to be measured by their numbers. The first break in the river line was made at Tikang on the evening of April 20. Garrisoning this town were the 80th and 88th divisions, the latter a crack outfit and one of the three army units originally known as "Chiang's Own." Both divisions revolted on the eve of the battle. On April 21, the Communists landed at Kiukiang midway between Nanking and Hankow. A day later, forces of the People's Liberation Army were in the Kiangyin fort area, supposedly the strongest point in Kuomintang defenses. The garrison batteries in the Kiangyin fort opened fire, not on the People's Liberation Army, but on Kuomintang gunboats so that the Communists could the more easily cross the river. Everywhere, the story was repeated: insurrection, surrender, disintegration. Formerly, military analysts had made distinctions between the fighting power of Central troops and Irregular troops loyal to the Kuomintang. The Yangtze crossing proved that such distinctions no longer existed. The revolution had brought all to the same level.

The advance of the People's Liberation Army was unbelievably swift. During the first week after the crossing, Communist troops captured an average of three cities per day. Within twenty-four hours, thirty thousand soldiers were at Wuhu, sixty miles southwest of Nanking. Within three days, they were at the walls of the capital of the republic.

The Kuomintang did not put up any fight for the capital of Chinese nationalism. As the Communists poured across the river, Chiang's officials and generals boarded American-made planes and flew in panic to Shanghai. A foreign diplomat who had come to say good-by noticed among the air-borne generals great piles of household furniture including one piano. With a whole world collapsing, the Kuomintang leaders, true to their nature, think only of saving their property.

When the officials sneaked away from Nanking, the city police took off their uniforms. Defenders of law and order, they had no desire to defend a dead regime. The common people emerged into the streets and began looting. So little affection did the crowds have for their departed rulers that they rushed to the house of President Li Tsung-jen and stripped it bare. In this they were aided by the departed president's housekeeper. Some American apologists for Chiang Kai-shek had often said he was a creative force in China because he had morally regenerated the people. Now, all the world could see just how deeply this regeneration had taken effect.

On April 24, the People's Liberation Army under the command of General Chen Yi and General Liu Po-cheng marched into Nanking. The Communist radio in a jubilant broadcast said: "This is the end of the reactionary rule of the Kuomintang. The government has passed out of existence."

Excited crowds gathered in the streets to see the army that had driven out their former rulers. While the crowds around them listened, the soldiers sang a number of anthems:

"We must think of the common man."

"Down with reactionaries."

"Mao Tze-tung is our savior."

Thousands of other soldiers moved hurriedly through the city without stopping and struck south and east in pursuit of Chiang's fleeing forces. General Chen Yi, conqueror of Nanking, ordered the publication of a seven-point policy which promised to protect lives, property, churches and schools, but demanded the confiscation of the bureaucratic capital belonging to the "rebel [sic] Chiang Kai-shek & Co." and prohibited the hoarding of arms and ammunition. Foreigners, including diplomatic personnel, would be protected "unless they indulged in law violations or subversive activities."

(continues on next page)

The next day, at 6:45 o'clock in the morning, twelve soldiers invaded the United States embassy and entered the bedroom of the American ambassador J. Leighton Stuart, who was lying in bed, half awake. After rudely addressing the seventy-two-year-old diplomat, a fluent Chinese scholar and a lifelong resident of China, they pointed to articles in his room and said, "These will soon belong to the people." As they were leaving, they told a servant of the embassy that Stuart should not be allowed to leave the residence compound. These simple soldiers, armed creators of the revolution, were no respecters of persons. They were probably a portent of the shape of things to come in the Orient. . . .

꒰꒱

During the crossing of the Yangtze River, there occurred an incident which pointed up the significance of the whole China war in a fashion more revealing than a dozen political dissertations. The Yangtze, one of the world's great rivers, which has its source in Tibet and its mouth three thousand miles away in the China Sea, is navigable for its last thousand miles by ocean-going steamers. On this stretch of the river, foreign warships have been maneuvering for nearly a hundred years, with no Chinese government able or willing to keep them out. As the battle over this great waterway began, British naval authorities, with a sublime indifference to the new realities in China, ordered the sloop *Amethyst* to move out of Shanghai with supplies for British embassy officials in Nanking. This action was definitely, though perhaps not purposely, provocative. Later both Kuomintang and British authorities were to declare that the ship had a perfect right on the Yangtze because of treaties concluded with the Chiang government. But it was just these treaties which the Communists were fighting to destroy. As might have been expected, Communist soldiers in the midst of a battle with the Kuomintang fleet and Kuomintang soldiers on the opposite shore opened up with their American-made batteries on the *Amethyst*. She was severely damaged and ran aground fifty miles from Nanking. From that city another British warship, the destroyer *Consort,* headed downstream but was beaten off by Communist guns. Adding folly to arrogance, two other British warships moved upstream from Shanghai; they too were heavily shelled and turned tail and fled. In all, the British suffered forty-four seamen killed, eighty injured.

The significance of this great event is tremendous. Thirty years earlier, the mere presence of the British warships on the Yangtze would have been enough to turn the tide of any civil war. Twenty years ago, such an incident would have sent every foreign warship on the China station scurrying up the river to silence the insolent Chinese; diplomats would have sternly demanded apologies; the foreign press would have thundered for revenge and editors would have written philosophic dissertations on the need for "law and order." But 1949 was not 1929.

The crossing of the Yangtze—like the crossing of so many other river barriers in history, from the Rubicon to the Rappahannock or the Rhine—may stand as a decisive date in world history.

It is likely to stand [remarked the *New York Herald Tribune*] as the day on which Chinese Communist gunners, learning how to use American equipment, brushed the Royal Navy contemptuously aside. It is likely to stand as the day when a bankrupt old regime in China was forced finally to confess itself impotent, and when the Western policies, founded upon hopes of its survival, were compelled to admit they could not save that regime and that new and different forces had assumed dominant power over the Chinese millions. It is proof certainly the old order is done, that neither the Chinese monied classes, British imperialism nor the American "open door doctrine" have sufficed to open a pathway through the tangled problems of the times which the Chinese people could follow.

This day is also likely to stand, the newspaper might have added, as the day which sounded the death knell of imperialism in Asia. The crossing of the Yangtze rang down the curtain on an era of history. It was an era that had opened one hundred years ago when the forces of reaction in Europe were crushing the Revolution of 1848 and beginning a ruthless expansion eastward into Asia. It was an era which saw Perry's opening of Japan, the Crimean War, the Indian mutiny, Russian czarist expansion to the Amur. It was an age which witnessed the Taiping and Moslem rebellions in China, the Meiji Restoration in Japan and Civil War in the United States, and the freeing of the Russian serfs. It was an age in which the British blew down the back doors of China, when the French grabbed Indo-China and Hainan, the Japanese seized Korea and Formosa and even little Portugal sliced off Macao from China. It was an age during which imperialism forced opium on the Chinese people, set up foreign concessions in China's cities and ruled her by special and unequal treaties. It was an era which saw Western capitalism devour itself in two costly wars, the first resulting in the Russian Revolution and the rise of a rival Asiatic imperialism in Japan, the second bringing about the Chinese Revolution and crushing blows to all imperialism in the Far East.

~Jack Belden, *China Shakes the World*

decades. China, which had been half-heartedly leaning toward the Soviet Union, surged into the socialist camp and became a standard-bearer for world revolution. The United States became engaged: They threw full military and political support behind the Nationalists in Taiwan and branded China another Cold War enemy and the compatriot of the evil Soviet Union. The world's most populous nation was barred from the U.N., and all official communication between the United States and the PRC stopped.

For the American missionaries in China, the Korean War made their already delicate position impossible. In the months before the war's outbreak, PRC authorities had begun to assert greater control over the American-financed churches, schools and hospitals. These efforts remained haphazard, however, until November 1950 when the government began its Resist America, Aid Korea campaign. Americans were the enemy, and many were forced to resign from their posts and relinquish their comfortable homes and apartments. The anti-American campaign extended to the tens of thousands of Chinese who had worked and studied in American institutions; they found themselves jobless, homeless and often imprisoned. The situation became more untenable a few weeks later, when the U.S. froze all PRC assets and outlawed all transfers of U.S. currency to China. American financial support of hundreds of Chinese institutions came to an end, and the mission boards ordered the Americans home.

USS Missouri *shells Chong Jim, Korea in an effort to cut North Korean communications, October 1950*

Harriet Mills, a victim of "thought reform" in a Chinese prison, meets the press in Hong Kong, 1955

It was rarely as easy as the boards assumed. The missionaries first had to apply for an exit visa and, before it was granted, be investigated for all type of political and economic sins against the proletariat. The Americans were frequently the target of spiteful informers who accused them of spying and sabotage. Those that were convicted were thrown in prison and compelled to undergo the brutal Communist "thought-cleansing" process to eradicate all vestiges of their capitalist thought-patterns. They were eventually released, but it often took years to recover from their ordeals. By the end of 1952, nearly every American citizen had fled the country, leaving in Beijing only a handful of long-time American supporters of the Revolution, such as Anna Louise Strong. For the first time since the 18th century, the United States was out of China.

Except for Hong Kong. The colony was now the West's only foothold on the Chinese mainland, and the U.S. and Britain were determined to hold on to the "Gibraltar of the East." Britain reinforced its garrison, and the United States dropped all talk of returning Hong Kong to China. By 1949, U.S. had established its first intelligence post for China-watching and was advising on the colony's defense. If China invaded, they did not guarantee any direct military action but said that they would bring the matter before the U.S.-dominated United Nations—not an idle threat considering the U.N. army then fighting in Korea.

The American refugees from the Civil War had begun trickling in to Hong Kong in 1948. For most of them, this was only a way station: They were either heading back to the States or waiting out the war in the safety of Hong Kong until they felt it was safe to return. However, Western refugees were only a drop in the bucket compared to the flood of Chinese. In 1949 and 1950 well over two million Chinese poured into the colony, most of them from Canton but many also from Shanghai and other Chinese cities. The colony's services were strained to the utmost as streets and parks were jammed with homeless people.

Only a fraction of the new American arrivals joined the American Club. Most of these were members of the Shanghai American Club, which may have had a cross-arrangement with the Hong Kong club. According to John Potter, the new arrivals (of which he was one) were a distinctly "raffish" set compared to the local American community. Many of them young and adventurous WWII veterans, they crowded the bar every lunchtime, playing liar's dice and drinking and, after the meal, sleeping it off in the library. Hong Kong's economy was undergoing a brief boom—the wealthy Chinese refugees were investing locally—and a number of the Shanghai American crowd were hired by American corporations to handle the new business.

The more reputable of this group were quickly invited into the American social whirl, at the center of which was Bill Harper, the local head of Pacific Far East Lines. An avid party-giver, he kept files on female guests and their party dresses, encouraging them to wear "that blue number," for example, at his next bash. Harper encouraged many newcomers to join the American Club, sponsoring them there and at other institutions, including the Shek O and Royal Hong Kong Golf Clubs.

The refugees were joined by new arrivals from the United States coming over for corporations and government agencies beefing up their Hong Kong operations. For many, the American Club was almost literally the first stop. Peg Bordwell came out as a secretary for a new section in the consulate (all right, the CIA) and spent the night in Kowloon's International Hotel:

"I went down for breakfast and ordered cornflakes. The first spoonful had a cockroach. I put it down, went straight to the office and told them. They sent me up to the American Club, and that's where I had my first breakfast in Hong Kong."

"Everybody went to the American Club," she said. "You just joined immediately."

For Phyllis Ross, the new arrivals made it a livelier and more active club—no more "you can't do this and you can't do that"—as the new blood began to shake up established American Club practices. Tired of sweating through Hong Kong summers in heavy business suits, Ross's father Wallace Harper decided to challenge the club dress code.

"Three of them—my father, John Paulin and Bob Landis—dressed up in safari suits and went up to the club," she said. "They said, 'We're sorry, but you can't wear those here.' So that's why you still have to wear business suits at the club."

Other challenges were more serious but took years of campaigning and angry meetings to change club policy. Many new members were shocked by the club rule against accepting not only Chinese as members but also against Americans who had Chinese wives. Up in Shanghai, the American community had been far more accepting of Chinese as equals not only in business but in social life. The Shanghai American Club had allowed Chinese since the late 30s, and the Shanghai set wanted the same at the Hong Kong club. It was absurd: Y.C. Wang had been a member of the Shanghai club but was refused in Hong Kong.

The policy also caught flack from new arrivals from the United States. The executive ranks of many American corporations in Hong Kong included a small number of Chinese-American managers, and at least one consular officer was Chinese-American. For many of their fellow citizens, it was extremely embarrassing that these respected Americans could not join the American Club.

Often bucking their home offices, which did not want them to rock the boat, the newcomers spearheaded the drive to allow Chinese-Americans into the club. It did not happen overnight. First, an American with a Chinese wife was

Leon Zigal (1900-1962) giving a demonstration of the first Opel in Hong Kong. A member since 1948, Zigal was the Managing Director of Triangle Trading Company Ltd., the General Motors' automobile concession in Hong Kong

American Marines at Stanley Cemetery at the headstone of U.S. Consul R. Engdahl, who died in Hong Kong at the age of 34, six months after the Occupation began

accepted as a member. The next step was harder. Probably influenced by the colonial atmosphere, the Hong Kong American community had always been more snobbish and conservative than its Shanghai counterpart. After much heated debate, around 1951 the club by-laws were changed and the first group of Chinese was sponsored and accepted as members. All four—Y.C. Wang, K.K. Tse, Jack Soong and Wilfred Wong—were prominent businessmen, Y.C. Wang with his family textile business and the others in insurance, oil and air-conditioning.

The acceptance of Chinese members was a major milestone for Americans in Hong Kong. Not all of the British-dominated clubs allowed Chinese, and one or two continued to implement a discriminatory policy over membership for years to come. As the Chinese came to dominate the world of Hong Kong business, the standing of the American Club and the corporations its members represented was enhanced.

While this debate was underway, upper crust Hong Kong was diverted by a controversy involving two very high-ranking Americans. Lady Maurine Grantham was the Nancy-Reagan-esque—petite and intensely social—wife of Sir Alexander Grantham, Hong Kong's Governor-General. When Government House was moved at the end of the 1940s, she oversaw the new residence's decoration and proceeded to spend far more than was budgeted. She was joined in Hong Kong by her sister, Mrs. Jane Scott, who began using her family influ-

ence to steer business deals in friends' directions. The two scandals broke concurrently, and much diplomatic note paper was spent on assuaging British sensibilities and reining in the two ambitious Americans.

The debate over allowing Chinese to join was only a minor part of members' worries in the early 50s. Events in China and Korea were threatening to overrun Hong Kong. In January 1951, the U.S. consulate posted on the American Club bulletin board a notice advising all non-essential citizens to leave the colony. The combined Chinese and North Korean armies had pushed the U.N. force back to south of Seoul; the United States feared not only that the entire Korean Peninsula would be captured but the war would spread to Taiwan and Hong Kong. The colony's feeling of isolation was heightened by the imposition of U.S. and U.N. embargoes on all trade with China. Business plummeted and Hong Kong's future looked very, very dim.

The consulate's advisory was voluntary, but hundreds of Americans left, including nearly every woman and child. Some American businesses also decided they had had enough of the Far East, most prominently the Chase Bank. With the advantage of 20-20 hindsight, it is possible to see that 1951 was a dividing line for Americans in Hong Kong. Those that stuck out the crisis and put down stakes made long and lucrative careers in the colony. Those that fled and then returned had to struggle and often left again for good.

THE FLOWERY KINGDOM

The tender which bore us to the Bund had no allotted slip or jetty; it merely tied up in slapdash fashion against five other boats each moored to the one adjoining it, and the passengers swarmed over the lot like ants over a sugar bowl. In effect, what you had was a Bronx subway rush with water jumps. One moment I was braced against a stanchion gaping at the skyline; the next, I was caught up in a swirl of coolies and shot forward down into a barge full of stones. I clawed my way across it, sprang down a dark companion-way, stumbled over three citizens stuffing themselves with bean curd, and landed in a perilously tossing sampan. As I straightened up to catch my breath, the second wave hit me. I saw Hirschfeld go past, flailing and kicking, his beard high in the air. "Hirschfeld!" I screamed piteously, *"To-varisch!"* He paid me no attention; he had other fish to fry. I lowered my head like a bull and, with two Cantonese encircling me, did a line plunge. I reached terra firma a broken man, my collar in shreds, eyeglasses twisted, streaming with perspiration. Hirschfeld was nursing a wrenched knee, having slipped and fallen between two boats in the melee. He had a bloody nose and had lost a shoe, but otherwise he was as fit as a fiddle.

To regain some measure of poise, we proceeded to the Cathay Hotel, reputedly Shanghai's finest, and had a drink apiece. The bill came to $39,000 Chinese National Currency—about $3.36—and we left a tip of $5000, or 41 cents. The exchange rate at the moment was twelve thousand Chinese dollars to the American one, and prices had more or less kept abreast. Our room, for instance, was $120,000 a day—slightly over ten dollars—and our breakfast $14,000. The real drawback, though, was the complete lack of any form of heat. A ton of coal cost three hundred U. S. dollars —in any case, a purely academic consideration at the Cathay, as the Japanese had stripped it of radiators and boilers. That night will linger in my memory as one of the most agonizing I have ever endured. Our teeth chattered so loudly that several Americans resident there phoned the Embassy to report gunfire. Just to indicate how cold it was, I left a tumbler of water at my bedside and when I woke up, it was gone. Hirschfeld had drunk it and also had eaten the glass. That was one cold night.

The following day we embarked on a shopping tour of the antique bazaars in the Kwantung Road, charmed at every turn by the indescribable wealth of imagination the Chinese lavish on their art. Surrounded by so much beauty,

it was difficult to determine what to choose; Hirschfeld finally settled on an imitation cloisonné cigarette stand complete with match receptacle and ash-trays, and I bought three ivory back-scratchers you could not duplicate in San Francisco for less than a quarter. About mid-afternoon we traced our steps to the American Club, a pleasant establishment in Foochow Road made doubly delightful by the circumstance that it had the only heated bar in town. Five whiskey sours drove the chill from our bones, and we decided to have a drink. There then ensued a hazy interval during which I seem to recall the sound of a cupful of poker dice being thrown repeatedly against a board and a playful attempt on my part to comb Hirschfeld's beard with a back-scratcher. From time to time strange faces swam into my field of vision; I remember a laborious, protracted recital by an UNRRA official of his difficulties in persuading the Chinese to eat canned peaches, but part of it was being given in Russian and some men were accompanying him on balalaikas. It suddenly grew much colder and I found myself in a very dim night club, teaching an exophthalmic Hungarian girl the Cubanola glide. The next morning I felt remarkably listless and there was an outbreak of beef Stroganoff on my tie as though I were coming down with a fever, but these symptoms soon passed, and by noon I was able to keep down a little clear broth made of Angostura, lemon peel, and bourbon.

What with the penetrating cold and the cost of living in Shanghai, it seemed on the whole inadvisable to tarry, and folding our hands submissively we journeyed north once more to Chinwangtao on the *Flier.* It took four interminable days to get rid of our cargo; my companion mooned in the cabin buffing his nails and I made a short excursion to Shanhaikwan to see the Great Wall. The Great Wall can also be seen facing page 556 of the Encyclopaedia Britannica by simply stretching your hand toward the bookcase, though the chances of picking up a flea are very much smaller. Shanhaikwan, it is interesting to note, has the smallest fleas in China; they are much prized by collectors, but I was fortunate enough to secure three or four fine specimens. As the Chinese Government strictly forbids their export, I had to smuggle them out in my clothing, but I managed to get them through to Singapore safe and sound.

~S. J. Perelman, *Eastward Ha!*

Impatient youngsters disembark for the American Club picnic at Silvermine Bay, Lantau, July 4, 1957

Chase came back in 1957, but its competition had established itself as the dominant American bank. It took Chase many years to rebuild its business.

Despite the danger over the border, life in the American Club continued at its customary pace. Businessmen still played liar's dice for drinks and lunch at the bar, and on July 4th the club hired a ferry to take the (almost all male) community out to Silvermine Bay for hot dogs, hamburgers and potato salad.

Normality such as this holiday ritual was elusive in early 1950s Hong Kong. The colony had become a focal point of Cold War tensions. In the eyes of many, the enemy was not the PRC, which had been recognized by Britain, but the United States, whose embargo was devastating local business. The U.S. demanded total compliance, even over the most absurd issues. Cases in point were the "Red Prawns" and Chinese ducks scandals. The shrimp were netted in Hong Kong waters, but they could have swum there from beyond territorial boundaries, making them Communist shrimp and therefore prohibited. The Chinese ducks had

hatched in Hong Kong from eggs laid in the PRC; the philosophical debate over whether that made them Communist raged for weeks.

This illegal trade went both ways. In 1953, the Associated Press's David Roads broke the story that U.S. sailors were selling strategic equipment such as engine parts, electronics tubes and even a cryptographic machine to Communist agents. These exchanges took place in Wanchai's seedy bars, which were gaining a worldwide reputation as a center of the red light trade. Although the trade was quickly stopped, for decades Wanchai remained a hub of information on U.S. fleet movements—bar girls knew when a warship was due to arrive well before the local Navy attaché.

The center for the anti-Communist side was the U.S. consulate, whose staff had ballooned to 115 serving a local American population of less than 1,300 (the 1938 staff was four). China, not Hong Kong, was their main concern. Their work was divided between research and operations. Along with the British, the consulate sent teams down to the refugee camps to interview recent arrivals about conditions in China. Other researchers produced digests of PRC books and periodicals, and their Survey of Mainland China Press reports became one of the most respected sources for information on China through the early 1970s. On the operations side, CIA agents recruited refugees to return to China to collect information and foment anti-revolutionary movements. The vast majority of these efforts failed, and most operatives ended their lives in Communist jails.

Spies and intelligence became part of the Hong Kong scene, and nearly every American knew someone working for the CIA or other intelligence organizations. Those that wanted a thrill could always visit Pop Gingles' bar on Nathan Road in Kowloon and drink with the CATF pilots who used it as their second home (the CATF offices in the Peninsula were their first). These colorful characters were always just back from or just about to leave on another perilous mission over China. When they were deep in their cups, and the stories began to fly, it was just like "Terry and the Pirates."

At the end of the Korean War, Hong Kong life was still running on colonial time. Westerners' social life revolved around the old Hong Kong Hotel, the Hong Kong Club, the Peninsula, the Repulse Bay Hotel and, for (hard) drinking, the Foreign Correspondents' Club. The colony's biggest social functions were the charity balls, such as the Red Cross Ball, held at either the Peninsula or Repulse Bay Hotel.

"At 4 P.M. you could go to the Peninsula and meet everybody you wanted to meet," said Sonny Sales. "They were all there drinking gin and tonics."

Nevertheless, the Americans were beginning to have an influence. According to Sales, the British would say:

"It was all very peaceful until you Americans came on board. Now we have to work on Saturday mornings."

After the Hong Kong Hotel was torn down in 1953, the center of social life moved across the bay to the Peninsula. In response, the hotel opened Gaddi's Restaurant, which today still sets Hong Kong's standard for fine French food. The most popular Western restaurants outside the hotels were Jimmy's Kitchen, where Jerry O'Donnell ate "2,000 meals," and its sibling, the Parisian Grill, better known as the "P.G."

"If you took your girlfriend to the Parisian Grill," said Felix Bieger, "it was an engagement."

For Americans, the other social circuit was home entertaining. This was frequently more rigorous than the hotel and restaurant scene, because they often had invitations to five or more dinner parties a week. For the hosts, this was not as difficult as it sounds: They all had cooks and servants, and they frequently did not know what would be served until they saw it on the table. The guests normally arrived at eight, dinner was served around nine and nobody went to bed before midnight. The next day they were expected to be in the office for regular business hours.

Cameraman and longtime Hong Kong resident, Marvin Farkas, captures Clark Gable for Movietone News, as the star arrives in Hong Kong for the filming of "Soldier of Fortune," 1955

"The way we were"—two views of Hong Kong in the early 1950s

(top) Roy Farrell, co-founder of Cathay Pacific, in the airplane he called "Betsy," 1946; (above) A delegation of General Motors officials from Asia leaving Kai Tak, ca. 1950

"How did we do it and why?" asks Peg Bordwell.

On weekends, Americans played golf, either at Shek O, which was very exclusive and very British, or at Fan Ling. If you became "island-happy"—driven stir-crazy by spending too much time in Hong Kong—the best option was boating, cruising by either sail or motor around Lantau or to the more obscure parts of the New Territories' coast. For less reputable pursuits, the destination was always Macau, where Hong Kongers spent "dirty weekends" having affairs with other people's spouses.

Another escape hatch were the American President Lines passenger ships, which were frequently docked at Kowloon. While they were in port, Americans could visit the ships' bars and buy good American beer and liquor for low American prices. Down-and-out Yankees also used them as a way to return home. More than one attended the going-away cocktail party and then hid on the ship until it was far out at sea, at which point they gave themselves up as stowaways.

Almost all American Club members from that time remember the mid- and late 1950s as a golden era. The American community was small, friendly and very close—the club only had around 200 members. The cost of living was low, the services excellent and the pace relaxed.

"Living in Hong Kong was delightful," said Peg Bordwell, "because we were very privileged."

"We had all the advantages of the Orient—servants and inexpensive living," said George Bell, who was working for an American oil company, "together with the very fine police and civic organization they had in Hong Kong."

The scene on the streets was a dramatic contrast to the comfortable world inside Hong Kong's Western clubs and offices. As a young government official, Burton Levin arrived in town in 1955 from Taiwan, where the economic disparity was not so great—nearly everybody in the Nationalist stronghold was desperately poor:

"Hong Kong then was a very disturbing place. As a Caucasian, you could not escape being constantly badgered by beggars, a solid crowd of them. The refugees from China

Reception of General Motors executives from around Asia at the American Club, ca. 1950s. In the top photo: Leon Zigal, third from left, and T.K. Ann, fourth from left. In above photo Alfred Hsieh, third from left. (opposite) The Hongkong and Shanghai Bank Building, 1950

in the back seat of his car, so it was always clean and safe.

For many of the poor Chinese refugees, "Americans could do no wrong," said Nora Sun, who escaped from Shanghai as a child. They saw Americans as open, friendly and not discriminatory compared to the British. Many young Chinese made a conscious effort to gain American rather than British accents by watching the Hollywood movies that filled Hong Kong theaters. This trend toward the United States increased as Hong Kong prospered and many Chinese sent their children across the Pacific for their education.

As the 1950s progressed, Americans back home began to recognize Hong Kong as a unique and enticing place. Cruise ships docked at Kowloon to disgorge hundreds of tourists eager to scour the colony for souvenirs and bargains (Shanghai refugee tailors had recently put Hong Kong on the world custom suit-making map). Hong Kong also received its share of celebrities, and they all had to be fêted at the American Club, including Charles Lindbergh, Lowell Thomas, Cardinal Spellman, humorist S.J. Perelman and the actor William Holden, who was a Hong Kong regular and had many friends at the club.

were truly desperate; streetwalkers were all over the place, even pitifully young girls; and people were sleeping on Queen's Road Central by the hundreds. I had a very mixed view of Hong Kong. On the one hand you could get a good steak, a cold draft beer and a good hotel room, unlike in Taiwan. On the other hand, there was incredible poverty in the streets."

In Central, office doorways became bedrooms for groups of homeless people, and many businesses agreed to let refugee families sleep in the offices at night in return for cleaning and running errands (during the daytime the refugee families lived in the parks). David Roads had a refugee living

The biggest American VIP to come through Hong Kong was Vice President Richard Nixon on his 70-day Asia tour in late 1953. "He was a breath of fresh air to old colonial Hong Kong," said Sonny Sales. The highlight of his visit was a lunch given in his honor by the local Jaycees and Rotarians in the Peninsula's ground floor restaurant. The American Club hosted him at a cocktail party, and, as club president, it was Jerry O'Donnell's job to introduce the Vice President to the members:

"I had to move him around in the club, which was not an easy job when you have a crowded room like that. You need someone who can move in and out of groups, but Nixon kept getting into long discussions with people. Cardinal Spellman, on the other hand, was the opposite; he was very quick and easy to move."

In 1957, the American Club had the good luck to hire Mario Prata as its manager. He had been a maître d' with Hong Kong and Shanghai Hotels and succeeded a Mr. R. Sales as manager (before that the position had been filled by a Russian). Prata seems to have been universally popular with the members, perhaps because he finally managed to secure a steady supply of American steaks—a great improvement on the locally grown beef. He also reorganized the annual 4th of July excursions.

In the morning the members and their families would pile on a chartered ferry boat and head out to one of the outlying islands. There they would be met by the bangs of firecrackers (before the boat landed, so the children would not get involved), a tent and a gramophone with two speakers blaring patriotic tunes. Lunch would be hot dogs, hamburgers, chicken, Coca-Cola (provided by the Henningsen family Coke franchise), ice cream and watermelon. After various games, the revellers would stagger back to the ferry in the late afternoon and steam for home.

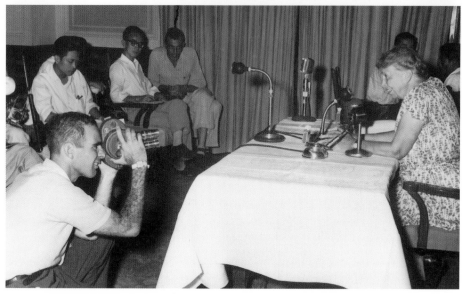

(top) Nixon's first visit to Hong Kong, 1953; (above) cameraman Marvin Farkas filming Eleanor Roosevelt during a press conference in Hong Kong

In the 1960s, Hong Kong began to blossom; all that hard work was finally paying off. It became Asia's center for inexpensive manufacturing, particularly clothing, and one of the Far East's busiest ports. The new money wanted a new, more opulent type of entertainment, and the early 60s ballroom scene was born.

The premier venue was the Paramount Ballroom, which featured one of the first European bands under the baton of Gian Carlo. For the rest, Filipino bands were the norm, usually belonging to offshoots of the colony's dance band favorites, the Carpio Family. Couples also went to the Ritz Ballroom, with its 18-piece orchestra in North Point, to the Luna in Causeway Bay, or to the Champagne Room in the Winner House Hotel where they danced to the Three Bubbles band.

By this time the American Club community included a number of children who were reaching an age when their parents thought it proper for them to learn the social graces of the ballroom. After school and on weekends, the children's free time was filled with dance classes taught by Gordon Campbell and his wife. The dress code of dresses and white gloves for girls and jackets and suit shorts for boys was mandatory. For small boys, it was not an easy time.

Leon Zigal at a Halloween party on an American Presidents Line crossing between Hong Kong and San Francisco

"I was petrified of the American Club," said Daniel Zigal. "My kids these days are absolutely fearless. In my youth, kids were seen and not heard. At the dances, everything was arranged by the mothers, starting when you were five or six years old. When it came time for me to hold a girl, I was scared stiff."

The culmination of the young Americans' year came at the December Cotillion, usually held in a rented ballroom. The participants' deportment was judged at every step of the process, beginning with the invitations.

"You had to send your responses back really fast," said Cathy Braga. "To give you practice writing back to people, the organizers noted who was on time and who was late. At the dance, the girls had a card with a little pencil, and the poor guys would have to go around and ask us for dances. We weren't allowed to have the same person twice. My male cousins hated it because they got so hot in their suits, and there were chaperones everywhere. It was a real zoo!"

The dance classes filled another important role for the children—it gave them something to do in a city purely oriented toward commerce. After school, home or friends'

houses (if they were nearby) were usually the only place to go. Occasionally they would be taken to the movies, particularly if it was a Disney film, or to the Parisian Grill or one of the floating restaurants for dinner. When the Hilton opened in 1963, its Coffee Shop became the "in" hangout for teenagers. Nevertheless, Hong Kong offered little diversion for expatriate children.

These peaceable pastimes took place during an era of increasing tension in the Far East. The United States was becoming heavily involved in the Vietnam conflict, and Hong Kong became an important supply station for the U.S. Navy. The colony also developed into one of the favorite rest and recreation spots for American troops. The American Club welcomed naval officers at its bar; many American women volunteered at Fenwick Pier, the Navy's Hong Kong supply station; and almost all American Thanksgiving and Christmas parties included servicemen on their guest lists.

The idea of thousands of American soldiers and sailors swarming over Hong Kong did not make the PRC happy. Chinese pressure forced the British to ask the U.S. to limit

(continues on page 184)

Marvin Farkas again filming the action, this time at the Macau Grand Prix, ca. 1950s

Since the earliest days of the American Club, games of chance have been a popular recreation—and an easy way to decide who pays for drinks and lunch. The 1950s were the heyday of liar's dice and here the Five Aces Club are seen demonstrating their prowess at the game. Anyone who rolled five aces—the ones on the dice—was treated to a meal and had his name engraved on a silver plaque (see page 189).Since the 1970s, liar's dice has been supplanted by backgammon in McKay's Bar

The American Club could not run without the remarkable skills and tireless service of its staff. Many have served the club for decades, and absent members can always count on seeing familiar faces tending bar or overseeing the dining rooms. (top right) Independence Day Picnic, Lantau, early 1970s. The American Club staff take time out for a group picture. From left: Johnny Choy, Otto Chan, Wilson Chu, W. C. Hung, Mike Mak, Sing Leung, Kwok Leung; (top left) same event and group as above; (middle right) staff picnic , Pui O, Lantau Island, 1968; (bottom right) the staff, grown larger in keeping with the club's expansion, pose at the Independence Day picnic at Lyemun Barracks, Shau Kei Wan, ca. 1980

*American Club dinners
al fresco on the beach at
Shek O, ca. 1958*

*Children's activities
have always been a part of the
American Club. Christmas and birthday
celebrations, the annual Children's Party, movies, Halloween
parades, even an ad hoc children's choir (right) aboard an
American Presidents Line ship—there is always something to
look forward to for club members and their families*

It's not just the kids that have all the fun . . .

Opening of the Children's Library at the American Club, August 25, 1948

Cub Scouts, ca. 1955

THE AMERICAN WOMEN'S ASSOCIATION

Like many of Hong Kong's American institutions, the American Women's Association grew from modest beginnings to become one of the territory's most important presences. When its 53 charter members founded the AWA in 1956, none of them could foresee that it would grow to become the powerhouse of fundraising and community service that it is today, boasting 1,800 members from over 40 countries worldwide and granting over HK$ 1.3 million in aid per year.

American Club member Audrey Shoemaker, new to Hong Kong in the '50s, recalls that the roots of the AWA, like those of many great ideas, began around the dinner table in social gatherings: "Everybody felt a responsibility in those days, and we used to talk about the need to do something for the Hong Kong community." As these discussions developed, three main areas of concern were identified which became the basis for the nascent organization: the blind, immigrant children and US servicemen.

In the small-town atmosphere of 1956, well before reclamation and skyscrapers altered the face and pace of Hong Kong, the thousands of refugees from China were a conspicuous presence. The colony's infrastructure could not absorb the influx, leaving many children and young adults with little or no prospects. The AWA's Workshop stepped in to provide vocational training, and this was the seed for today's Education and Scholarship Committee which annually contributes HK$300,000 in student loans and scholarships.

At about the same time, the United States armed services were also becoming an increasing presence in Hong Kong. Arriving by the thousands for R&R stops, Hong Kong provided dazzling but intimidating respite for these often very young men. Recognizing their bewilderment, a fledgling core of the AWA set up an information center at Fenwick Pier. Servicemen were always invited to Thanksgiving and Christmas celebrations—a tradition maintained by the AWA membership and the Servicemen's Guides, who still gather at Fenwick Pier to greet and orient the Seventh Fleet.

The third branch of the nascent AWA was Project for the Blind. AWA members pooled their resources to buy brailling machines and paper and to train teachers to instruct the blind on how to use these machines. This group laid the foundation for the AWA's fundraising, which has

(continues on next page)

since donated millions of dollars to scores of Hong Kong charities.

Possibly the greatest landmark in the AWA's history was its decision in 1980 to purchase its own premises. While the Association had until then been able to support its running costs entirely from its membership dues, the growing price of rents in Hong Kong forced its executive board to consider purchasing an office space. Led by the then President and American Club member Gretchen Willoughby, the board wanted to insure that every cent of the money it raised would go directly to charities and education funds. After finding a suitable property, an apartment in a residential block on 48 Kennedy Road, Willoughby spent many late nights poring over spread sheets and sat in many fraught meetings with bank managers in her efforts to secure a low rate mortgage.

In April 1996 Willoughby and other AWA members had the gratification of triumphantly burning the mortgage. This symbolic act also marked the occasion of what was until that time the only American organization to fully own its premises, a remark-

able fact in that it is an entirely voluntary organization with the exception of a paid staff of seven part-time workers. It is from its own home that the AWA now coordinates its many charitable ventures, as well as a wealth of cultural activities that its 53 pioneer founders could never have imagined.

~Anastasia Edwards

their permanent military presence in the colony and sharply curtail the number of military flights from Vietnam landing at Kai Tak. Naval personnel not stationed in Vietnam were not affected by this agreement, so from 1966 on sailors with the Seventh Fleet far outnumbered all other servicemen.

One of these servicemen was Doug Holtz, the General Manager of the American Club since 1995, who at the time was a young Second Lieutenant with the 101st Airborne Division stationed in Vietnam. Little did he know that years later he would return to make Hong Kong his home.

"My first stops were to check in at the old President Hotel and find a tailor shop," he said. "Twelve shirts, three sports coats, a mohair topcoat and eight or ten pairs of slacks were the basic load for most visiting officers. If you were really smart, you

also picked up a solid gold Rolex watch for US$50. Then it was off to Wanchai and a visit to the wonderful world of Suzie Wong."

A protest outside the Bank of America, 1967

Riot police became part of Hong Kong's landscape as protesters threatened the colony's peace during the summer of 1967

1966 was also the beginning of China's Cultural Revolution, a chaotic mass movement that cost 20 million lives and destroyed much of China's irreplaceable heritage. That year the movement struck as close as Macau, where rioting Red Guards were fired upon by Portuguese troops. Some saw the hand of Communist agitators in April's Star Ferry riots, but the Cultural Revolution's chaos did not really reach Hong Kong until May 1967.

An industrial strike turned into a summer-long series of riots, demonstrations and bombings. This time, the guiding hand of the Red Guards (now ruling in Canton) was obvious. The demonstrators waved copies of Mao's "Little Red Book" in policemen's faces, and huge speakers were set up on the roof of the Bank of China building, the PRC's *de facto* Hong Kong headquarters. American Club members had to hear the blared propaganda not only on their way to and from work but while they were playing dice and drinking in the club, because the Bank of China was directly east of the Hongkong and Shanghai Bank Building.

The disturbances shook the foreign community; many of the demonstrations were directed against British and American targets, including Goverment House, the U.S. consulate and that symbol of American cultural might, the Hilton Hotel. To get to the American Club, members had to pass through lines of protesters; luckily, these were usually well-behaved (these were Hong Kong Red Guards, not Canton or Shanghai Red Guards). When Americans were harmed it was usually by accident: Stanley Freedman was hit by a camera accidentally dropped from the roof of the Hilton by a photographer. For most, the demonstrations were the daily drama which they could watch from the windows of the Hilton or the American Club. Wives and children rarely ventured downtown, because one never knew when a bomb would go off.

The riots wounded Hong Kong's economy; business faltered and some Americans thought they would have to leave. For the second time since the war, they discussed evacuation strategies. The employers of Hal Archer, Club Secretary for 1995-96, planned to evacuate their Chinese employees (who were in greater danger from the Communists) on the company boat, while the Europeans stayed behind to guard the business.

"We were quite serious," he said. "It was a very uncertain time. Bodies were floating down the Pearl River from Canton, and there was fighting at the border."

Life member Russell Blando became P.C. Blando of the Hong Kong Marine Police Auxiliary. He served 33 days in a row, carrying his uniform to work in a bag that also contained a shotgun (which he never had to use).

The canny followed the advice of their Chinese friends and bought property from those that had decided to leave the colony. This fire sale produced extraordinary bargains— houses on the Peak went for US$5,000—which, after real estate skyrocketed, provided the basis for some extremely comfortable retirements.

The Cultural Revolution was not an auspicious time to be plotting big changes at the American Club. Nevertheless, circumstances could not wait. The mid-60s had seen a boom of major American corporations, such as Dow Chemical, moving in to Hong Kong. All the new arrivals wanted to join the club, but there was no room. Membership already was about 1,000, and the waiting list was years long. At the same time, Hongkong Bank desperately wanted the club's floor back for offices; they could not raise the rent but could raise the air-conditioning fees, which increased exponentially. The club consensus was that Hong Kong would weather the riots. Now it was time to find a larger space.

The first idea was to move the club into the building of the Club Lusitano, the Portuguese version of the American Club. This was squashed when a member stated that he thought the club could get a better deal from the Kadoorie family, who were planning to build the St. George's Building in Central. The project was handed over to a select committee of Ed Burrell from Bank of America, Esso's Fred Westphal and John Shoemaker, who owned the Fenwick Tailor shop in the Hilton among other businesses. Both Shoemaker and Westphal had strong ties to the Kadoorie family—Westphal had come out to help them develop a power station— and knew that they needed a high-profile tenant to attract big American corporations to the prospective St. George's Building. The American Club fit the bill. The Kadoories offered what the committee thought were favorable terms, and they presented it to the membership, who accepted. Esso, Merrill Lynch and Bank of America soon followed.

The contract for the new club's architecture and design was given to International Design Limited, which was owned by Lane Crawford. Their bid had been low and their design called for an attractive American-colonial-style space that the membership appreciated. It was an engineering challenge to fit a club with a large kitchen and beverage operation into an office building. There was no provision for drainage, so the kitchen floor had to be raised. Where would all the stove exhaust go? They tapped into the bathroom ventilation and widened the pipe.

Finally, after three years of committee meetings and one year of construction, on April 8, 1969, the new American Club in the St. George's Building was formally inaugurated.

CHAPTER SIX

Flying the Flag

In 1969, the United States was everywhere in Hong Kong. American citizens were the largest group of foreign tourists. U.S. Naval ships filled the harbor; military planes crowded Kai Tak, disgorging thousands of GIs and sailors on their one-week R&Rs. The U.S. Consulate had become one of the largest in the world, with a constant stream of military and political VIPs walking through its doors. An aggressive American Chamber of Commerce, many of whose charter members had longstanding connections to the American Club, was founded to coordinate ties between the business community and the U.S. government. The American businessmen and military officers who thronged the bars and restaurants of the Hilton had money and power; locals could make millions cutting a deal with them.

In the midst of this ferment, the new American Club opened in the St. George's Building. "It reeked of Americana," according to Daniel Zigal. The look was Mt. Vernon-esque—early American plush with wood panelling and burgundy wallpaper—and larger and more formal than the club in the Hongkong Bank Building. The rattan furniture was gone, replaced by wooden colonial-style chairs and tables. The only objects remaining from the old club, such as the Presidents' photos, were those literally carried from the old building to the St. George's by the decoration committee (Irene Saunders, Nikki Scully, Mary Ketterer, Mary Patterson and Kay Proper).

The Select Committee as lampooned by architect David Crowe: John Shoemaker as a monkey, Fred Westphal as a jackass, and Ed Burrell as a goose. These panels formed part of a mural which hung in the Colony Room at St. George's Building

(top left) Dedication of the Club at St. George's Building on April 9, 1969; (above center) the lounge at St. George's Building; (right) staircase leading from the 12th to 14th floor

(top right) Patrons of the American Club Cotillion, March 21, 1970; (above) another view of the lounge at St. George's Building

For some, the new club was too big and too elegant; they missed the old cozy, homey feel. For others, generally the more recent arrivals, the new club was a perfect fit —a reflection of their community's new prominence in Hong Kong. The elevator opened onto the 12th floor lobby which was dominated by a grand staircase sweeping up to the floor above. To the right, a door led to the Stag Bar, notable for its portrait of a bounteous reclining nude over the bar, and the Grill Room. The latter was a male-only sanctum during lunch-time—they rolled dice and ate around big round communal tables—but women were allowed at night and on weekends, when it became a popular family luncheon spot.

The Stag Bar regulars included many of the hard-living garment and jewelry executive crowd—one habitué arrived every day at 3:45 P.M. and always began with a double Tan-queray martini and two Bufferin. If their careers fell on hard times, the bar became their office, and Samson, the bar-tender, fielded their calls until they got back on their feet.

"I started my own business in the St. George's club," said Joe Champagne, American Club President in 1992. "Samson was my secretary. I worked out of my home and the Stag Bar and ended up with seven offices in Asia and 50 employees."

To the left from the elevator stood the Mayflower Lounge, which women could patronize. Evenings, entertainment was provided first by Fred Carpio on the guitar (and sometimes his trio) and later by the piano-playing of Larry Allen, who was a fixture for years. Through the lounge lay the Colony Room, the club's main dining room. During the 70s, the club was determined to improve the quality of the food (and evening attendance) with special events such as Mexican Night and German Octoberfest. This drive was led by William Mortson, the head of the food and beverage committee, with the help of ex-British Army sergeant Roscoe Triplett, who in 1969 succeeded Mario Prata as manager.

The centerpiece of the Colony Room was a mural painted on wood panels by David Crowe, a British architect commissioned by the American Club. The theme was colonial America, and while he worked, the artist received regular visits from the select committee of John Shoemaker, Fred Westphal and Ed Burrell. In fact, Crowe became so annoyed by these visits that in the last two panels he added satirical portraits of the select committee: The monkey with the tape measure was John Shoemaker; the goose, Fred Westphal and the jackass, Ed Burrell. The mural was expertly restored by Gerri Holtz, wife of current General Manager Doug Holtz, and now hangs in the Boston Clipper; the last two panels remain in storage. From both the Colony Room and the Stag Grill, members could step out onto a terrace overlooking Ice House Street and Chater Road.

St. George's Building

Up the grand staircase you found the Chuckwagon coffee shop which featured a jukebox and was decorated with antique rifles, a buffalo head and a photo of John Wayne. Serving hamburgers, milkshakes and the like, the Chuckwagon was a favorite of the younger set, the only place where they did not have to wear formal jackets or dresses. NFL football films flown in by Pan Am were shown here every week during the season, as well as occasional films of U.S. golf and boxing matches. Off the Chuckwagon lay four function rooms—Ante Room I and II, the Williamsburg Room and the Plantation Room.

The other end of the floor was largely occupied by the library—far larger than the present one at Exchange Square—and the reading room. Men used the latter for their postprandial naps, so women and children were barred during these hours (the men liked to take their shoes off). This caused a simmering resentment among the women members, eventually leading to the club's first brush with the feminist movement. The teenagers of this era were a rambunctious set, and their most frequent crime was sneaking beers in the library.

The club newsletter (the full magazine had not yet started) often had admonitions to parents to keep their children under control. Next door to the library stood the sauna and massage rooms and the diminutive gym.

Catalog introducing St. George's Building together with an assortment of Five Aces Club paraphernalia, including a set of silver cups belonging to Ronnie Ross and Jack Keenan's dice cup

The new American Club immediately became the community's focal point, its favorite downtown meeting place.

"If there were riots on the streets," Daniel Zigal said, "your parents told you to go to the club. If you went to the dentist, your mom would meet you at five at the American Club."

This era was probably the last one in which Hong Kong's American community could be called a village. In 1970, there were less than 5,000 Americans in the colony, and while you could not know everybody anymore, it still felt that way.

"Almost every American corporation had its office in Central," said Glendon Rowell, American Club President from 1985 to 1987. "You would go to out to a restaurant or bar, and you would know everybody there. On weekends, you would go out to Lamma Island on a junk, and you would see familiar faces on all the other boats."

As in most villages, it was still important to protect your reputation in the community.

"What other people said about you made a difference," said Cathy Braga. "Rebels were always gossiped about. If you set up a business, others would sit back and wait and watch for a year and only then begin to do business with you. Once you were established, they would be faithful to the end."

The first few years in the St. George's Building were shaky ones for the club, because they had stretched their finances to the limit in making the move. These were also nervous years for the local economy; it had not completely recovered from the 1967 riots, and there were serious questions about the colony's future viability.

After the Cultural Revolution spent its force, Chairman Mao realized that the years of chaos had severely wounded China. The Soviet Union (now its most powerful enemy) had reinforced its troops along the border, and during the long isolation, China's technology had fallen behind the West. Mao wanted to rejoin the world community and finally gain membership of the United Nations. He needed the help of the United States, which had long supported Taiwan over the PRC at international forums.

During 1970, the Chinese sent the United States a series of carefully coded messages indicating that they wanted to open talks on normalizing relations. These led to the groundbreaking visit by the U.S. table tennis team in April 1971 followed by Henry Kissinger's secret trip in July. A few months later, the United Nations voted to oust Taiwan from their seat and give it to the PRC. Finally, on February 21, 1972, President Nixon landed at Beijing where he was greeted by Zhou Enlai and whisked off to meet Chairman Mao.

Nixon's China visit was of huge symbolic importance: It marked the end of the PRC's 20-year isolation and the faint beginnings of a more pragmatic Chinese leadership. Immediately, however, there would be little change. Radical forces led by the Gang of Four were still ascendant, and the next years would bring massive campaigns against capitalism, individualism and other Western values. Nevertheless, Mao and Nixon did sign a communiqué calling for exchanges in science, technology, culture, sports and journalism. Through this little window, Western businessmen once again heard the siren song of the China market, now grown to one billion potential consumers strong.

The US table tennis team visits China in 1971 and opens ping pong diplomacy. Zhou Enlai greets a team member (middle), and team members pose in front of a poster evoking the Cultural Revolution (bottom)

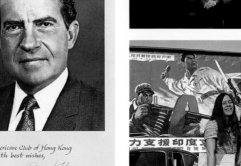

To The American Club of Hong Kong
With best wishes,

Taco Proper, Sr. with former President Gerald Ford, ca. 1973

The British government heard that tune as well. Nixon's visit was followed by Anglo-Chinese meetings at which Hong Kong was the main sticking point. The British had already decided that Hong Kong was indefensible and (in the Immigration Act of 1971) that the vast majority of its citizens had no right to live in the United Kingdom. The New Territories lease would be up in 1997, and when given the choice between trade with the world's most populous country or protecting their tiny colony and its four million inhabitants, the British chose the former. The two sides signed a communiqué establishing embassies in their capitals and agreeing to respect each other's "sovereignty and territorial integrity." From now on, Hong Kong would not be a "colony" but a "territory," losing the stigma—or honor—of possession by a foreign state.

The beginnings of the British retreat from Hong Kong were lost in the uproar of the opening to China. No place on earth was better suited than Hong Kong to become a staging area for forays into the China market. The territory had location, contacts, language skills, business expertise and a vast resource of cultural knowledge.

Since 1957, Westerners (but not Americans) had been travelling up to Canton for its annual trade fair and brief contacts with the PRC's state business community. They all stayed at one of two bad hotels and could tell whether the fair would be good or bad by the quality of beer served in the bars—Tsingtao (good) or a watery Cantonese product

(bad). In 1972, the Canton veterans were joined by a handful of Americans and other aggressive businessmen eager to cash in on the new frontier. The hotels and organizational skills of the Chinese bureaucrats were taxed to the limits. Both sides quickly discovered that they had much to learn about each other.

Although the dream of vast wealth from tapping the China market would not materialize overnight, American corporations were determined not to lose the opportunity. While China became organized (and overthrew the lingering legacy of the Cultural Revolution), U.S. businesses poured millions of dollars into Hong Kong. The fastest growth took place in the financial services sector, led by Citibank, which was to become the territory's fourth largest bank. In 1983, Citibank moved into their new office tower in Causeway Bay, beginning the rush of building outside of Central. No longer was Americans' work, shopping and socializing concentrated within a few blocks of downtown Hong Kong. U.S. corporations brought in thousands of new employees, and the American community mushroomed—and fragmented, as the village became a city.

This influx of new faces in the early 1970s included many women coming out as executives in their own right and not merely following their husbands. Some of these women joined the American Club, and they began to challenge the club's conservative, male-dominated traditions. During this period the centers of the controversy were the male-only territories of the Grill Room, the sauna and the library, where the men liked to take off their shoes and settle in for siestas. A woman bank executive demanded that they be opened to all and threatened to ask her corporate home office to stop paying its employees' club dues.

Comfortable with colonial traditions of segregation and isolated from the feminist movement then sweeping across the U.S., many men were outraged. Most of the other American women did not want to go to the Grill Room; on the library, however, they agreed. The club leadership stonewalled, giving in only on opening the sauna to women for a few hours during the day. The controversy finally ended when the woman executive returned to the States. When the American Club moved into new quarters, however, they would finally be forced—still grudgingly—to recognize women as equals.

Kay Proper, Bob Hawley and Bill Mortson

In early 1975, Bill Mortson, who in 1973 had been club president, replaced Roscoe Triplett as the American Club's manager. A great gourmet, Mortson worked indefatigably to improve the club cuisine, helping to open Hong Kong's first salad bar in the Grill Room and finally attracting an evening crowd for dinner. Mortson moved on to run the American Chamber of Commerce in 1977. He was succeeded by Bob Sanders, currently General Manager of the Foreign Correspondents' Club, who had been a member since 1971 and was lured back from a brief stay in South Africa.

The Bund, 1979. A kung fu master demonstrates his art in front of a poster hailing the "Four Modernizations"

The 1976 Bicentennial celebrations, staged jointly by the American Chamber of Commerce and the American Club, were probably the apex of American influence during the 1970s. The gala fortnight featured the then-current Miss America, Terry Meeuwsen of Wisconsin (now a host on the "700 Club"), and the Rangerettes, a crack all-girl drill team from Texas. These special guests participated in parties and receptions all over town culminating in the American Club's mammoth picnic out at Chi Ma Wan.

The picnic was well under way, with the guests enjoying their usual hamburgers, hot dogs, sodas and beer, when the Redcoats arrived. Dressed in Revolutionary War uniforms and firing muskets, the British invaded by land and by sea on the Hilton's replica brigantine. Unfortunately, there was no Paul Revere to warn the Americans; they were taken by surprise and captured. The lure of free food and drink dis-

tracted the aggressors, however, and led them to ransom their prisoners for a share of the celebration. Of all the American Club July 4th parties, this was by far the most memorable.

Two months later, Chairman Mao died after a long illness. His eulogy was given by Hua Guofeng, a recently elevated party boss from Hunan, with the radical leaders Jiang Qing, Wang Hongwen, Zhang Chunqiao and Yao Wenyuan at his side. Less than a month later these radicals were behind bars, accused of forming the "Gang of Four" that allegedly committed a long list of crimes, including forging Mao's statements. Hua Guofeng emerged as the new leader, while from Canton Deng Xiaoping engineered yet another return from political oblivion.

Although Hua styled himself a doctrinaire Maoist, the cornerstone of his regime was the "Four Modernizations", an effort to bring China up-to-date in agriculture, industry, science and technology, and defense. In 1978, an advance guard of almost 500 students were sent to study in 28 countries, including the United States, to convey this information back to China. At the same time, a party congress recognized that these modernizations, especially in agriculture, could not succeed without loosening state control of farming and markets. The door to free enterprise inched open.

Through 1978, China and the United States held talks normalizing ties, culminating in a mid-December announcement that the two countries would open full diplomatic relations on New Year's Day, 1979, and that the United States would close its embassy in Taiwan. Four weeks later Deng Xiaoping flew to Washington to embark on a triumphant media tour of the United States. He was photographed wearing a huge cowboy hat in Texas. Corporate executives could do business with him; they flocked to build contacts with China. Two companies already had: Boeing and Coca-Cola had signed agreements to sell planes and soda in the world's biggest market. Old China hands such as John Shoemaker were also helping companies like Pan Am tap into the China trade.

Shortly after Deng returned, the PRC announced the formation of four special economic zones, Shenzhen, Zhuhai, Shantou and Xiamen—the last two the old treaty ports of Swatow and Amoy—to jump-start China's economy. The door to the China market now yawned wide open, and one

Dick Ross greeting former First Lady, Rosalyn Carter, 1988

wanted to join the American Club as associate members, but overcrowding meant that the waiting list was years long.

Americans could join immediately, but by 1978 there were 1,300 members (roughly 1,000 voting and 300 associate) crowded into the club. Complaints rose about getting seats and service in the Grill Room. Many of the recent arrivals were young executives with families; they appreciated the club as a business luncheon spot but also wanted somewhere their wives and children could swim and socialize. The older members did not share this need, because they had already joined one of the sport and recreation clubs. This was expensive for those with growing families, and in any case many of the recreation clubs had closed their books to newcomers—except those with the right connections, of course —to preserve their exclusivity. The younger set began to speak out on the need for the American Club to expand its facilities.

of the greatest benefactors was Hong Kong. Those who had toiled in Hong Kong sweatshops now became managers of Shenzhen sweatshops. As the territory became the main conduit of investment in Chinese industry, the financial services sector boomed, and numerous U.S. financial institutions, including Salomon Brothers and Manufacturers Hanover, moved in to take a piece of the pie.

Once again, the American Club faced the problem of not enough room and too many people waiting to become members. The waiting list now included many non-Americans working for U.S. corporations. The Carter Administration had changed the U.S. tax code so that foreign benefits were treated as salary and taxed; it was significantly more expensive to hire Americans than local Hong Kong citizens or third-country nationals. The executive ranks of companies such as IBM and Citibank were suddenly filled with Australians, British, Chinese, Germans, Canadians and Dutch. They all

The American Club's sporty side: (top) Col. Jim Culbertson and Karl Kirchner congratulate Rick Kroos on winning the 1985 President's Cup golf tournament; (above) photos hang in the American Club Box at the racetrack; (left) badges and pendants from the track

One reason for the club's popularity was the sudden improvement in the quality of the food. In 1980, Bob Sanders hired Philippe Seiler, a young but highly-trained Swiss chef, away from the Peninsula Group. The meat-and-potatoes crowd saw their old-standby dishes transformed by Seiler's nouvelle cuisine presentation. The American Club favorites —steak, iceberg lettuce salad and ice cream—remained on the menu, but the other offerings ranged through the world's cuisines. Lunch at the American Club now competed with the Hong Kong Club or the Royal Hong Kong Jockey Club, and, in the minds of many, far outdid its competition.

The push for change in the club was also helped by the economic climate. The late 70s were the go-go years, when Hong Kong acquired its reputation as the capitalist paradise, and speculation, particularly in real estate, was driving prices through the roof. Although the influx of new members was helping its bank balance (entrance fees were HK$2,000 in 1978), the club was still fighting a losing battle with rising labor costs and rent. Aggressive young executives (the word "yuppies" had not yet been coined) argued that it was time to buy, time for the club to own an asset other than its name and prove to the community that it was here to stay. After years of marginal profitability or losses, they said, it was time for the club to make some real money.

"We were sitting on a very good asset," said Patrick (Rick) Kroos, American Club President in 1982. "We were the American Club, with a big presence in the American community. We had to leverage that."

As an engineer, Kroos had worked on the construction of new facilities for the Hong Kong Club and the China Fleet Club. He had seen how these clubs had been able to use their name and reputation to convince a major developer (Hongkong Land) to cover many of the expenses of construction in return for using the club's prestige to draw other tenants to the building. The American Club had leveraged its name to move into the St. George's Building, and Kroos saw no reason why they could not do it again.

Inertia—the stubborness of the old guard and the apathy of the majority—held off any dramatic change until early 1982, when they were forced to take advantage of a rare opportunity. At the negotiations for the lease renewal, the Kadoories notified the club that in May 1983 the rent would rise from HK$7.50 a square foot to HK$21. 50 a square foot. Everybody, even the old timers, realized that it was time to talk about the club's future. At the same time, the balloon that was Hong Kong real estate had burst, sending prices

tumbling. Suddenly, it was the perfect time to buy. On February 25, 1982, club president Donald Griswold convened a general meeting to discuss the options.

About 100 members attended the meeting. The range of ideas was wide. Some were less than likely to succeed: The Kowloon gang wanted to move the club across the harbor, where rents were low and life was more free-wheeling (that idea was quickly shot down—the majority wanted the club to remain in Central). As Griswold saw it, there were three main options: Do nothing and increase dues to meet rising rent and other costs. Shrink the club by attrition, reducing it to a small, purely American luncheon club—essentially reverting to its prewar character. The most ambitious proposal was to buy a new facility in Central with enough space to handle 2,000 members and a wider range of facilities. Estimated to cost HK$75 million, the latter plan would be financed by selling debentures to corporations and individuals. Griswold suggested that the club explore the last option, and, in a vote, the attendees agreed. A select committee would have one year to come up with a deal to make the idea work.

The Premises Sub-Committee—and the core of the group that would see the project through to completion—were future Presidents Patrick Kroos, Terrence Ahearn and Thomas Greer. They were respectively an engineer (J. Roger Preston and Partners), a lawyer (Exxon) and a banker (Citibank), and together they possessed the skills and contacts to make this extremely complicated and daring idea a reality. They also had time on their hands to work on the project— business was slow. When they finally could rest on their laurels three years later, they realized that they had hit the market at exactly the right time with exactly the right proposal. Slightly later, Robert Lusher and Donald Greco joined the sub-committee and played important roles in seeing the project to fruition.

At the same time as this meeting, Bob Sanders resigned (despite much pleading) to pursue a career as a restaurateur. He was briefly replaced by James Kelley, Jr., who in December was succeeded by John Firrell, ex-manager of the mess at the H.M.S. Tamar. Firrell managed the club through the most turbulent years of its expansion and had the unenviable task of riding a constantly changing situation.

On April 1, 1982, Rick Kroos succeeded Don Griswold as club president. He hired a polling firm to survey all the American Club members to gauge their support of the purchase idea—82% agreed. The survey also identified the demographics of the club and what its members wanted from

Wanchai and Central, 1980

a new facility. Kroos, Ahearn and Greer spread out through the corporate community to introduce them to the concept of a new, bigger American club. U.S. corporations would be the largest purchasers of debentures and it was crucial to know what they needed for their Hong Kong employees.

Rick Kroos and Terry Ahearn also contacted Hong Kong's major downtown developers to find out what property they had available and what kind of deal they were willing to make. One of the major sticking points was that the American Club wanted to buy rather than rent, which would force the developers to give up total control—something they previously had been reluctant to do. In the depressed real estate market, however, any customer was better than no customer.

At the end of September, Kroos called an extraordinary general meeting to report on the progress, to raise the entrance fee from HK$6,000 to HK$10,000, and to ask the membership's opinion of a refinement of the plan. The survey of the American corporations had shown broad support of a new facility with one addition. While they recognized

the importance of a larger downtown club, what they and their employees really needed was a recreation club, preferably on the south side of the island where most of the managers resided. Once again, the club membership was polled. They agreed to expand the search for a new facility to include a country club as well. Jones Lang Wootton, the estate agents who had been advising the club on a contingency basis, were appointed to aid in the search and valuation of potential sites.

Shortly before this meeting, Hong Kong had been rocked by an event that would begin the end of almost 150 years of British rule. Riding a wave of success—the victory in the Falklands—Margaret Thatcher visited Beijing to discuss Hong Kong's future after the termination of the New Territories lease on June 30, 1997. Unfortunately, she seems to have been less than well-prepared and did not understand Chinese resentment of years of unequal treaties and gunboat diplomacy. For Deng Xiaoping, an extension of the lease was out of the question; he demanded nothing less than the complete return of Hong Kong and the New Territories in 1997. The details would be worked out over the following two years.

Thatcher's visit shook Hong Kong and flattened the still-moribund local economy. The planners of the new American Club, however, viewed it not as a setback but as an opportunity.

"We saw the hand-over as a positive," said Rick Kroos. "If Hong Kong becomes part of China, U.S. corporations could show their long-term commitment to China by building this new American Club."

None of them doubted Hong Kong's viability, and the short-term real estate crisis was an advantage for those looking to buy. Developers were even more desperate to move their property; they upgraded their buildings to attract tenants with deeper pockets and became open to any deals, even allowing customers to buy rather than lease. The search for sites now went into high gear.

The addition of a recreation club outside Central made the task significantly more difficult and limited the suitable developers to the handful that controlled both a downtown building and a country site. The Sub-Committee visited properties as far afield as the New Territories and briefly considered a golf club until they realized the extravagant cost. Downtown, the shortlist included Hongkong Land's Exchange Square (then in the planning stages), the Hong Kong Club's temporary quarters in Worldwide House, Harbour Centre, Wheelock House and even the St. George's Building.

Tai Tam in the late 1980s

Exchange Square was always at the top of the shortlist. Planned for one of the last remaining sites—before more recent landfills—on the Central waterfront, the twin 50-story towers of Exchange Square 1 and 2 would have a commanding view of the harbor and dominate the downtown skyline. Remo Riva of P & T Architects and Engineers HK had designed Exchange Square to be Hong Kong's first Class A office development. The 22,000 square feet of the top two floors of Exchange Square 2 would put the American Club

on the map. There was only one difficulty: Hongkong Land did not have an appropriate site for the country club. Even then, the available sites in Hong Kong—and particularly on the south side of the island—were few and far between.

Then, one day Bob Lusher arrived for a committee meeting and off-handedly announced that he had found a site on the south side of Hong Kong. Nobody believed him. Yes, he insisted, it was in Tai Tam and consisted of three abandoned villas overlooking the bay. The problem was, Hongkong Land did not own the site; its ownership was divided between Stanley Ho and Sun Hung Kai. The committee told Hongkong Land that they would only sign on for Exchange Square if they could get the Tai Tam site as well.

Hongkong Land succeeded. They gave Stanley Ho a deal in the Mid-Levels, and Sun Hung Kai received the site immediately north to build the present Tai Tam Villa apartment building. Normally, buildings on the water side of Tai Tam Road were limited to three stories, but the American Club agreed to restrict their height and not put in residences. In return, the government allowed Sun Hung Kai to build his tower. The government had also planned to build a road across the north end of the current club grounds; instead, they granted the club a year-by-year lease of the property, now the site of tennis courts.

The town and country club package was now complete. On February 28, 1983, Rick Kroos called an extraordinary general meeting to present and vote on the proposal. The purchase of the sites would cost HK$100 million; construction and outfitting were estimated to cost up to another HK$100 million. The committee proposed to borrow up to HK$200 million through selling debentures in denominations originally priced at HK$300,000 for full debentures and a limited number of HK$75,000 town-only debentures—not all corporations wanted the recreation facilities. February 1, 1984 was established as a "no-go" date; if the club could not raise enough money by then, Hongkong Land would refund their initial deposits minus interest.

Rick Kroos gave the initial presentation, followed by Tom Greer and Terry Ahearn with details on the finances and the debentures plan. The discussion was lively, occasionally heated, but a vote was held and the measure to go ahead was passed. The expansion of the American Club would become a reality.

The plan went ahead on two fronts. Ads were placed in the *Asian Wall Street Journal* and the *International Herald Tribune* soliciting architectural proposals for the town and country clubs. To kick off the debenture sales, Rick Kroos hosted a champagne reception at the home of M. L. Lo for the corporate manager set. A number of Fortune 500 companies had already committed themselves to specific numbers of debentures, and the committee was optimistic that they would reach their goal before the no-go date.

Thirty-five packages arrived from architects around the world, each containing pictures of their previous work and descriptions of their philosophy and approach to comparable projects. As the committee leafed through the proposals, they realized there was a big difference in quality between the town and country proposals. Over some strenuous ob-

Architect's rendering of the Grill Room, Tai Tam

jections, the committee decided to hire two architects. In June, a shortlist of seven was asked to come to Hong Kong at their own expense to meet the committee.

After a grueling (for the architects) series of interviews, the building committee announced its decision: For the town club, they chose Warren Platner, who had designed Windows on the World at the top of New York's World Trade Center, and for the country club they selected William Turnbull, a San Francisco architect known for his ability to work buildings and landscapes together. Platner was given the brief to extend his Windows on the World concept—a premium and ultramodern restaurant atop New York's tallest building—to an elegant two-story space that would encompass not just a restaurant but full club facilities. Turnbull's task was more complicated.

"My concept was a big house in the sense of Newport, Rhode Island in the 1890s," he said, "a big house at the seaside with the capacity to enfold not just family but extended family and the family friends. We were looking for a big, convivial image, something comfortable and non-formal. It would be a place where American businessmen far from

The view from the Tai Tam site before building

Architect's rendering of the Tai Tam Club

home with their wives and kids could feel at home. The difficulty was to fit that concept into a unique site while trying to save as much landscape as we could. It was a wonderfully challenging problem."

Platner's first act was to convince the club that they should not accept the eight-foot ceilings planned for their Exchange Square quarters. This was easy, because club members had long complained of the low ceilings in the St. George's Building. Hongkong Land was a much harder sell. They would have to talk to the building department, perform new wind shear studies and consult the architect and the engineers. Afterward they said yes, but it would cost the club another HK$4.5 million. This was actually a bargain because Bob Lusher convinced the facade contractors to significantly reduce their rates. Hongkong Land also received permission to add another floor to Exchange Square 1, because both towers had to be the same height.

A few weeks after his hiring, negotiations between the American Club and Warren Platner fell apart. Essentially, he asked more than the club was willing to pay. Tom Greer went to Connecticut to tell Platner the contract was terminated, and the club immediately turned to their second choice for the town facility, Gary Whitney of 3D/International in Houston. In August, Whitney and Turnbull both

View of the Tai Tam site before building

flew to Hong Kong to hold intense discussions with various club committees about their specific needs for the town and country facilities. A month later, the architects returned with detailed plans.

Whitney had recently completed the Tower Club in Dallas, another opulent private club atop an office tower overlooking the city's downtown. His idea for the American Club was to reproduce that elegance with a Hong Kong twist.

The Empress of China dining room

The President's Room

"I came up with a design scenario that reflected both cultures: wholly American and heavily influenced by Asia. For example, the Empress of China restaurant—of course named after the first American ship in China—has a ceiling shaped like a Chinese fan. Under our art program, the objects and paintings we displayed reflected the trade between the continents. I wanted a space that reflected the best of both worlds."

Some of the members had wanted more of the colonial Williamsburg look, as in the St. George's club, but Whitney felt that colonial decor did not blend with the ultramodern curtain wall and glass construction of Exchange Square. In the new club, only the President's Room would retain the old style.

While the projects went ahead, the club did not stand still on other fronts. During Terry Ahearn's presidency, the American Club finally abolished the Lady Member status, which allowed them to participate essentially as associate members without voting status, even if they had American citizenship.

"We were getting a lot of pressure from corporations," said Ahearn. "A lot of American women were getting involved in business in Hong Kong and wanted to entertain clients at the club. As part of the whole deal to start the new club and get all the corporations on board, I knew it was necessary. We had a big fight in the committee, but we finally got it passed that women could become full members."

At the same time, women also won the right to lunch in the Grill Room. At a July 1983 open meeting to discuss the issue, some old-timers exploded at the disappearance of exclusively male space. To protect their terrain, it became the unwritten rule that the two round communal tables (now in McKay's Bar) were men-only at lunchtime, and they were partitioned off from the rest of the room.

Through October and November, Turnbull and Whitney fine-tuned their plans with the aid of their local architectural associates—Moira Moser for the country club and Jay Bouton of Design Phase Limited for the town club. Negotiations and discussions with Hongkong Land and government land and building departments took place constantly (the extra height for the town club took months to resolve). The Exchange Square towers were already well under way—the frame approached the American Club level—and the club was anxious to break ground for Tai Tam.

In early December, however, Terry Ahearn and the building committee realized that they were facing problems on the financial front. The debentures—then priced at HK$350,000 —were not selling as well as expected, and the numerous changes, particularly at Exchange Square, had raised the total construction cost. If they continued at the current rate, they would not have enough to cover their obligations to Hongkong Land by the February 1, 1984 no-go date. Ahearn wrote to David Davies (not to be confused with David Davies of First Pacific Davies), the new managing director of Hongkong Land:

"The 1997 question, the problems of other clubs of Hong Kong at the moment and the lowering of the property market all seem to have contributed to a reluctance by the local community to give us the kind of support we expected. Therefore, it is highly likely that our fund raising will fall short of the mark by the "no-go" date, although I am confident that if we can work out a solution to some of our financial problems, we can continue to attract additional debentures over the next year or so before the Club opens."

The committee had good relations with David Davies' predecessor, Trevor Bedford, as well as with Hongkong Land executives Nigel Rich and Ian McFadzean among others. In mid-December, the building committee went to see David Davies.

"He had his feet up on his desk and he was smoking a big cigar," said Rick Kroos. "We explained the situation to him, and he said, 'You guys are like a kid in front of a candy store on Fifth Avenue with only a nickel in your pocket, and you want the candy costing a dime.'"

Davies said no: no money, no deal. The committee left, angry and disappointed. In the following weeks, Nigel Rich and Ian Mc-

The Grill Room, Tai Tam

Tai Tam and environs today

Topping out at Exchange Square, July 4, 1984

Fadzean worked to change Davies' mind. Hong Kong real estate was still depressed, and their company still needed this deal. Finally, Davies relented and in January 1984 agreed to give the American Club an extension in the form of a bridge loan. The building committee negotiated a sweetheart deal—a HK$60 million loan payable in seven years with the first three years interest-free, guaranteeing the construction of the two facilities.

"What a deal we got!" said Rick Kroos.

The cash crunch nevertheless had an effect, particularly on Tai Tam. The two-level parking lot under the tennis courts became only one (the reason parking is so difficult there), and plans were scrapped for a structure housing function rooms at the site of the north tennis court. To make up for the lost space, the floor of the big dining room was raised and the function rooms were put in below.

On January 22, 1985, ground was finally broken at the Tai Tam site. The ceremony began with the lighting of joss sticks and a lion dance to ensure good luck. Then the spadework began, with Tom Greer, Don Greco, Lynn McPheeters, Bob Giss, Bill Turnbull and Moira Moser each digging into the dirt. Within months, the site was cleared and the excavation of the foundation was completed.

Over at Exchange Square, the frame was nearly completed, and the club and its architects were working out the fine

points of the design. Dr. Andrew Wong, American Club President in 1990, was then on the General Committee and pointed out that it was absurd for the Hong Kong American Club, with its significant Chinese and Chinese-American membership, not to have a Chinese restaurant. The proposal was heatedly debated, but Dr. Wong's logic won the day. The designers created the Trade Winds restaurant featuring gourmet Cantonese cuisine, which is still one of the club's most popular dining spots.

On July 4th, Hongkong Land held a topping out ceremony at Exchange Square in which they and the American Club interred time capsules in the building's roof. The brave who attended the ceremony included Richard Williams, the acting American Consul-General, as well as Lynn McPheeters, Terry Ahearn, Rick Kroos, Bob Lusher and John Firrell. In a small box, they placed a 1931 American Club debenture for HK$50.00, a "tombstone" for the new financing deal, a debenture invitation, a plan of the Exchange Square Club, a membership list and a copy of a *South China Morning Post* article on the new club.

While construction proceeded at both sites, British and Chinese diplomats in Beijing engaged in lengthy top-secret negotiations to hammer out the future of Hong Kong. Finally, in September 1984 the Joint Declaration was signed and the details of the "one country, two systems" agreement were revealed. The Hong Kong Chinese felt set adrift, and the

Architect Moira Moser at the Tai Tam ground breaking ceremony, January 22, 1985

Taco Proper, Sr. and Sir Run Run Shaw, ca. 1985

United States, in the person of Consul-General Burton Levin, hastened to reassure them that the U.S. would retain a presence in Hong Kong and treat it as a separate trading partner.

In the context of this new situation, the construction of the luxurious American Club facilities at Exchange Square and Tai Tam became a symbol of the American business community's confidence in Hong Kong. The American consulate pointed to the huge American Club investment as the best proof that the United States was in Hong Kong to stay. The club was not slow to use this as a lever to sell more debentures: If companies wanted to show they were committed to Hong Kong long-term, the club told them, the best way to broadcast this was to buy more debentures.

Finally, in July 1985 the American Club was ready to take possession of their new face. Operations in the St. George's Building club began to wind down at the end of June, and the 4th of July was the final closing date. That night, the old club closed with the bang of an auctioneer's gavel; they sold most of the furnishings, including the lobby chandelier, leather booths from the Stag Bar, the bar itself, the Chuckwagon's photo of John Wayne, an exercise cycle and the manager's electric fireplace. These pieces decorated members' Hong Kong apartments, and many ended up back in the States (a rolling bar graces Don Greco's home in Brooklyn). What happened to the nude painting from the Stag Bar remains a mystery. Mark Blacker bought the bar stools, and Tom Greer bid on all the club doorknobs and do-

nated them to the club to be given (suitably plaqued) for meritorious service—the first one went to John Firrell.

The new club opened the following day with a huge invitation-only party celebrating not just the new premises but the American Club's 60th anniversary. The next day, a local newspaper reported:

"The opening of the American Club was one of the most extravagant bashes in recent history. Some 1,400 people turned up on the 48th and 49th floors of Exchange Square and thoroughly pigged it right through the evening. Enough salmon to empty a Scottish river was washed down by a lake of champagne."

The revellers were treated to guided tours of the lavish new club. A lion dance troupe performed for good luck, with club president Lynn McPheeters dotting the eyes, and a letter of congratulations was read from President Ronald Reagan. McPheeters then proposed the toast and cut the huge birthday cake. While eating and sipping (over 400 bottles of champagne were consumed), the members wandered through their new facilities, admiring the elegant decor blending American and Chinese motifs and marveling at the stupendous view of Hong Kong harbor.

You reached the new American Club from special elevators that took you up from the 47th floor, then leased by IBM. Facing the 48th floor elevator lobby was reception, with a much-reduced library shoe-horned into the space behind. To the left lay the main Empress of China dining room, occupying the space of today's Grill Room and lounge. To the right was a waiting room—now the Portside Bar—and, next

President Reagan, among others, acknowledged the celebration of the Club's 60th anniversary

Dr. Dominic Kam, Don Greco, and Col. Jim Culbertson

door, McKay's Bar squeezed into the site of the current President's Room. McKay's was named after an early clipper ship captain and, by overwhelming vote, would continue the men-only tradition of the old Stag Bar. At the end of the corridor lay the Grill Room, now the Empress of China dining room (they were switched in 1995).

The staircase up to the 49th floor commenced next to a Gary Whitney-designed fountain decorated with a huge ball symbolizing the Earth with water burbling out the North Pole. Up on 49, the main attraction was the Forty-Niners coffee shop, named for the date of the California gold rush (and in 1995 one of the few rooms to retain its original function). Opposite, the space now occupied by McKay's Bar was the gym and locker rooms, which members discovered were far smaller than they looked in the plans. Through the elevator lobby lay the administrative offices and the Trade Winds Cantonese restaurant, which also doubled as the function room or rooms.

The new American Club was almost twice the size (over 24,000 square feet) of the old club and far more luxurious. It would take time for the members to get

used to the facility and to discover if it fitted their needs. Why, for instance, did the bar in McKay's only have space for four stools? In the meantime, management begged for patience until they decided on what renovations to make. Over the next few years, the members would change the club and they themselves would be changed by the opulent new surroundings.

Club President F. Lynn McPheeters opens Exchange Square, 1985

The Tai Tam club, meanwhile, was delayed. The responsibility for overseeing its construction fell to Glendon Rowell, who in September began a Rooseveltian multiple term as president after Lynn McPheeters was transferred back to the States. Tai Tam's problems began below ground-level. After part of the foundation had been poured, the government changed the environmental laws to say that facilities such as this had to include their own sewage treatment plant. Back to square one. The entire foundation had to be torn out so that two sewage holding tanks the size of squash courts could be installed. That took a couple of months.

A view of Exchange Square and Central in the 1980s, long before reclamation altered the landscape

Then the steel roof arrived, custom-cut in Britain and shipped over in prefabricated parts. When they began to put it on, they discovered that the contractor had not built the side walls according to plan. The roof did not fit. An expert from Britain was flown over, and after weeks of cutting the roof and altering the walls, it was finally installed. Other problems followed—the locker room floor, the sprinkler system, the loading dock ramp. They were not as serious but they all delayed the opening.

Through these delays, the club members demanded that Glendon continue as president.

"I got re-elected twice," he said, "because I knew more

than anybody else about Tai Tam and nobody else wanted the grief. I also had the great good fortune to have people on the committee like Rick Kroos, Bob Lusher, Don Greco and others who were very helpful."

During the Tai Tam construction, the General Committee decided that it was time to renovate the club's management. John Firrell had been working in tandem with a club management firm, but it was not enough to handle the complexity of bringing the two facilities up to par. Glendon Rowell launched an international search for the world's best club manager. After numerous interviews, the committee chose Colonel Richard Ross, who was director of business operations for the U.S. Army's worldwide network of 723 clubs, 16 hotels and 43 golf courses.

"I could not go any higher where I was," said Ross. "And I needed a new challenge."

"Dick had a mandate," said Rowell. "To make the club the best in Hong Kong, the best in Asia and outstanding in the world in food, service and ambiance."

Dick Ross welcoming Governor Patten at the Town Club

Ross's tasks were legion: reorganizing operations to make them more efficient and cost-effective; altering the new club space so that it was more suitable to members' needs; and attracting members to all the new facilities so that they received the fullest possible use.

View from the pool area of the Tai Tam Club

Shenzhen, China—Nowhere is the economic boom currently sweeping Southern China more evident than in Shenzhen, the first Special Economic Zone to be established in China, and just over the border from Hong Kong in the Pearl River Delta. Green hills and an expanse of traditional fishponds contrast with a scale of modern highrise development indistinguishable from that of Hong Kong—evidence of the growing economic integration between the territory and Guangdong Province. The meandering Shenzhen River marks the border between Hong Kong and China. In the foreground, the Lok Ma Chau Border Crossing carries over 11,000 vehicles daily.

McKay's Bar, before it was moved to the 49th floor

Trade Winds—one of Hong Kong's best Chinese restaurants

The first problems were financial. Accounting's computer was an abacus, and the most important billing records were kept in a cigar box. After an audit, he discovered that the club was losing money hand over fist.

"For the first 90 days, I couldn't draw a paycheck," said Ross. "Our cash flow was terrible—business, membership and sales were all declining—and I couldn't even afford to pay myself."

From the manager's office outward, he computerized, streamlined and professionalized the club's operations. Now he could track the movement of every can of soda and tell what facilities were making or losing money and why. He was so efficient that a 1988 fire in the ventilation system only closed the grill for four days, not enough time to collect business interruption insurance. After decades of marginal financial health, the club finally began to build a comfortable cushion in its bank account.

Dick Ross's next task was to attract members to Exchange Square, particularly during the non-lunchtime hours. Although everybody was impressed with the luxurious new quarters, few were taking full advantage of the facilities. At the same time, many members were concerned that the club was losing its American character. They counted on Ross, the club's first American manager since Bill Mortson, to bring back that missing ingredient and inject new excitement into the club's social life.

He began by throwing the American Club's first Superbowl Party in January 1987. Team banners decorated the 48th-floor reception area, and the early-morning live broadcast attracted a standing-room-only crowd. He followed by rejuvenating the Greet the Fleet program of receptions for U.S. Navy officers—he estimates he has met over 700 ships and 14,000 officers in nine years—and by turning the Christmas party into a distinctly American oversized bash. After Santa Claus arrived on a fire truck at the 1987 Christmas party, the question every year since has been "how will Santa arrive?"

His vehicles have included a helicopter, rickshaw, rappelling down a rope, parachute, and a Harley-Davidson escorted by bikers.

Dick Ross's last mandate—altering the club to suit members' needs—would take longer, nine years, in fact. Nothing could be done to the town club until Tai Tam was finished, because there was not enough money. Meanwhile, he went over plans, using his long experience to visualize whether what they were constructing would work or not.

Tai Tam had a "soft," or partial, opening at the end of 1986. The "hard" opening came on July 4, 1987 with a big party at which Glendon Rowell cut the ribbon and Bill Turnbull and Moira Moser were thrown in the pool.

For Moira Moser, this was one of the crowning events of her career:

"An architect feels rewarded when you feel a place you designed is being used in the way that you intended it to be used. That moment came the evening of the opening when two young girls came out and started to turn cartwheels on the lawn."

In the nine years following its opening, the Tai Tam club changed far less than the town facility. An adult bar was opened upstairs, while the pro shop moved downstairs. The gym and family lounge were expanded, as were the number of eating facilities, including a poolside barbecue and the Fireside Lounge. The most innovative change was Dick Ross's invention of the Country Store as a shop to sell American food products and the like. Under the management of Steven Ma, the store expanded rapidly and outgrew its space a number of times.

Tai Tam was almost too popular. Parking became difficult to find, and summer weekends found the poolside crawling with kids—too many, griped the old-timers.

Club President Glendon Rowell cuts the ribbon at the Tai Tam opening, July 4, 1986

Glendon Rowell with Walter Mondale

In May 1988, the club membership finally allowed Glendon Rowell to retire after two and half terms as president. In recognition, the club presented him with a plaque stating:

"Presented to Glendon Rowell at the termination of his seemingly perpetual term as President of the American Club in Hong Kong on May 17, 1988."

One of the unforeseen side effects of having these expensive new facilities and the debenture program it took to build them was that it changed the nature of the membership. Only rich corporate types could afford to join. On the Membership Committee, a group comprising Dave Murray, Russ Blando and Don Greco realized that the young Americans were being squeezed out of club membership.

"I was approached by a lot of young Americans in the softball league," Russ Blando said. "They wanted to join but couldn't afford it. I realized that we were losing that part of the American community."

A survey commissioned by Don Greco found over 100 Americans wanting to join. The Membership Committee suggested that a Young American program be instituted in which U.S. citizens between age 21 and 35 could join for HK$30,000. The General Committee agreed after some debate but set the age limit at 33 and raised the entrance fee to HK$50,000. The Young American program ran from January 1, 1987 to October 1988, revitalizing the club with about 230 new members and their families and adding over HK$10 million to club coffers as well as some unforeseen consequences

—a horde of kids providing the next generation of American Club members. Afterward, the admission books were closed until August 1989, when the Club began the current (and more expensive) American Individual Membership program.

Under the presidencies of Gordon Chang and John (Jack) Keenan, the work began on altering the Exchange Square club to fit the membership's needs. 1989 saw the first major renovations. The 48th floor waiting area became the Portside Bar; McKay's was moved up to its present larger quarters on the 49th and the President's Room was moved down. Jack Keenan also began negotiations with IBM, the club's downstairs neighbor, for subletting the 47th floor. IBM was willing, but the company was undergoing a reorganization and Hongkong Land did not look favorably on the sub-lease deal. The sorely-needed space on 47 would have to wait.

1989 was also one of those watershed years in China. Like 1967, 1951 and 1949, it was a year when many Westerners made the decision to either stay in Asia or return home. The Tiananmen demonstrations and the incidents of June 4 were a stunning display of where power really lay in China. Many Western hopes about the future of China were shattered, and now they would have to decide whether they could accommodate themselves to this new reality or not.

More immediately, American companies working in China and Hong Kong had to deal with the U.S. Congress's threat to withdraw China's most-favored-nation status. The American Chamber of Commerce fought this proposal by pointing out that over 900 American companies had offices in Hong Kong. Any harm to China's foreign trade would hurt Hong Kong and the bank balances of all those American businesses.

The local American community suddenly realized how important it was to Hong Kong: The 22,000 U.S. passport holders constituted the second largest expatriate community (after the Fil-

ipinos). American companies had US$7 billion invested in Hong Kong; a further US$99 billion was deposited in the local branches of U.S. banks. And the United States was by far the largest market for Hong Kong goods.

"Hong Kong is an American outpost," said Amcham President John Kamm.

China's most-favored-nation status was not withdrawn, but over the following years this continued to be a threat, particularly around election time.

On a more mundane level, the post-Tiananmen insecurity hit the club in the bank balance. The club was hoping to finance the renovations by further debenture sales, but the market collapsed as corporations reassessed Hong Kong as the base of their Asian operations. Luckily, a worldwide eco-

The Boston Clipper, before it switched locations with the Empress of China

nomic recovery picked up Hong Kong in its wake, and corporate managers began making too much money to back out of the territory. Debenture sales soared, driving up their value; by the mid-1990s, full debentures reached the astronomical price of HK$1.8 million. The club would have enough money for the 47th floor.

In 1991, Fred Heeney and his Board of Directors (the club had gone from a committee to a board system under Jack Keenan) made a controversial decision that still rankles some today. The American Club's male-only territories had been an issue since the late 1960s; Heeney and his directors decided that it was time for the club to move into the modern era: Without consulting the greater membership, they voted to allow women into McKay's Bar.

Dick Ross, Pat O'Brien, Doug Holtz, and Mark Blacker, September 1996

"We voted unanimously for the change," said Frank Martin, who was on Heeney's board. "Nobody thought there would be any opposition."

They were wrong, of course. Five years later, there are still angry mutterings from members around the big round tables in McKay's that are the last bastion of an all-male preserve. The opening to women had been going on too long to change, however. In 1996, the consensus was that although the move had perhaps been unfairly imposed, there would be no going back to the old policy.

In 1992, the American Club finally realized that it had almost 70 years of history in Hong Kong; it was time to recognize the achievements of its veteran members. The first five Senior Life Member inductees, George Ross, John Shoemaker, Robert Thompson, Lydia Arcus and Russell

Fourth of July celebrations at Tai Tam, 1992

Blando—all with over 39 years as club members—received special privileges and mementoes in the form of plaques mounted with the St. George's Building doorknobs. Every year since then, five members with over 39 years in the club have been inducted into the program.

The American Club's move down to the 47th floor began under the presidency of Frank Martin, when IBM and Hongkong Land finally gave the go-ahead to the project. A renovation sub-committee under soon-to-be president Daniel Sullivan generated an in-depth financial analysis of the project that showed it was feasible. Almost 50 applicants were waiting to buy debentures at the HK$1.8 million price; that would pay for the move. All they needed was the approval of the membership.

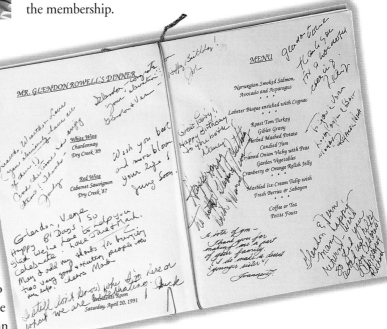

"We learned our lesson from the McKay's Bar episode," he said. "We made absolutely certain that communication with membership would be very open. I had two open membership forums and commissioned a survey that found 92% approval for the move."

In September 1994, Daniel Sullivan replaced Frank Martin as club president and William Allen Wright was hired as the project designer. Essentially, the 47th floor would be the site of everything they could not fit anywhere else—a large and well-equipped gym, function rooms, storage facilities and better administrative offices. Dick Ross promised that the work would be completed by April 1, 1995.

"No one believed I could get it done by then," he said, "but they didn't realize that once the structure is in place the decoration is a snap."

He had a special reason for this timing: After nine years as the American Club's most dynamic General Manager ever, Dick Ross had decided to retire. The man with a unique gift for understanding the present and future needs of the membership and making them a reality would try his hand at opening American Clubs across Asia.

A few weeks before, Daniel Sullivan had hosted a gala retirement dinner for the man who turned the American Club into the largest and most popular and profitable club in Hong Kong. The party was attended by Consul General Richard Mueller, the Admiral of the Seventh Fleet, many past club presidents and dozens of members. They gave him numerous gifts, including a Baccarat crystal eagle and a flight jacket covered with naval insignia. In return, all the past presidents received a thick tome titled "Everything I

The Membership Committee before Consul General Richard Williams' departure from Hong Kong, 1993. From left to right: Dr. Richard Walters, Consul General Richard Williams, Mark Blacker, Dr. Andrew Wong, Stanley Jacobson, Dr. Henry Y. Wong, Russ Blando, Dean Harden, and Dick Ross.

Know About Private Club Management" by Richard Ross: Inside, all the pages were blank.

Dick Ross's successor was Douglas Holtz, who came from the Mid-Pacific Country Club in Hawaii. Not coincidentally, he had also been Colonel Douglas Holtz, Director of Business Operations for the U.S. Army's worldwide club facilities following Dick Ross's tenure in that post. The American Club would continue under another efficient and highly-trained General Manager.

In 1996, during the presidency of Mark Blacker the American Club has reached a plateau of excellence. Ten years of work have finally adapted the Exchange Square club to the membership's needs. There is still work to be done at Tai Tam—a new children's play facility—but its popularity is the best mark of its success. The question is, with June 30, 1997 fast approaching, where will the American Club go from here?

The answer is found in the American Club's history. Since 1925, the club has been an integral part of Hong Kong's American community, which has grown from a few hundred to over 36,000 American citizens and 1,100 U.S. firms. Through all those years, and numerous wars and crises, the American Club has remained dedicated to Hong Kong and its people. The club has also never wavered in its commitment to its American identity. This means not just a gathering of passport-holders but a commitment to American heritage, traditions and ways of doing business.

Today, the American community has shown in numerous surveys that it is very optimistic about Hong Kong's future. The American Club reflects that optimism. Beyond 1997, the club will continue to grow, keeping its American identity and constantly improving its service to members and to the larger community as well. The American Club will be in Hong Kong as long as there are Americans in Hong Kong.

POSTSCRIPT

What goes before gives insight as to where in the future we are likely to be. As so well described in the foregoing pages, the American Club, and indeed Hong Kong, has witnessed several important changes over the past 70-plus years. No doubt as we proceed into the next millennium both the club and Hong Kong shall experience further significant changes, but perhaps changes not so dissimilar to those of the past. People, and by extension their organizations, tend to resist change and are frequently slow to recognize change. It often takes observation by an outside, impartial observer who chronicles experiences and events to show us that indeed the times and environments of the past are very different from what we enjoy today.

When the founders first gathered to establish our club, life in Hong Kong was much more austere. Rickshaws were everywhere, but roads were few and those that did exist outside of Central and Kowloon were not so well maintained. Educational opportunities for the great majority of the populace were scarce, commerce was limited to relatively few products and services, trading partners were restricted to a modest number and, perhaps most notably, the population was sparse. Today, Hong Kong is a leading commercial and financial center, trading with virtually every nation in the world. Highways abound throughout the Territory, cars fill our roads, and formal, quality education is available to everyone. Our population today well exceeds six million. Where to from here?

During the past 70 years Hong Kong has moved to the forefront of the world's leading economies. Its people, indigenous and immigrants, have prospered. Participating in, and to some extent leading this prosperity has been the American Club. Both Hong Kong and the club seem well positioned to move into the next century, confident and enthusiastic. There is much that we can be proud of, and equally there is much about which to be encouraged in looking forward.

If the members who assume club leadership in the next century can find inspiration and guidance from the achievements of those who brought our club to its present condition, and if they can apply these insights with energy and benefit, the club's future will be assured. We are reminded by Sir Joshua Reynolds in *Discourses* that: "Nothing is denied to well-directed labour; nothing is to be attained without it."

Pat O'Brien

Patrick D. O'Brien

AMERICAN CLUB PRESIDENTS

1926	Gordon Duclos		1966	Peter Wodtke/
1927	Gordon Duclos			Stephen Y.N. Tse
1928	C.E. Meyer		1967	Stephen Y.N. Tse
1929	H.H. Pethick		1968	Frederick Westphal Jr.
1930	D.M. Biggar		1969	William H. Allman
1931	E.W. Duggan		1970	John F. Shoemaker
1932	T.B. Wilson		1971	John Holt/Matthew J. Burvett
1933	J.A. Shaw		1972	Matthew J. Burvett
1934	J. Oram Sheppard		1973	William Mortson
1935	C.M. Benson		1974	Roy G. Schwerdtman
1936	Captain George Anderson		1975	Edwin H. Burrell
1937	J.B. Emmert		1976	Edwin H. Burrell/
1938	Charles M. Gee			M. Wayne Coon
1939	—		1977	M. Wayne Coon
1940	D.L. Ballantyne		1978	Michel R. Dahrouge
1941	A.M. Kirby		1979	David M. Murray
1947	F.F. Booth		1980	George E. Betts
1948	R.M. Gordon		1981	Donald B. Griswold
1949	Charles T. Carroll		1982	Patrick R. Kroos
1950	R.A. Wabraushek		1983	Terrence J. Ahearn
1951	John G. O'Donnell		1984	Thomas F. Greer Jr.
1952	Roy R. Pearson		1985	F. Lynn McPheeters/
1953	David H. Rowsome			Glendon Rowell
1954	Gwyn M. Hughes		1986	Glendon Rowell
1955	Guy T. Harden		1987	Glendon Rowell
1956	Arthur A. Chase		1988	Gordon G. Chang
1957	George A. Bell		1989	John J. Keenan
1958	Henry M. Sperry		1990	Andrew W.H. Wong
1959	E.B. Ash		1991	Fred S. Heeney
1960	Guy T. Harden		1992	Joseph R. Champagne
1961	David M. Kowalke		1993	Francis G. Martin
1962	Gordon W. Vaughn		1994	Daniel J. Sullivan
1963	Thomas B. Hitchcock		1995	Mark C. Blacker
1964	John J. Bordwell		1996	Patrick D. O'Brien
1965	John L. Soong			

TIMELINE

1773	USA/WORLD	Boston Tea Party
1776	USA/WORLD	Declaration of Independence
1781	USA/WORLD	Articles of Confederation proclaimed; Defeat of British at Yorktown
1783	USA/WORLD	Articles of Peace ratified (Treaty of Paris)
1787	USA/WORLD	Constitutional Convention meets in Philadelphia
1787-88	USA/WORLD	Alexander Hamilton *et al. The Federalist*
1788	USA/WORLD	Constitution ratified
1789	USA/WORLD	George Washington elected first U.S. President
1790	USA/WORLD	First census shows population of 3.9 million
1791	USA/WORLD	Bill of Rights adopted
1793	USA/WORLD	Eli Whitney invents cotton gin
1800	USA/WORLD	Thomas Jefferson elected third U.S. President
1803	USA/WORLD	Louisiana Purchase extends U.S. border to Rockies
1807	USA/WORLD	African slave trade to U.S. abolished
1812-14	USA/WORLD	War of 1812
1815-17	USA/WORLD	Collapse of Federalist Party
1823	USA/WORLD	Monroe Doctrine
1824	USA/WORLD	John Quincy Adams elected sixth U.S. President
1825	USA/WORLD	Erie Canal links Hudson River and Great Lakes
1828	USA/WORLD	Andrew Jackson elected seventh U.S. President
1831	USA/WORLD	Nat Turner uprising in Virginia
1832-33	USA/WORLD	Nullification crisis leads to scaling-down of tariffs on imported goods.
1833	USA/WORLD	American Antislavery Society founded
1840	USA/WORLD	Abolitionists launch Liberal Party
1840-42	CHINA	Opium Wars
	USA/WORLD	William Harrison becomes President
1841	USA/WORLD	John Tyler becomes President upon Harrison's death
1842	HONG KONG	Treaty of Nanjing; Hong Kong ceded by China to Britain and declared a free port
	USA/WORLD	Webster-Ashburton Treaty settles disputed US-Canada boundary
1843	USA/WORLD	First overland caravans to Oregon
1844	USA/WORLD	James K. Polk elected President
1845	HONG KONG	U.S. Consul appointed
	USA/WORLD	Texas enters Union as slave state
1846	HONG KONG	Hong Kong Club opens in Queen's Road Central
	USA/WORLD	Beginning of Mexican War; Treaty with Britain divides Oregon Territory along 49th parallel
1848	HONG KONG	Sir Samuel Bonham appointed Governor
	USA/WORLD	Gold discovered in California; Zachary Taylor elected President; Treaty of Guadeloupe Hidalgo ends Mexican War
1849	HONG KONG	Completion of St. John's Anglican Church
	USA/WORLD	California Gold Rush
1850	HONG KONG	Population reaches 33,000
	USA/WORLD	Taylor dies and is replaced as President by Millard Fillmore
1851	HONG KONG	Cricket Club established
1852	HONG KONG	Taiping Rebellion refugees arrive in Hong Kong
	USA/WORLD	Franklin Pierce elected President
1854	HONG KONG	Sir John Bowring appointed Governor
	USA/WORLD	Commodore Perry opens Japan to American trade
1855	HONG KONG	Last public execution
1856	USA/WORLD	John Brown's raid at Pottawatomie Creek; James Buchanan elected President
1857	HONG KONG	British Consul declares war on China (Arrow War)
1858	HONG KONG	Treaty of Tianjin signed, legalising opium sales in China
	USA/WORLD	Lincoln-Douglas debates
1859	USA/WORLD	John Brown's raid on Harper's Ferry
1860	HONG KONG	Kowloon Peninsula chosen as a camp for Allied Expeditionary Forces to China Convention of Peking ratified—Kowloon Peninsula and Stonecutters Island ceded to Britain in perpetuity
	CHINA	China accepts Russian annexation of eastern Siberia
	USA/WORLD	Democratic Party divides along sectional lines at Baltimore; Abraham Lincoln elected President; South Carolina secedes from Union
1861	HONG KONG	Hong Kong General Chamber of Commerce founded; Population approaching 100,000
	USA/WORLD	Rest of deep South states secede, as well as Virginia, North Carolina, Tennessee and Arkansas; Jefferson begins presidency of Confederate States of America; Beginning of Civil War
1862	HONG KONG	Battle of Tsim Sha Tsui between local Punti and Hakka groups
	CHINA	French forces invade Indochina
1863	HONG KONG	Hong Kong issues silver dollar coins
	USA/WORLD	Lincoln issues final Emancipation Proclamation; Confederate victory at Fredericksburg
1864	HONG KONG	Gas street lighting introduced
	CHINA	Taiping Rebellion crushed
	USA/WORLD	Grant named Union General in Chief; Lincoln re-elected President; Sherman marches from Atlanta to the sea
1865	HONG KONG	Hong Kong and Shanghai Banking Corporation founded
	USA/WORLD	Lee surrenders at Appomatox; Lincoln assassinated; Andrew Johnson becomes President; Thirteenth Amendment ratified
1866	HONG KONG	Hong Kong Royal Mint opens
	CHINA	Sun Yat-sen born in Guangdong Province
	USA/WORLD	Congress approves Fourteenth Ammendment; Ku Klux Klan formed
1867	HONG KONG	The Blockade of Hong Kong by Chinese customs vessels
	USA/WORLD	Congress passes Tenure of Office Act and Command of Army Act to reduce Johnson's power

1868	HONG KONG	Tung Wah Hospital opened
	CHINA	Russia annexes Bokhara and starts eastward moves into today's Xinjiang Autonomous Region
	USA/WORLD	Former Confederate states adopt new constitutions granting universal suffrage; President Johnson impeached; Ulysses S. Grant elected as President
1869	HONG KONG	Visit by HRH Duke of Edinburgh
	CHINA	Suez Canal opened
	USA/WORLD	Congress passes Fifteenth Amendment
1870	HONG KONG	Hong Kong-Amoy-Shanghai cable opens for traffic; Completion of submarine telegraphic cable to China
1871	HONG KONG	Hong Kong-Singapore cable begins operation
1874	HONG KONG	Typhoon kills and wounds thousands
1876	USA/WORLD	Genral Custer's defeat at Little Bighorn; Alexander Graham Bell transmits first telephone message; End of Reconstruction
1877	HONG KONG	Budget exceeds HK$1 million
1880	HONG KONG	First rickshaws used; Telegraphic link with the Philippines established
	USA/WORLD	Garfield elected President
1883	HONG KONG	Cable connects Hong Kong to Shanghai and Fuzhou; Canton-Kowloon telegraph line opens
	CHINA	Franco-Chinese War starts
	USA/WORLD	Garfield assassinated; Arthur becomes President
1884	HONG KONG	Riots caused by Sino-French War; Hong Kong Jockey Club founded
	USA/WORLD	Cleveland elected President
1885	CHINA	French defeat Chinese in Indochina
1888	HONG KONG	Peak Tramway connecting Cathedral to Victoria Gap is opened
	USA/WORLD	Harrison elected President
1890	HONG KONG	Praya reclamation begins; Public telephone service offered by China and Japan Telephone Company
	USA/WORLD	Sherman Antitrust Act; Sherman Silver Purchase Act; "Battle" of Wounded Knee; McKinley Tariff
1892	HONG KONG	Gas lighting introduced in Kowloon
	USA/WORLD	Cleveland re-elected President
1893	CHINA	Mao Zedong born in Hunan Province; France extends its rule to Cambodia and Laos
1893-97	USA/WORLD	Depression
1894	HONG KONG	Bubonic plague breaks out
	USA/WORLD	"Coxey's Army" Pullman Strike
1894-95	CHINA	Sino-Japanese War—China forced to cede Taiwan to Japan
1896	HONG KONG	Second outbreak of bubonic plague
	USA/WORLD	McKinley elected President
1898	HONG KONG	Convention of Peking—New Territories ceded to Britain for 99 years
	CHINA	Hundred Days Reform under Emperor Guangxu; Dowager Empress Cixi imprisons Emperor and returns to power
	USA/WORLD	Spanish-American War—U.S. annexes Philippines; Hawaiian Islands annexed
1899	CHINA	Zhou Enlai born in Jiangsu Province
	USA/WORLD	National Consumer's League founded; Open Door Policy
1900	HONG KONG	Hong Kong serves as base for Chinese Expeditionary Force during Boxer Uprising; Chinese General Chamber of Commerce founded
	CHINA	Boxer Rebellion; Russia builds Port Arthur
	USA/WORLD	Gold Standard Act; McKinley re-elected
1901	HONG KONG	Worst bubonic outbreak since 1894; Population at 265,000
	USA/WORLD	United States Steel Corporation formed; Platt Amendment; McKinley assassinated—Theodore Roosevelt becomes President; Hay-Pauncefote Treaty
1902	CHINA	Anglo-Japanese Alliance
1903	USA/WORLD	Departments of Commerce and Labor established
1904	HONG KONG	Electric Tramways on Hong Kong Island begin service
	CHINA	Russo-Japanese War (ends 1905): Japan gets Port Arthur, Dairen, Russia's concessions in South China and additional "rights". Sun Yat-sen forms Revolutionary Alliance Society in Tokyo
	USA/WORLD	Roosevelt Corollary to Monroe Doctrine; Roosevelt elected President
1906	HONG KONG	Worst typhoon in recorded history
1907	USA/WORLD	Gentlemen's agreement with Japan
1908	USA/WORLD	Taft elected President
1910	HONG KONG	All opium dens in Hong Kong and New Territories closed; British sections of Kowloon-Canton Railway opened; First automobile in Hong Kong
1911	HONG KONG	Chinese section of Kowloon-Canton Railway open; First airplane flight in Hong Kong at Shatin
	CHINA	Republican Revolution overthrows Manchu power in Central and Southern China; Sun Yat-sen declared President of Chinese Republic; Student Mao Zedong enlists in rebel army
1912	HONG KONG	University of Hong Kong opened
	CHINA	Qing Dynasty falls and Puyi abdicates as Emperor of China; Sun Yat-sen resigns as President of Republic of China
	USA/WORLD	Wilson elected President
1912-14	CHINA	Yuan Shikai accepts Japan's "Twenty-one Demands"; Japanese sieze Qingdao
1913	USA/WORLD	Sixteenth Amendment: the Income Tax; Seventeenth Amendment: Popular election of U.S. Senators; Underwood Tariff; Federal Reserve Act
1914	USA/WORLD	Federal Trade Commission Act
1915	CHINA	Yuan Shikai tries to re-establish monarchy with himself as Emperor
	USA/WORLD	Sinking of the *Lusitania*
1916	CHINA	Second Republican Revolution: Yuan Shikai overthrown and his acceptance of Japanese demands nullified. Era of warlords begins
	USA/WORLD	Wilson re-elected
1917	CHINA	Beijing's shadow government declares war on Germany; Sun Yat-sen, heading a separate provisional regime in Canton, also declares war
	USA/WORLD	US enters World War I

1918	HONG KONG	Hundreds killed in Happy Valley Racecourse fire
	USA/WORLD	Fourteen Points; Sedition Act; War Finance Corporation; Armistice Day, November 11
1918-19	CHINA	175,000 Chinese laborers sent overseas to help allies; 400 "Work-study" student interpreters include Zhou Enlai (and Deng Xiaoping); in Hunan Mao forms pro-Russian Revolution
1919	CHINA	May Fourth Movement: Nationwide student demonstrations against Versailles Treaty award of Germany's China concessions to Japan—beginning of modern nationalist movement.
	USA/WORLD	Prohibition Amendment ratified
1920	HONG KONG	Population reaches 600,000
	CHINA	Mao Zedong organizes Hunan Branch of Socialist Youth Corps
	USA/WORLD	Red Scare leads to mass arrests of labor agitators
1921	HONG KONG	Crown Prince of Japan (later to become Emperor Hirohito) visits
	CHINA	Chinese Communist Party (CCP) first organized at First Congress—Mao participates and is chosen first secretary of Hunan Communist Party
1922	HONG KONG	Seamen's strike
	CHINA	Sun Yat-sen forms a United Front with Chinese Communist Party—Communists may now hold joint membership in Guomindang (GMD)
1924	USA/WORLD	Immigration Restriction Act; Coolidge elected President
1925	HONG KONG	Guangzhou-Hong Kong strike starts (ends 10/26); **American Club opens**
	CHINA	Mao returns to Hunan and organizes peasant support for Nationalist (Liberation) Expedition; Sun Yat-sen dies
1926	CHINA	Nationalist Revolutionary Expedition launched from Canton under Chiang Kai-shek; Nationalist-Communist coalition forces conquer most of South China
1927	CHINA	Chiang Kai-shek leads anti-Communist coup—Communist membership reduced by four-fifths
	USA/WORLD	Charles Lindbergh flies across the Atlantic
1928	HONG KONG	Peninsula Hotel opens
	CHINA	Chiang Kai-shek establishes nominal centralised control over China under GMD; Mao Zedong forms first "Red Army" of China
	USA/WORLD	Hoover elected President
1929	USA/WORLD	Black Thursday, October 24, stock market crashes
1930	HONG KONG	First commercial flight from Hong Kong to Guangzhou
	CHINA	Red Army led by Mao captures Changsha; Chiang Kai-shek launches first major offensive against the Reds; Mao's wife and sister executed in Changsha
1931	HONG KONG	Anti-Japanese riots
	CHINA	Japanese invasion of Manchuria; Mao elected chairman of first All-China Soviet Government; End of great famine (1929-31) in Northwest China
	USA/WORLD	Hoover Debt Moratorium

1932	HONG KONG	Charlie Chaplin visits
	CHINA	Japan attacks Shanghai; Chiang Kai-shek extirpates underground Reds from Shanghai
	USA/WORLD	Franklin Delano Roosevelt elected President
1933	HONG KONG	George Bernard Shaw visits
	CHINA	Chiang Kai-shek begins a new campaign against Communists
	USA/WORLD	"Hundred Days" session of Congress; Emergency Banking Act; U.S. recognizes Soviet Union; Prohibition repealed by Twenty-first Amendment
1934	HONG KONG	China Fleet Club opened
	CHINA	Second All-China Soviet Congress re-elects Mao Zedong chairman, but Party leadership falls to "Twenty Eight Bolsheviks"
1935	HONG KONG	New Hong Kong and Shanghai Bank Building opened
	CHINA	Long March; Japanese move into Chinese Inner Mongolia.
1936	HONG KONG	Arrival of Imperial Airlines flying boat, carrying first airmail from Britain to Hong Kong; Pan-American Clipper service between U.S. and Hong Kong inaugurated
	CHINA	Xi'an incident—Chiang Kai-shek is arrested by Marshall Zhang who insists that Chiang accept national united front against Japan. GMD opens negotiations with CCP.
	USA/WORLD	Roosevelt re-elected
1937	HONG KONG	Passenger air service between Hong Kong and Manila started; Beginning of Sino-Japanese War; Japanese bomb Bias Bay area 1938
	CHINA	Japan invades China; agreement signed for joint Nationalist-Communist war of resistance against Japan.
1938	HONG KONG	Visit by Madam Chiang Kai-shek; Imperial Airways plane fired on by Japanese near Hong Kong; Fall of Guangzhou—flood of Chinese refugees enter Hong Kong
	CHINA	Mao becomes undisputed leader of CCP; Japanese armies overwhelm North China; Nationalists retreat to West
	USA/WORLD	Munich agreement
1939	HONG KONG	Japanese occupy Hainan Island; Lo Wu bombed by Japanese, 12 killed; Conscription for British subjects; Registration of British women and children; 44 Vickers tanks arrive in Hong Kong
	CHINA	Rapid expansion of Communist cadres and military forces; China's struggle begins to merge with the Second World War; Yan'an blocked by Nationalist troops
	USA/WORLD	War breaks out in Europe
1940	HONG KONG	General Norton appointed "Acting Governor"; Population at 1.6 million
	USA/WORLD	United States preparedness and defense measures; Battle of Britain; Roosevelt re-elected
1940-41	CHINA	Breakdown of cooperation between Nationalists and Communists

1941	HONG KONG	Japanese bomb Kai Tak and invade Hong Kong on 8 December; British surrender to Japanese
	USA/WORLD	Battle of the Atlantic; Atlantic Charter; Japanese attack Pearl Harbor
1942	HONG KONG	Japanese forces occupy Hong Kong; Allied troops incarcerated in POW camps; Civilians interned at Stanley
	CHINA	Mao consolidates power in CCP through "rectification" campaign, gaining ascendancy over "Moscow" faction
	USA/WORLD	Battle of Coral Sea; Allied Campaign in North Africa
1943	HONG KONG	Japanese rebuild Government House; Seven British civilians beheaded at Stanley for possession of radio
	CHINA	GMD and fighting capacity rapidly decline; Zhou Enlai claims 800,000 Party members.
	USA/WORLD	Casablanca Conference; Allies invade Italy; Teheran Conference
1944	CHINA	U.S. Army "observers" arrive in Yan'an, Communist "guerilla" capital
	USA/WORLD	Invasion of Europe; Landing at Normandy, June 6; Roosevelt re-elected; Battle of the Bulge
1945	HONG KONG	Allied planes bomb Hong Kong; Japanese surrender on August 30; Hong Kong resumes normal trading
	CHINA	After V-E DAY, Communist-led forces flood North China and Manchuria, competing with American-armed Nationalists. U.S. Ambassador Hurley flies Mao to Chongqing to negotiate with Chiang Kai-shek; Yalta Pact promises Taiwan to China
	USA/WORLD	Yalta conference; Roosevelt dies—Truman becomes President; Germany surrenders; Atomic bomb dropped on Hiroshima; Japan surrenders; United Nations formed; Potsdam Conference
1946	HONG KONG	Civil government restored
	CHINA	Communist War of Liberation begins
1947	HONG KONG	China insist on right of access to Kowloon Walled City
	CHINA	Mao calls for general offensive against Nationalists
	USA/WORLD	Marshall Plan proposed; Taft-Hartley Act; Truman Doctrine
1948	HONG KONG	U.K. Treasury control over Hong Kong's finances ends
	CHINA	Nationalists defeated in Manchuria
	USA/WORLD	Truman elected President; Berlin Blockade
1949	HONG KONG	Communists take Guangzhou and reach Hong Kong border
	CHINA	Chiang Kai-shek flees to Taiwan as his armies disintegrate; People's Liberation Army is successful all over China; Chinese People's Republic formally proclaimed in Beijing
	USA/WORLD	North Atlantic Treaty Organization founded; U.S. withdraws its diplomats from China
1950	HONG KONG	Left-wing political demonstrations; China National Aviation Corporation planes held at Kai Tak; Korean War begins; U.S. imposes an embargo on selected exports to and from Hong Kong
	CHINA	Mao concludes Sino-Soviet treaty of alliance
	USA/WORLD	Korean War begins; Rise in popularity of anti-communist Senator Joseph McCarthy
1951	HONG KONG	UN Embargo on trade with China; Population passes 2 million
	USA.WORLD	Truman fires General Douglas MacArthur
1952	HONG KONG	Chinese planes grounded at Kai Tak since 1949 returned to U.S.; GMD attacks communist offices and personnel in Hong Kong
	USA/WORLD	Eisenhower elected President
1953	HONG KONG	Squatter fire in Shek Kip Mei makes 58,000 homeless—Public Housing program starts
	CHINA	U.S. forms alliance with Chiang Kai-shek, making Taiwan a U.S. protectorate. First Five-Year Plan announced
	USA/WORLD	Korean ceasefire; Rosenbergs executed
1954	CHINA	Agricultural cooperatives lay basis for collectivization; State establishes partnerships with remaining private enterprise
	USA/WORLD	South East Asian Treaty Organization; Geneva Conference on Indochina; Senate censures Joseph McCarthy; Communist Control Act
1955	HONG KONG	Han-Dynasty tomb discovered in New Territories
	USA/WORLD	Geneva Summit Meeting
1956	HONG KONG	Double Tenth arrivals at Sham Shui Po—Chinese arrivals surge
	USA/WORLD	Eisenhower re-elected
1957	HONG KONG	Television started by Rediffusion
	CHINA	Beginning of breakup of Sino-Soviet Unity
	USA/WORLD	Eisenhower Doctrine
1958	HONG KONG	Kai Tak Airport runway completed
	CHINA	Second Five-Year Plan announced; Great Leap Forward; Beijing's threat to liberate Taiwan provokes Sino-American crisis
	USA/WORLD	National Defense Education Act; First U.S. satellite launched
1960-63	CHINA	PRC slowly recovers from near-famine conditions
1960	HONG KONG	Population reaches 3 million
	CHINA	Moscow recalls all Soviet advisers from China
	USA/WORLD	Kennedy elected President
1961	HONG KONG	Population surpasses 3 million
	USA/WORLD	Bay of Pigs; Peace Corps established
1962	HONG KONG	Over 70,000 illegal immigrants flood into Hong Kong from China
	CHINA	Sino-Soviet clashes foreshadow wide international ideological fight
	USA/WORLD	Cuban Missile Crisis
1963	HONG KONG	Chinese language TV services commences
	CHINA	Mao issues a declaration calling upon "the people of the world" to unite against American imperialism and support American Negro struggles
	USA/WORLD	Test Ban Treaty; Kennedy is assassinated—Lyndon B. Johnson becomes President

1964	HONG KONG	Sir David Trench becomes Governor	1976	HONG KONG	Zhou Enlai's death mourned in Hong Kong
	CHINA	Breakdown in Sino-Soviet relations almost complete		CHINA	Mao Zedong dies
				USA/WORLD	Carter elected President
	USA/WORLD	Gulf of Tonkin Resolution passed; Johnson elected President; Civil Rights Act	1977	HONG KONG	Second Lion Rock Tunnel opened
				USA/WORLD	Panama Canal Treaties
1965	HONG KONG	Influx of U.S. troops on "R&R" from War in Vietnam; Major bank run halted by government intervention	1978	HONG KONG	Opening of Shatin racecourse
				CHINA	Deng Xiaoping comes to power; First American tourists arrive
	CHINA	The United Nations vote on the admission of the PRC ends in a tie		USA/WORLD	Camp David Agreements
			1979	HONG KONG	Direct train service to Canton resumes
	USA/WORLD	Voting Rights Act; Medicare; U.S. forces in Vietnam approach 500,000 men		USA/WORLD	Three Mile Island Nuclear Disaster
			1980	HONG KONG	Population reaches 5.2 million
1966	HONG KONG	Kowloon riots sparked by proposed Star Ferry fare increase		CHINA	Gang of Four imprisoned; Shenzhen Special Economic Zone opened
	CHINA	Mao launches Cultural Revolution; China sends small arms and food to North Vietnam		USA/WORLD	Reagan elected President
			1980-1	USA/WORLD	Iranian hostage crisis
1967	HONG KONG	Riots and bombings provoked by Cultural Revolution sympathisers; Five Hong Kong policemen killed by PLA soldiers at the border	1982	HONG KONG	Prime Minister Thatcher visits Beijing to discuss future of Hong Kong; Vietnamese boat people confined to closed areas
1968	HONG KONG	City district offices set up by government		CHINA	Talks on Hong Kong open with Britain
	CHINA	U.S. Ship *Pueblo* is boarded by North Korean sailors while intelligence gathering off North Korean coast—in crisis which follows China calls for a united front in support of North Vietnamese forces		USA/WORLD	Equal Rights Amendment fails to gain ratification
			1983	HONG KONG	Formal rounds of Sino-British talks begin; Hong Kong dollar linked to U.S. dollar at conversion rate of HK$7.80 to US$1
	USA/WORLD	Tet offensive in Vietnam; Martin Luther King assassinated, April 4th; Nixon elected President		USA/WORLD	241 United States Marines killed in Beirut; United States invades Grenada
1969	HONG KONG	Shatin— first New Territories satellite town	1984	HONG KONG	Mrs Thatcher signs Sino-British Joint Declaration in Beijing; Opening of the unified Stock Exchange in Exchange Square
	USA/WORLD	Moon landing, Apollo 11		USA/WORLD	Ronald Reagan elected President
1970	HONG KONG	Population reaches four million; Arrival at Kai Tak of first Boeing 747	1985	HONG KONG	First elected members to Legislative Council
	USA/WORLD	America invades Cambodia	1987	HONG KONG	Hang Seng Index falls from 3,207 to 2,241 in one day. Hong Kong Stock Exchange closed for four days
1971	HONG KONG	Prevention of Bribery Ordinance			
	CHINA	China admitted to U.N.	1988	HONG KONG	Permanent office of Sino-British Joint Liaison Group set up in Hong Kong
	USA/WORLD	Kissinger's secret trip to Beijing		USA/WORLD	George Bush elected President
1972	HONG KONG	Influx of Vietnamese boat people; Cross Harbour Tunnel opens	1989	HONG KONG	Mass rallies take place in support of the democratic movement in China
	CHINA	U.S. recognises China		CHINA	Tiananmen Square massacre
	USA/WORLD	Nixon re-elected; Equal Rights Amendment passed	1990	HONG KONG	Basic Law for the SAR of Hong Kong promulgated by the National People's Congress in Beijing, to come into effect 1 July 1997
1974	HONG KONG	ICAC set up to enforce Prevention of Bribery Ordinance	1991-92	USA/WORLD	Crisis in the Gulf
	USA/WORLD	Nixon impeached—Ford becomes President	1992	USA/WORLD	Los Angeles Riots; William Clinton elected President
1975	HONG KONG	Queen Elizabeth II visits			
	CHINA	Gang of Four come to power; Chiang Kai-shek dies			

BIBLIOGRAPHY

Alsop, Joseph, *I've Seen the Best of It* (W.W. Norton and Company, New York, 1992).

Anderson, Irvine, *The Standard-Vacuum Oil Company and United States East Asian Policy* (Princeton University Press, Princeton, 1975).

Belden, Jack, *China Shakes the World* (Harper & Row, New York, 1949).

Booker, Edna Lee, *News is my Job* (Macmillan and Company, New York, 1940).

Booker, Edna Lee, *Flight from China* (Macmillan and Company, New York, 1945).

Breslin, Thomas A., *China, American Catholicism, and the Missionary* (Pennsylvania State University Press, University Park, Pa., 1980).

Brown, D. Mackenzie, *China Trade Days in California* (University of California Press, Berkeley, 1947).

Cameron, Nigel, *Hong Kong, the Cultured Pearl* (Oxford University Press, Hong Kong, 1978).

Candlin, Enid, *The Breach in the Wall* (Macmillan, New York, 1973).

Carew, John, *Hostages to Fortune* (Hamilton, London, 1971).

Christman, Margaret, *Adventurous Pursuits, Americans and the China Trade, 1784-1844* (Smithsonian Institution Press, Washington, D.C., 1984).

Clifford, Nicholas, *Spoilt Children of Empire* (Middlebury College Press, Middlebury, 1991).

Colling, John, *The Spirit of Yenan* (API Press Ltd., Hong Kong, 1991).

Collis, Maurice, *Foreign Mud* (Faber and Faber, London, 1946).

Cottrell, Robert, *The End of Hong Kong: The Secret Diplomacy of Imperial Retreat* (John Murray, London, 1993).

Courtauld, Caroline, *Odyssey Illustrated Guide to Hong Kong* (The Guidebook Company, Hong Kong, 1996).

Crossman, Carl L., *The Decorative Arts of the China Trade* (Princeton Pyne Press, Princeton, 1972).

Crouch, Archie, *Scholars' Guide to China Mission Resources in the Libraries and Archives of the United States* (Princeton University Press, Princeton, 1983).

Daggett, Brigadier-General A.S., *America in the China Relief Expedition* (Hudson-Kimberly Publishing Company, Kansas City, 1903).

Davies, Shann, *Odyssey Illustrated Guide to Macau* (The Guidebook Company, Hong Kong, 1993).

De Leeuw, Hendrik, *Cities of Sin* (Willey Book Company, New York, 1947).

Endacott, G.B., *A History of Hong Kong* (Oxford University Press, Oxford, 1964).

Endacott, G.B., *Hong Kong Eclipse* (Oxford University Press, Oxford, 1978).

Espey, John, *Minor Heresies, Major Departures* (University of California Press, Berkeley, 1994).

Fairbank, John King, *Trade and Diplomacy on the China Coast* (Harvard University Press, Cambridge, 1953).

Fairbank, John King, *The Cambridge History of China* (Cambridge University Press, Cambridge, 1983).

Fairbank, John King, editor, *The Missionary Enterprise in China and America* (Harvard University Press, Cambridge, 1974).

Ferguson, Ted, *Desperate Siege* (Doubleday, Garden City, N.Y., 1980).

Finch, Percy, *Shanghai and Beyond* (Scribners, New York, 1953).

Gittins, Jean, *Stanley: Behind Barbed Wire* (Hong Kong University Press, Hong Kong, 1982).

Goldstein, Johnathan, *Philadelphia and the China Trade* (Pennsylvania State University Press, University Park, 1978).

Griffin, Eldon, *Clippers and Consuls* (Edwards Brothers Inc., Ann Arbor, 1938).

Hidy, Ralph and Muriel, *Pioneering in Big Business* (Harper and Brothers, New York, 1955).

Howard, David S., *New York and the China Trade* (New York Historical Society, New York, 1984).

Howe, Christopher, editor, *Shanghai, Revolution and Development in an Asian Metropolis* (Cambridge University Press, Cambridge, 1981).

Hughes, Richard, *Borrowed Place, Borrowed Time* (Deutsch, London, 1976).

Hunt, Michael, *The Making of a Special Relationship: The United States and China to 1914* (Columbia University Press, New York, 1983).

Hunter, William C., *An American in Canton (1825-44)* (Derwent Communications Ltd., Hong Kong, 1994).

Hutchison, James, *China Hand* (Lothrop, Lee and Shepard Company, Boston, 1936).

Johnson, Robert E., *Far China Station* (Naval Institute Press, Annapolis, 1979).

Johnson, Linda Cooke, *Shanghai: from Market Town to Treaty Port, 1074-1858* (Stanford University Press, Stanford, 1995).

King, Frank H. H., *The History of the Hongkong and Shanghai Banking Corporation* (Cambridge University Press, Cambridge, 1987-1991).

Lambot, Ian and Gillian Chambers, *One Queen's Road Central* (HongkongBank, Hong Kong, 1986).

Latourette, Kenneth Scott, *A History of the Expansion of Christianity* (Harper & Brothers, New York, 1944).

Latourette, Kenneth Scott, *A History of Christian Missions in China* (Society for Promoting Christian Knowledge, London, 1929).

Liu, Kwang-Ching, *Americans and Chinese* (Harvard University Press, Cambridge, 1963).

May, Ernest R. and John King Fairbank, editors, *America's China Trade in Historical Perspective* (Harvard University Press, Cambridge, 1986).

Miller, G.E. (pseudonym), *Shanghai, The Paradise of Adventurers* (Orsay Publishing House, New York, 1937).

Perelman, S.J., *Eastward Ha!* (Simon & Schuster, New York, 1948).

Powell, John, *My Twenty-Five Years in China* (Macmillan, New York, 1945).

Priestwood, Gwen, *Through Japanese Barbed Wire* (D. Appleton-Century Company, New York, 1943).

Reynolds, Quentin, *Officially Dead* (Random House, New York, 1945).

Rickman, John, *Journal of Captain Cook's Last Voyage to the Pacific Ocean* (E. Newberry, London, 1781).

Roberts, Elfed V., *Historical Dictionary of Hong Kong and Macau* (Scarecrow Press, Metuchen, N.J., 1992).

Shaw, Samuel, *The Journals of Major Samuel Shaw* (William Crosby and H.P. Nichols, Boston, 1947).

Spence, Jonathan, *God's Chinese Son* (W.W. Norton & Company, New York, 1996).

Spence, Jonathan, *The Search for Modern China* (W.W. Norton & Company, New York, 1990).

Spence, Jonathan, *To Change China* (Little, Brown, New York, 1969).

Steurt, Marjorie Rankin, *Broken Bits of Old China* (Thomas Nelson, Nashville, 1973).

Swisher, Earl, *China's Management of the American Barbarians* (Far Eastern Publications, New Haven, 1951).

Thomas, James, *A Pioneer Tobacco Merchant in the Orient* (Duke University Press, Durham, N.C., 1928).

Tolley, Kemp, *Yangtze Patrol* (Naval Institute Press, Annapolis, 1971).

Tucker, Nancy B., *Taiwan, Hong Kong, and the United States, 1945-1992* (Twayne Publishers, New York, 1994).

Ukers, William H., *The Romance of Tea* (Knopf, New York, 1936).

Varg, Paul A., *The Making of a Myth: The United States and China, 1897-1912* (Michigan State University Press, East Lansing, 1968).

Varg, Paul A., *Missionaries, Chinese, and Diplomats* (Princeton University Press, Princeton, 1958).

Wakeman Jr., Frederic, *Policing Shanghai 1927-1937* (University of California Press, Berkeley, 1995).

Waterford, Van, *Prisoners of the Japanese in World War II* (McFarland, Jefferson, N.C., 1994).

Welsh, Frank, *A Borrowed Place: a History of Hong Kong* (Kodansha, New York, 1993).

White, Theodore H. and Annalee Jacoby, *Thunder Out of China* (William Sloane Associates, Inc., New York, 1946).

CREDITS & ACKNOWLEDGMENTS

PHOTOS & ILLUSTRATIONS: **Airphoto International** 18, 195, 196, 204, 206-207, 211 (bottom), 215; **The American Club** 109, 166, 187, 189 (catalog), 190 (left), 191 (bottom), 193 (bottom: racing pictures), 197, 198, 199, 200, 202 (bottom), 208, 210, 213; **Magnus Bartlett** 211; **The Beaton Estate** 123; **Alan Birch** 133 (top); **Russell M. Blando** 174 (top); **Jack & Peg Bordwell** 179 (middle and bottom), 181 (left column and top right); **Butler Institute of American Art** 27 (top); **Cathay Pacific Airways** 171 (top); **Otto Chan** 178; **John Colling** 139, 142, 143, 153; **Marvin Farkas** 164, 169, 174 (bottom), 176; **Frank Fischbeck** 190 (right); **Bob Gordon, Sr.** 182 (top); **Thomas Gorman** 72; **The Guidebook Company** 192 (bottom); **Arthur Hacker** 50, 83, 108, 119, 121; **Susan Hess** 57 (bottom); **The Historical Society of Pennsylvania** 19, 24, 26 (bottom); **John J. Keenan** 189 (bottom); **Patrick R. Kroos** 193 (middle); **Hong Kong Land** 189 (top); **Hong Kong Museum of Art** 28 (bottom), 30-31, 34-35, 53; **The Hongkong and Shanghai Banking Corporation Limited** 4-5, 13, 20-21, 22, 23, 25, 28 (top), 29, 32, 33, 36, 38 (top), 38-39, 41, 43, 45, 46-47, 51, 52, 53, 58, 60, 62, 68, 76, 77, 90, 98 (bottom), 100-101, 103 (bottom), 111, 113, 133 (bottom), 134, 172; **Hong Kong University Library** 138; **The Library of Congress** 89, 94, 151; **The Billie Love Historical Collection** 67, 73, 74, 82; **Massachussets Historical Society** 26 (top); **Museum of History and Industry** 102; **National Archives and Records Administration** 75, 88, 96, 125, 132, 141, 148, 150, 154, 155 (bottom), 158, 159; **Naval Historical Center** 65 (top), 78, 79, 92, 93, 103 (top), 104, 105, 106, 107 (top right), 110, 116, 120, 124, 130, 140, 146-147, 163; **The New York Public Library** 59, 63 (bottom); **Peabody and Essex Museum** 54, 55. 63 (top), 65 (bottom), 84; **Philadelphia Museum of Art** 27 (bottom); **Pictorial Histories Publishing** 126 (bottom); **Taco Proper, Sr.** 191 (top), 192 (top), 202 (top); **Malcolm Rosholt** 140, 144; **George R. Ross** 189 (bottom); **Richard H. Ross** 193 (top), 205 (top), 211 (top); **Glendon Rowell** 209, 211 (bottom); **Ruttonjee Estates Continuation Ltd.** 107 (bottom); **San Francisco Maritime NHP** 57 (top); **John and Audrey Shoemaker** 179 (top), 181 (middle right); *South China Morning Post* 98 (top), 126 (top), 127, 152, 184 (bottom), 185; **Russell Spurr** 170; **John Swire & Sons Limited** 48; **Union Pacific Museum Collection** 64; **Yale Divinity School** 86 (top), 107 (top left), 128, 155 (top), 160 (top); **Yale University Library** 85, 86 (bottom), 160 (bottom); **Wattis Fine Art** 14, 16-17; **Frederick C. Westphal, Jr.** 188; **Dr. Andrew Wong** 212; **Daniel Zigal** 117, 165, 168, 171 (bottom), 173, 175, 177, 180 (all except middle right), 181 (bottom right), 182 (bottom), 183, 184 (top), 193 (bottom: racing badges).

The Publisher wishes to make special mention of the generosity of the Hongkong Bank in making available the material (including the front cover painting) from their archives.

LITERARY EXCERPTS: Grateful aknowledgement is made to the following authors and publishers for permissions granted: **Thomas Nelson:** *Broken Bits of Old China* ©1973 Marjorie Steurt Rankin. **Macmillan Publishing Co., Inc.:** *The Breach in the Wall; A Memoir of the Old China* ©1973 Enid Saunders Candlin; *My Twenty-Five Years in China* ©1945 John B. Powell; *News Is My Job: A Correspondent in War Torn China* ©1940 Edna Lee Booker. **Harper & Row:** *Foreign Devils in the Flowery Kingdom* ©1945 Carl Crow; *China Shakes the World* ©1949 Jack Belden. **Lothrop, Lee and Shepard Company:** *China Hand* ©1936 James Lafayette Hutchison. **Alfred A. Knopf, Inc.:** *Prisoner of the Japs* ©1943 Gwen Dew. **H. Smith and R. Haas:** *Cities of Sin* ©1933 Hendrik de Leeuw. **Random House:** *Officially Dead: The Story of Commander C.D. Smith* ©1945 Quentin Reynolds. **The Literary Executors of the Late Sir Cecil Beaton:** *China Diary and Album* ©1945. **API Press Limited:** *The Spirit of Yenan* ©1991 John Colling. **Simon and Schuster:** *Eastward, Ha!* ©1977 S.J. Perelman.